# STRANGE INHERITANCE

# STRANGE INHERITANCE

## JOHN COLVILLE

MICHAEL RUSSELL

© John Colville 1983

First published in Great Britain 1983
by Michael Russell (Publishing) Ltd
The Chantry, Wilton, Salisbury, Wiltshire

Set in Sabon by The Spartan Press Ltd, Lymington
Printed and bound in Great Britain
by Biddles Ltd, Guildford and King's Lynn

*All rights reserved*
ISBN 0 85955 104 0

# Contents

|    | Preface | vii |
|----|---------|-----|
| 1  | The Seymours | 1 |
| 2  | The Sheridans | 21 |
| 3  | The Queen of Beauty | 35 |
| 4  | Prelude to Tragedy | 50 |
| 5  | Disaster | 66 |
| 6  | The Aftermath | 83 |
| 7  | Gilded Youth | 98 |
| 8  | The Socialist | 115 |
| 9  | The Suffragist | 127 |
| 10 | The Philosopher | 133 |
| 11 | The Cavendish-Bentincks | 143 |
| 12 | The Diplomatic Ladder | 152 |
| 13 | Exacting Assignment | 167 |
| 14 | Warsaw | 176 |
| 15 | The Crash | 189 |
| 16 | Picking up the Pieces | 195 |
|    | Index | 199 |

# Preface

This is the story of Ruth St Maur, illegitimate daughter of a half-gipsy kitchenmaid and a duke's eldest son, and of her son Bill, whose experiences in life have been neither ordinary nor dull.

Heredity and environment both influence our development. Which is the dominant factor varies from person to person, but perhaps distant ancestors affect the personality of their descendants more by tradition than by physical inheritance. Those whose forbears were of high distinction in one walk of life or another may believe they possess ancestral characteristics with which family history makes them familiar, whatever the genetic reality.

Ruth descended directly from the formidable Protector Somerset, from Richard Brinsley Sheridan and Georgiana, Queen of Beauty at the Eglinton Tournament, as well as from an untraceable line of humble Suffolk labourers and the mysterious, wandering Romany people. To this strikingly mixed ancestry Bill added the line of William Bentinck, William III's Dutch favourite, of Robert Harley, Earl of Oxford and Jacobite statesman, and of that notable matriarch, Bess of Hardwick. Of course, looking backwards, ancestors multiply by geometric progression and the famous are but a small handful of those from whom Ruth and Bill derived. All the same there is much in a name and a proud descent carries a conscious or subconscious influence. So it seems appropriate to trace briefly the story of the Seymours, the Sheridans and the Cavendish-Bentincks, for it was where these lines met and crossed that the two principal characters in this book emerged. I have tried, too, to give an account of the totally dissimilar environments in which mother and son were born and brought up.

All but one of the families described in separate chapters of this book have their history told in detail in great tomes lying dustily on the shelves of libraries and country houses. Ruth's brother,

Harold St Maur, wrote a massive work which unravelled with literary grace the intricate and often confusing story of the Seymours and the many branches that spread from the two wives of the Protector Somerset. In 1893 Lady Guendolen Ramsden and W. H. Mallock published the papers of the 12th Duke of Somerset, having already had many of the letters of Earl St Maur and his brother, Lord Edward, privately printed. The Cavendish-Bentincks are still more bewildering than the Seymours; but their later history has been succinctly told in A. S. Turberville's *History of Welbeck Abbey and Its Owners*. The Sheridans, less illustrious in origin but scarcely less notable in achievement, tend to concentrate attention on that bright star in the political and theatrical firmament, Richard Brinsley Sheridan, though his father, grandfather and three sparkling granddaughters all demand attention in their own right.

Family trees are confusing to all but dedicated genealogists. I have done my best to simplify their roots and branches, conscious that each provides material for a separate volume and that I offer impressionist sketches rather than full-scale paintings. My hope is that collectively they provide a background canvas against which the portraits of Ruth and Bill stand in relief.

For the account of the Eglinton Tournament I owe much to the admirable description of that costly anachronism written by Ian Anstruther in *The Knight and the Umbrella*.

I am deeply indebted to Brinsley Ford and Joseph Hoare for the loan of many hundreds of Ruth's expressive notes, letters and articles. Gainsborough's painting of Elizabeth Sheridan is reproduced by permission of the National Gallery of Art in Washington. I thank Mr Edward St Maur for the loan of photographs and original documents, the Duke of Northumberland for permission to reproduce the pictures of the Protector's two wives now hanging at Syon, and the Duke of Portland and Group Captain Brian Thynne for other photographic reproductions. Lady Christina Hoare drew the title page illustration; Mr A. T. Harrison of the Northern Irish Public Record Office kindly extracted letters relating to the three Sheridan 'graces' from the Dufferin papers in Belfast. Lord Hankey and Sir John Russell were good enough to vet the chapter on Warsaw; and it would be impossible to write accurately about Intelligence in the Second World War without reference to F. H. Hinsley's excellent official history.

Above all, I am indebted to the Duke of Portland for encouragement, information and wise counsel. I am grateful, also, to Mrs Anthony Berry for her patience in typing my untidy pencil manuscripts.

# 1
# The Seymours

The mists shrouding the legends and traditions of Europe in the dark centuries after the fall of the Roman Empire will never disperse. It is reasonable to suppose that many of those legends have a basis of fact, even if fact has been richly embroidered by the fancy of succeeding generations.

It is said that in the seventh century A.D. a fugitive Abyssinian prince, descended from King Solomon and the Queen of Sheba, took refuge as a hermit some twenty miles south of the river Loire. He was a man of piety and the local inhabitants called the village near his cell Saint Maure, since to them all Africans were Moors. It is today a fair-sized township on the road leading from Tours to Poitiers. The family which owned the village were known as de Saint Maure. It is possible, if improbable, that they were the offspring of the holy man, a possibility for which they later sought corroborative evidence in the fact that they sometimes had dark eyes and a swarthy complexion. They were even so presumptuous as to claim that with the blood of Solomon and the Queen of Sheba in their veins they were heirs to all the wit and wisdom of the world. Modesty was seldom a characteristic of the family.

Even before the year 1000 their name appears in surviving historic documents. One of them, Guillaume, settled in Normandy and in 1066 his son, Wido, accompanied William the Conqueror to England. He was handsomely rewarded, for the Conqueror cheerfully made free with the lands of the routed Anglo-Saxons. Thus in 1086 Wido's son held ten manors in what are now the counties of Somerset, Wiltshire and Gloucestershire.

The family prospered. A St Maure became master of the Knights Templar and another, Milo, was one of the barons who confronted King John with Magna Carta. They married with a consistent eye to the main chance. In the fifteenth century Roger de Saint Maure won the hand of an important heiress in

Somerset. His grandson, who anglicised his name to Seymour, inherited great estates and added to them a domain in Wiltshire called Wolf Hall.

When the Wars of the Roses ended, the Seymours, having prudently avoided affiliation with either the Red Rose of Lancaster or the White Rose of York, were in a strong position to win favour from the new Tudor dynasty. John, who succeeded to the family estates in 1492, wasted no time. He went with Henry VII to fight an army of Cornish rebels and so distinguished himself at the Battle of Blackheath that he was knighted on the field. He fought valiantly in France and Flanders. He was never out of royal favour and attended the meeting of Henry VIII and Francis I of France at the Field of the Cloth of Gold. In 1535 he received the signal, if expensive, honour of entertaining the King and his huge retinue at Wolf Hall for the best part of a week.

Sir John became still grander by marrying Margery Wentworth, a descendant both of Harry Percy, known as Hotspur, and of John of Gaunt, 'time-honoured Lancaster'. One of their sons, Edward, became the Protector of the Realm and first Duke of Somerset. Another, Lord Seymour of Sudeley, was Lord High Admiral of England and the husband of Henry VIII's widow, Catherine Parr. A daughter, Jane, was Queen of England and one of their grandchildren became a king.

In that generation the family's illustrious fortunes, and equally famous misfortunes, stemmed from Henry VIII's deep and sincere love for Jane Seymour, who was lady-in-waiting both to Catherine of Aragon and to Anne Boleyn.

The ambassador of the Emperor Charles V described her as 'of middle stature and no great beauty', but he did praise her for her intelligence which was matched by a high moral sense unusual at Henry VIII's court. When her father entertained the King at Wolf Hall, Henry, who had not hitherto taken much notice of her, was impressed by her intellectual gifts and her charm of manner. He began to single her out for attention at Court functions, much to the indignation of Queen Anne Boleyn.

In March 1536 the King sent Jane a purse full of sovereigns together with a letter containing dishonourable proposals. To his astonishment she returned the letter and the purse, asking the messenger who had brought them to tell the King there was no treasure she valued as much as her honour and on no account would she lose it, even if she were to die a thousand deaths. If the King wished to make her a present of money, let him reserve it for when she made a respectable marriage. This was not the kind of answer to which the King was accustomed, but he was unexpectedly pleased by her reply and his desire for the apparently unobtainable was not to be quenched. Anne Boleyn was an obstacle, but obstacles can be removed.

Jane was out of London when Anne Boleyn was arraigned for treason; but shortly afterwards she was lodged in a house on the Thames and there, on the very day Anne was condemned to death, the King visited her as a suitor, though not as a lover. She was summoned to Hampton Court and formally betrothed on the morrow of Anne Boleyn's execution. She then retired to Wolf Hall and when she was married, ten days later, she was still *virgo intacta*.

Dressed as a Queen, Jane, though excessively pale, improved in looks. Sir John Russell wrote that 'the richer Queen Jane was dressed, the fairer she appeared; on the contrary the better Anne Boleyn was apparelled the worse she looked'. Her good nature won affection, and in particular her maternal care of her stepdaughters. She reconciled the King to Mary, Catherine of Aragon's neglected child, and she cherished Anne's daughter, the two-year-old Princess Elizabeth. Moreover, intelligent though she was, she refrained from interfering in political or religious controversies.

In October 1537 Jane gave birth to a son at Hampton Court. She was delicate and the confinement weakened her. However, protocol demanded she should attend the christening of her little Edward, which took place by torchlight shortly after the birth and with all the ceremonies attached lasted till midnight. She caught a cold, fell seriously ill and, aged only twenty-eight, died twelve days after her son was born.

The King was grief-stricken, but at last he had a male heir. Jane was buried in St George's Chapel, Windsor, and in due course the coffin of Henry VIII was placed beside that of the only one of his six Queens whom he genuinely loved. It was alleged that at Hampton Court on the anniversary of Edward VI's birth Jane Seymour would be seen to ascend the stairs to her apartment, clad in flowing white garments with a lighted lamp in her hand.

Jane's untimely death did not diminish the standing of her family in the eyes of the King. One of her brothers, Thomas, acquired notoriety rather than fame. He was a swashbuckling brigand with limitless ambition. Indeed Bishop Latimer described him as 'a man furthest from the fear of God that I ever knew or heard of in England'. He made crude advances to Princess Elizabeth only a few weeks after her father's death. She snubbed him politely, saying that she must be in mourning for at least two years. He then tried his luck with Princess Mary and Anne of Cleves both of whom firmly said no; but he was nothing if not persistent and within two months of the King's death he succeeded in marrying, as her fourth husband, Henry VIII's last Queen, Catherine Parr, whom he made wretched by his continued advances to Princess Elizabeth. In September 1548 Catherine died in childbirth. Despite four marriages, she was still only thirty-six. Thereupon Thomas once again set his cap at Elizabeth who, from that fatal attraction women often feel for cads, did not discourage him as firmly as she should. The Council warned him off and his elder brother, by this time Protector of the Realm, tried to reason with him. Undeterred, he set about raising an army and stored large quantities of arms. In January 1549 he was arrested, attainted by Parliament and executed on Tower Hill. It must have been a disagreeable decision for the Protector to make about his brother, but no victim of the Tudors was more deserving of his fate.

Jane's eldest brother, Edward, had a far different personality. Born in 1506, he was knighted when he was only eighteen for gallant deeds in an army which penetrated deep into French territory and came within a few miles of Paris. He was also an expert at tilting, a sport in which Henry VIII delighted, so that when he was nineteen the King nominated him to accept challenges on the royal behalf.

In 1532 the King took Edward with him to France for a new meeting with Francis I. He was honoured with an expensive royal visit to his house in Hampshire. This, like the visit to his father at Wolf Hall, was regarded as a mark of special favour. The only cloud in the sky, and one which was to grow black fifteen years later, was an acrimonious dispute with John Dudley, the future Earl of Warwick and Duke of Northumberland, over the ownership of land in Somerset.

Thus, when his father, Sir John, died in 1536, Edward was already held in high repute. The curious chance of his demure sister Jane winning the love of the King transformed high repute into power. On marrying Jane the King made Edward a peer and gave him a number of manors to add to those he inherited. He was summoned to the Privy Council. At the christening of his nephew, the future Edward VI, he carried the infant Princess Elizabeth in his arms and was created Earl of Hertford. As senior uncle of the heir apparent, he was one of the greatest men in the land and the Seymours were as powerful a family as any in England.

A Knight of the Garter in 1541, chosen to reinforce the defences of Calais, a constant attender at the Council, Edward was deputed, with Archbishop Cranmer, to manage the Government's affairs when the King was away. Then in 1544 he was appointed Lieutenant General of the North with orders to punish the Scots for daring to make a treaty with France.

Hertford, as he now was, took his orders seriously. He who was always generous to his fellow Englishmen, and tolerant to an extent uncommon in those days, put the Scots in a different category. No Assyrian came down like a wolf on the fold with greater savagery than Hertford and his English army in Scotland. They stormed Leith and, blowing in the Canongate, captured Edinburgh apart from the castle, which was impregnable. They burned the city, destroying the Abbey and Holyrood. Hertford, asserting that he had punished the Scots for their 'detestable falsehood', was then recalled to accompany Henry to France where, partly by judicious bribery, Boulogne was seized. The French sent an army 14,000 strong to recapture it, but by a dawn sortie with 4,000 men and 700 horse Hertford routed the besiegers, who left their guns and stores behind in their flight. That was in January 1545. In the following July the French struck back, sending a large fleet to attack Portsmouth and invade the Isle of Wight. In full view of the King his great ship, the *Mary Rose*, capsized and sank with almost all her crew.

Hertford was away at that inglorious moment, preparing an army to seek further vengeance in Scotland where the angry lowlanders had soundly defeated the Earl of Shrewsbury. This time the reckoning was even harsher than in the previous year. Hertford marched through Jedburgh and Kelso, and in the course of a three weeks' campaign his troops sacked and burned market towns and 243 villages. The ruins of the border abbeys at Jedburgh and Kelso, Melrose and Dryburgh still bear witness to that September affray of 1545.

Meanwhile the Duke of Norfolk's son, Lord Surrey, who was a better poet than general, allowed the French to drive a wedge between the English garrisons in Calais and Boulogne. Surrey had been in trouble a few years before for breaking windows in the City and potting at peaceful citizens with a catapult. He was summoned before the Council, sternly admonished by Hertford and temporarily incarcerated in the Fleet Prison. Thereafter he disliked Hertford heartily, and his feelings were shared by his father, the Duke of Norfolk. Hertford went back to France to repair the damage Surrey had caused and reopened communications between Calais and Boulogne.

Returning to Windsor in the summer of 1546, he was leader of the Protestant faction. This brought him into still more bitter opposition to the Duke of Norfolk and Lord Surrey. The King veered this way and that on religious matters but by the time he died, in January 1547, he had inclined to the Protestant party. The Howards lost favour and Surrey lost his head. Norfolk was saved from the same fate by the King's death; nor did Hertford, when the power was his, pursue a vendetta against him.

With Henry dead, the new King's uncle was the foremost man in the kingdom. Edward VI was only nine. The Council appointed Hertford Protector and he was made High Steward of England, Treasurer of the Exchequer and Earl Marshal. He was elected Chancellor of Cambridge University and created Duke of Somerset.

The Protector had supreme power, but his lot was not to be envied. The country was in disarray, with a debased coinage, acute religious antagonisms, a young and unhealthy King, avaricious nobles, hordes of unemployed vagrants and loud murmurs of war from both France and Scotland. He was a proud man, as his ancestors had been and his descendants were also to be. His pride sometimes bordered on arrogance, and he could be ill-tempered; but he had an unshakeable determination to do his best for the people of whatever standing they might be, a revulsion from personal violence (except, it seems, where the Scots were concerned) and a desire to allow as much freedom as was safe and practicable. In modern terms he was a liberal.

His first preoccupation was to resolve the religious dispute. He pronounced that the new Prayer Book and the Bible should be used in English translation. He allowed priests to marry, an innovation the value of which is proved by the high proportion of sons of the clergy whose names now appear in the *Dictionary of National Biography*. He provided for Communion to be taken in both kinds. Withal he was moderate in the promotion of his policy and tolerant of disagreement, allowing the devoutly Catholic Princess Mary to retain her Latin rite. There were no executions during his Protectorate and the fires which had burned at Smithfield in King Henry's time, and were soon to burn with redoubled fury under Queen Mary, were never lit while Somerset was Protector.

He dreamed of uniting England and Scotland by the marriage of his nephew, Edward VI, to the seven-year-old Mary, Queen of Scots. Their ages matched and they were but first cousins once removed. He spoke, a hundred and fifty years before it happened, of a single Kingdom of Great Britain, 'having the sea for a wall and mutual love for defence', with Scotland retaining its autonomy and free trade between the two countries.

It was not to be. Shortly after Henry VIII died, Francis I of France was succeeded by his bellicose son, Henry II, who declared his intention to regain Boulogne, marry his eldest son to Mary, Queen of Scots, and fight for Scotland. The Protector at once set sail for Newcastle with 18,000 men and 60 ships. He arrived too late. The little Queen had been carried off to Stirling. At Pinkie Cleugh, near Musselburgh, he was confronted by a Franco-Scottish army which he totally defeated, losing only 200 men against 10,000 casualties by his opponents. Then, proud though he might be, he set about fortifying Roxburgh and himself worked by hand for two hours each day in order to encourage his men. However, in the spring of 1548 the French spirited Mary, Queen of Scots away to France and married her to the King's son, the unprepossessing Dauphin.

Back in London, where news of the battle of Pinkie Cleugh had caused great rejoicing, the citizens gave Somerset a triumphant reception. He had no difficulty in persuading Parliament to reduce the severity both of the treason laws and of those suppressing heresy. He ordained that all religious works, whether Protestant or Catholic, might be freely printed and he encouraged open debate in Parliament, insisting that members should not be molested if they made proposals inconvenient to the Government.

The enclosure of common land was his gravest problem. It was encouraged by the landowners, who found pasture more profitable than arable land: it made good economic sense, but it brought unemployment. Somerset was determined to halt it. When the Council declined to support him, he issued an arbitrary proclamation forbidding further enclosures. He despatched Commissioners to enforce the decision. Joyfully welcomed by the people, they met strong antagonism from the landed interest and Parliament rejected an anti-enclosure bill which Somerset laid before them. Thereupon, there were uprisings by the disappointed peasantry and small farmers all over the country.

By the summer of 1549 he was losing control of the Council which insisted on prohibiting the Mass and voted for a radically Protestant prayer book. He failed to stop a new enclosure Commission organised to suit the landed gentry; and when the people took violent action he told the angry Council that 'he liked well the doings of the people. The covetousness of the gentlemen gave occasion to them to rise; it were better they should die than perish for lack of living.' Despite the Council, Somerset on his sole authority proclaimed that all illegal enclosures should be levelled to the ground and a free pardon given to those who had rioted. At this the lords and gentry armed their retainers and assaulted the would-be levellers. There was bloodshed and Somerset's influence with his colleagues plummeted. As Professor Pollard has written, the Council 'prepared to remove not the disease but the physician'. With the Earl of Warwick in the lead the hounds were unleashed.

Warwick was that John Dudley with whom the Protector had quarrelled over land in Somerset. It may be doubted whether any age has been marked by greater corruption and less scruple, more cruelty and less charity, than the century of the Renaissance, of the revised Classical culture and the new Enlightenment. Man has seldom been viler than in the generation of Copernicus and Galileo, Luther and Calvin, Holbein, Velasquez and Titian; but few, even then, were as cruel, corrupt and unscrupulous as John Dudley, Earl of Warwick and for two ignoble years Duke of Northumberland.

Because Somerset declined to use the forces at his disposal in Civil War, Warwick prevailed. He drew up a long list of charges, which were mainly inventions, and cajoled the young King, now almost twelve, into ordering his uncle's arrest and incarceration in the Tower. Religious persecution became the order of the day. Unfavourable peace treaties were made with France and Scotland. Boulogne was surrendered. Corruption flourished in the Law Courts, and the coinage, which Somerset had tried to restore to some degree of purity, was abjectly debased. Church plate was seized, enclosures flourished and the poor were reduced to despair.

Somerset sat in the Tower, studying moral philosophy and divinity and writing the preface to a book extolling patience. The time for sterner measures was not yet ripe. He was, after all, the King's uncle and his popularity with the people was undoubted. So a bill was laid before Parliament confirming his right to his property and it seemed that he would be allowed to retire in peace. Released from the Tower, he went to Syon, the splendid house he had created on the Thames. He was given a full royal pardon and was invited to dine with the King and Council at Greenwich. He was re-sworn of the Privy Council and restored to rank as its senior member. The House of Commons thought of petitioning for his reinstatement as Lord Protector.

Warwick took fright. He arranged for false tales to be whispered to the sickly but precocious King, who was gradually induced to believe them. Unfortunately the Lord Chancellor, who wanted Somerset restored as Protector, wrote him a letter detailing Warwick's intrigues. This letter was simply addressed 'To the Duke', and a servant delivered it in error to the only other Duke, Norfolk. It was at once shown to Warwick.

In making drastic religious innovations the new majority on the Council decided to remove Princess Mary's priests and compel her to use the new English service. Somerset alone took her part and at the same time urged general toleration. At this point Warwick, newly created Duke of Northumberland, found an accomplice in Sir Thomas Palmer, a false and venal man. Palmer alleged that in the preceding April Somerset had plotted a rebellion. He declared that the plan had been to seize the Tower, raise the City, incite the apprentices, carry off the Great Seal and have Warwick murdered at a banquet.

Months later when Northumberland himself was on trial, he admitted the evidence to be false and Palmer confessed that he had told the story at his behest. At the time, however, this outrageous falsehood was believed. Somerset was arrested and committed to the Tower with his wife and many of his supporters.

He was tried in Westminster Hall, being taken from the Tower at 5 a.m. to avoid a popular demonstration. But a crowd assembled at Westminster, all devoted to Somerset, all shouting abuse at Northumberland. Of a total of forty-seven temporal peers only twenty-six were summoned, those thought to be favourable to Somerset being excluded. The Lords decided there was no case for treason and he was therefore tried for felony. Obedient to Northumberland, the Lords found him guilty and condemned him to death. He had risen high in his forty-five years; his fall was precipitous. His dukedom was attainted; his lands were confiscated.

It was important to influence the King's mind against his uncle and to ensure that he was beheaded before Parliament met; for the House of Commons was unshakeable in its support of him. An order to the Council, written in the King's own hand, directing them to consider what action should be taken with regard to Somerset's confederates, was so amended by Northumberland as to include the Duke himself and to insert words which the King had not written, namely 'execution according to the laws'. An order for the examination of Somerset's confederates was thus changed into one for his execution.

The people of London disregarded instructions to stay at home on the day. A thousand armed men were brought to surround the scaffold, but the people came too, drawn for once by affection and sympathy rather than by the sadistic pleasure which normally ensured a large attendance at executions. The Duke, attired in his finest apparel, mounted the scaffold shortly before eight o'clock on the morning of 22 January 1552, the day before Parliament was due to meet. After kneeling in prayer he spoke in a clear and even voice, saying: 'I am condemned by a law whereunto I am subject, as are we all, and therefore to show obedience I am content to die.' He asked the people to pray for the King and did not say a word in condemnation of his judges. He knelt, laid his head on the block, said three times 'Lord Jesus save me'; and the axe fell. As for the ailing, adolescent King, great pains were taken to divert him and he was left no time to consider his uncle's plight. All he wrote in his journal on 22 January was: 'The Duke of Somerset had his head cut off upon Tower Hill between 8 and 9 o'clock in the morning.'

Those who did grieve for the Duke were the King's half-sisters, Mary and Elizabeth, both of whom made some effort to recompense his heirs.

It was Somerset's two marriages that were of special significance to the future of the Seymour family. His first wife, Catherine Fillol, daughter of an undistinguished knight, bore him two sons of whom only the younger, Edward, won his father's affection. On Catherine's death, he married a scheming woman called Anne Stanhope by whom he had nine more children. Anne persuaded her husband to make her children rather than Catherine's his heirs and contrived to have this arrangement confirmed by Act of Parliament. However, Somerset did insist on inserting a clause stating that if his line by Anne Stanhope should ever be extinguished, then the descendants of Catherine Fillol's younger son, Edward, should succeed. No doubt Edward VI, who had been only two when this Act of Parliament was passed, felt that Catherine's sons had been unfairly treated, for he later took pains to restore to them an extensive property at Maiden Bradley in Wiltshire which Henry VIII had bestowed on their father, and which is the home of the Duke of Somerset to this day.

Anne Stanhope's descendants had vivid careers. They also had an unfortunate propensity for becoming entangled in sensitive dynastic matters. Her eldest son, confusingly christened Edward like Catherine Fillol's child, was created Earl of Hertford by Queen Elizabeth; but he secretly married Lady Catherine Grey who was, by Henry VIII's will, next in succession to the Queen. Lady Catherine was soon pregnant and she ill-advisedly confided in Bess of Hardwick, that remarkable collector of rich husbands, who at once sneaked to Elizabeth. The loving couple were incarcerated in the Tower of London where two sons were born. When they were let out the Queen insisted they be separated and Lady Catherine died of a broken heart. Her little dog went to lie on her grave and did the same.

Hertford's grandson, William, was equally rash. He married against royal command another potential heiress to the throne, Lady Arabella Stewart, ten years his senior, painfully plain but notably intelligent. James I had them both clapped in the Tower. They escaped in disguise, but though William reached the Continent safely, Lady Arabella was caught in the Straits of Dover and sent back to the Tower where she died in frustrated misery.

William, however, became in due course one of Charles I's most loyal and successful generals in the Civil War.

When the Royalist cause collapsed and the King was taken prisoner, William and three fellow noblemen offered to stand trial in the King's stead. The offer was declined, but after Charles was beheaded they were allowed to take his body to Windsor for burial. They found St George's Chapel unrecognisable. Cromwell's troops had defaced the monuments and turned the Chapel into a stable. One of the mournful noblemen, striking the pavement with his staff, deduced from the hollow sound that there was a vault beneath. It was, by chance, that in which the coffins of Henry VIII and Jane Seymour lay. Alongside them they placed that of the decapitated Charles I, only to be disturbed when years later George IV authorised the opening of the vault and coffin to ensure that the King's head was there. It was.

William had won such a reputation that he was considerately treated, 'delinquent' though Parliament had pronounced him. Oliver Cromwell even invited him to dine. Having already spent enormous sums in supporting Charles I during the Civil War, he now regularly sent the exiled Charles II £5,000 a year, which was a huge sum in the 1650s.

When the Restoration took place, he was of course in high favour. He met the King at Dover and was made a Knight of the Garter. In September of that year, 1660, an Act of Parliament restored to him the dukedom of Somerset removed from his great-grandfather by Northumberland. Charles, in giving the royal assent, said that 'as this was an Act of an extraordinary nature, so it was done for an extraordinary person who had merited as much of his royal father and himself as any subject could do, and he therefore hoped no man would envy it'. He was styled the 2nd Duke of Somerset.

Six weeks later he died, having seen all that he had striven for achieved. His immediate successors were of no significance, but as his grandson died unmarried, most of the Somerset estates devolved upon the young man's sister, married to the Earl of Ailesbury. Amongst other Seymour properties Savernake Forest left the family for ever.

The dukedom descended to a penniless great-nephew who was shot while on holiday in Genoa by an irate Italian whose wife had been insulted by some of the Duke's French travelling companions.

This crime brought great advantage to the victim's younger brother, Charles. Equally impoverished, he had what was described as 'an expressive countenance'. He was selected by the old Countess of Northumberland as a suitable match for her red-headed granddaughter, Lady Elizabeth Percy, sole heiress to the immense fortune left by her father, the last Earl of Northumberland. She had been an orphan since she was four and at fourteen she had been married three times. Her first husband was the thirteen-year-old Earl of Ogle, who was heir to one of Bess of Hardwick's Cavendish descendants, the Duke of Newcastle. He died shortly after the unconsummated marriage. Her next husband, Thomas Thynne of Longleat, was murdered in Pall Mall when she was fourteen.

Her grandmother, undaunted by these setbacks, then married Lady Elizabeth off to Charles, the new Duke of Somerset. She brought him all the estates of the House of Percy in Northumberland, including Alnwick Castle, as well as Syon, Petworth and Northampton House at Charing Cross, soon renamed Northumberland House. It stood, until the 1870s, where Northumberland Avenue now joins Trafalgar Square. The impoverishment of the Seymours was a thing of the past; and though taking the surname of Percy had been part of the arrangement, Charles and Lady Elizabeth agreed that Seymour was just as good.

The Seymours were notorious for their pride, though a few of them were capable of humility. Charles outstripped all other members of the family and went down to history as 'The Proud Duke'. The vast access of wealth his wife brought him went to his head and stayed there all his life. His arrogance knew no bounds and he was the embodiment of all uncharitableness. His redeeming quality was political courage, for when they displeased him he confronted, and even insulted, James II, William III, Queen Anne and George I without hesitation. It was either courage or unassailable self-confidence. He was undoubtedly one of the least attractive noblemen of all times.

When he died in 1748, in affluent and self-satisfied tranquillity at Petworth, he was succeeded by his son Algernon, whose promising military and diplomatic career had been disrupted by gout. Algernon's heir had died of smallpox in Bologna on his nineteenth birthday – to the loudly expressed indignation of his grandfather, the Proud Duke; and so as soon as Algernon succeeded he busied himself with disposing of the family possessions.

He persuaded George II to make him Earl of Egremont with special remainder to his nephew, Charles Wyndham, to whom he left his palatial house and estate at Petworth. A greater problem was the name and the remaining property of the Percys, which included large tracts in Northumberland, Syon on the Thames and Northumberland House at Charing Cross. His obliging sovereign agreed to create him Earl of Northumberland as well as Earl of Egremont, and to decree that on his death the Northumberland title should descend to Sir Hugh Smithson, a baronet from Yorkshire of no particular distinction who had married his daughter, Lady Elizabeth Seymour.

Algernon died in 1750, having survived his unpleasant father by only two years. On his death the male line of the Protector and Anne Stanhope expired, unequalled in wealth but no longer steeped in glory. The Smithsons changed their name to Percy and a few years later Sir Hugh was created Duke of Northumberland, a title which must have made the Protector turn in his grave. Nevertheless he and Lady Elizabeth Seymour founded a new line of Percys which has been notable in succeeding centuries for continuity of intelligence and devotion to public service. Meanwhile the dukedom of Somerset reverted to the heirs of Edward, son of Catherine Fillol. At long last primogeniture triumphed, at least as far as the title was concerned.

Algernon had given no thought to his successor in the dukedom and thus for the second time in a century most of the Seymour estates were alienated. However, Maiden Bradley and the 15,000 Wiltshire acres surrounding it, which Edward VI had restored to Catherine Fillol's sons, had never belonged to the younger branch of the family; nor had Berry Pomeroy in Devonshire. They were the property of the new 8th Duke of Somerset, whose forbears were less bedecked with glamour, drama and melodrama than their cousins of the younger branch. Indeed, with one exception, they had made no impact on public affairs. They were, with monotonous regularity, called Edward.

The grandson of the Protector and Catherine Fillol was made a baronet by James I, who, starved of funds by grudging Parliaments, found the sale of this new form of hereditary knighthood a useful contribution to his exchequer. Edward Seymour was one of the eager takers; but he must have been a little naive, for he apparently did not realise he was expected to pay for the honour until he received a bill for £1,095, nominally to defray the costs of maintaining thirty men for three years' military service in Ireland.

His successor was an incorrigible buccaneer who, among other dastardly exploits, seized and sold goods from a French merchantman, captured an Irish barque and plundered another French vessel which, in his capacity as Governor of Dartmouth, he had brought under duress into an English port. He even owned a piratical man-of-war which he named *The Reformation*. But these activities did not deter him from diligent performance of his duties as a justice of the peace, Deputy Lieutenant of Devonshire and Member of Parliament for Totnes. When the Civil War broke out, he loyally set off with his son to fight for the King, and had the misfortune to be taken prisoner by a squadron of Parliamentary horse. He was only held captive for a few weeks, but when he returned to his castle at Berry Pomeroy, to the embellishment of which he had devoted his privateering gains, he found to his dudgeon that it had been occupied by another body of Parliamentary horse and the entire contents sold for £89.12s.6d.

He had ten children, for the Seymours were nothing if not fertile; and it was his eldest grandson, Sir Edward Seymour, 4th baronet, who won the only renown that can be claimed for any of Catherine Fillol's descendants before the nineteenth century. At the age of twenty-seven, this Sir Edward, who was tall and handsome (though also described by Pepys as 'proud and saucy'), entered the House of Commons and served there for forty-eight years. He was the first man not trained as a lawyer ever to be chosen as Speaker.

Greater in ability, marginally less unpleasant, but almost equal in pride to his cousin and near contemporary, the Proud Duke, he has one lasting claim to be remembered. Together with Lord Shaftesbury he was responsible for the Habeas Corpus Act of 1679 which is the linchpin of freedom from arbitrary imprisonment. He strongly opposed James II's desire to create a standing army, and in a speech of notable courage, heard in silence by a subservient and corruptly elected House of Commons, Sir Edward declared that 'it is a matter of vulgar notoriety, it is a matter which requires no proof, that the Test Act, the rampart of religion, and the Habeas Corpus Act, the rampart of liberty, are marked out for destruction.'

Disillusioned by James II, whose loyal supporter he had once been, he was prominent among those who turned their eyes towards William, Prince of Orange, and prayed for a Protestant wind to blow. In 1688 he went to meet William at Exeter. The Prince's attempt to be gracious was not a success. 'I think,' he said, 'you are of the family of the Duke of Somerset?' Seymour, who never forgot his was the elder branch of the family, replied: 'Sir, the Duke of Somerset is of *my* family.'

Few were so scrupulously honest in that corrupt age. He was public-spirited too. The country's finances being in a lamentable state, he lent £10,000 out of his own pocket to the Treasury. As a stern Tory he opposed King William's Whig Government and he shared with his cousin, the Proud Duke, a strong antipathy to the Dutch favourites, in particular William Bentinck, Earl of Portland.

Queen Anne favoured the Tories and when she came to the throne Seymour, by then an elder statesman of great repute, was given office. He refused a peerage for himself, but accepted a barony for one of his younger sons, who became Lord Conway and was father of the 1st Marquess of Hertford. However, he overdid his opposition to the Whig faction, which soon regained some influence, and in 1704 the Queen felt obliged to dismiss him. With his haughtiness undiminished, he sent word that he would return his staff of office by the common carrier.

In 1708 he died in a splendid new house he had built at Maiden Bradley, his death accelerated by an assault from a lady who forced her way into his study while his household were disporting themselves at a neighbouring fair. He had two wives, to whom he was faithful, and nine children, to whom he was dutiful if rarely amiable. Austere, often morose, he can seldom have allowed laughter to echo in the corridors. It is, however, to his credit that in an age when office was normally accompanied by large financial gain, he left at his death an estate scarcely more valuable than that he had inherited. Nor did he ever demand repayment of his loan of £10,000 to the Treasury.

His totally undistinguished eldest son, the 5th baronet, chose to live quietly at Maiden Bradley, though he was as a matter of course elected Member of Parliament for Totnes. He had twelve children, of whom the eldest was as undistinguished as his father. On succeeding as 6th baronet, he did feel obliged to become a Member of Parliament and was duly elected for Salisbury. However, his wife, Mary Webb, a Wiltshire heiress, died shortly after his election and, deeply grieved, he retired from the parliamentary scene. On the death of the Proud Duke's only grandson, it was evident that he was the ultimate heir and it was suggested that he might unite the two branches of the family, and retain some of the vast Seymour estates, by marrying one of Duke Algernon's daughters. He did not pursue the suggestion; nor did Duke Algernon.

In February 1750, when Algernon died, his unambitious heir was on his way to London. He had stopped to dine at an inn and was playing chess in the parlour. The innkeeper came in and told him the news. He finished the game without any comment, but he went on to London, proved his claim to the peerage and took his seat in the House of Lords. There were two things in which he differed from other dukes. Though second only to Norfolk in precedence, his sole title apart from Duke of Somerset was Lord Seymour, all the marquessates, earldoms and viscounties having become extinct. Secondly, by ducal standards he was remarkably poor. Some minor offices did indeed come his way and he was made a Knight of the Garter as well as Lord Lieutenant of Wiltshire. When he died, he left four impecunious sons of whom the youngest, Lord Francis, became Dean of Wells and is the ancestor of the present duke.

The two elder sons followed each other as 9th and 10th duke in rapid succession. The first, disappointed in love, developed a phobia about smallpox, refusing ever to touch a letter, but ordering a servant to hold it up outside a window through which he would read it. Secluded at Maiden Bradley, where he lived frugally, he did at least do something to accumulate the income from his estates, and George III, horrified that the second duke in his kingdom should be so impoverished, gave him a pension of £1,200 a year.

On his death in 1792 the next brother inherited, but died a year later having married the heiress to lands in Oxfordshire and, like his own father, produced four sons. The first two died young; the fourth, highly acclaimed in academic circles as a geologist and moral philosopher, never married; but the third was Edward Adolphus, 11th Duke of Somerset.

This admirable man had scholarly tastes. At Christ Church, Oxford he showed an aptitude for science and mathematics and, like his younger brother, won enough reputation as a geologist to be elected a Fellow of the Royal Society. He also wrote learned treatises on such abstruse subjects as the properties of the ellipse. Oxford thought him worthy of a D.C.L., the Society of Antiquaries made him a Fellow and he was President of the Royal Institution. University College, London, asked him to be their Vice-President and the Linnaean Society to be their President. The Seymours, so long immersed in politics, rose to eminence in the academic field.

He had a long face, a high forehead and a benign smile. He campaigned vigorously for free universal education, long before it was widely supported, and for other liberal causes. All the same he was no laggard when it came to extending his territorial possessions. His mother's estate in Oxfordshire and his grandmother's in Wiltshire had been added to Maiden Bradley and Berry Pomeroy. His minority and the inexpensive stewardship of his two predecessors had improved the family fortunes. His own marriage to Lady Charlotte Douglas-Hamilton brought him substantial possessions from her father, the Duke of Hamilton, including a magnificent collection of pictures. So he spread his wings. In 1810 he bought from the Duke of Portland Bulstrode Park, a long low house of classical design in a park of 800 acres near Gerrards Cross. In due course he replaced it with a vast and ugly mansion 'in the Tudor style', which his son made uglier still.

Good architectural taste was not included among his excellent qualities. He demolished two-thirds of the elegant house at Maiden Bradley which his ancestor, the Speaker, had built in the reign of William and Mary, leaving only one wing as a resort for hunting and shooting and a centre from which to administer the property. Two years later, in 1823, he bought Stover, an eighteenth-century house in Devonshire, near Newton Abbot. Luckily he did not rebuild it, and he and his wife hung the Hamilton pictures there. They, as well as Bulstrode and Stover, provided indigestible bones of family contention in the next generation.

There were few eighteenth and nineteenth-century dukes who were under-housed. Most of them had five or six houses at least. Now, though Petworth and Syon had been alienated and he owned no Chatsworth or Woburn, no Arundel or Blenheim, Somerset had made some strides towards equality with his peers. His liberal convictions helped, for, unlike most landed proprietors, he was sufficiently distressed by the plight of the starving Irish peasantry to give energetic support to the repeal of the Corn Laws. During the agricultural depression which followed, he acquired land in Lincolnshire, Cambridgeshire and Norfolk.

Wimbledon, although as yet scarcely suburban, was conveniently close to London and he bought Wimbledon Park from Lord Spencer. This meant that he had five large houses. However, the second senior duke must also have a suitably fine house in London. So, as a sixth residence he purchased 40 Park Lane and renamed it Somerset House. This was a shade presumptuous of him, for there was another more splendid establishment bearing the name between the Strand and the Thames. The original palace had been started by the Protector Somerset in 1549, but before it was completed he lost his head. It never returned to the Seymours, and in the eighteenth century it was replaced by the magnificent set of Government offices that today hold the wills and birth certificates of the British people. There were also domiciled in this new building the Fine Rooms of the Royal Academy and of two institutions to which Edward Adolphus belonged, the Royal Society and the Society of Antiquaries. It may therefore be judged that he went a little too far when he also called 40 Park Lane Somerset House.

An efficient and conscientious landlord, and a speaker in the House of Lords on social and educational matters, he was more attached to his scientific studies than to public affairs. However, he carried the orb at the Coronations of William IV and Queen Victoria, and he was made a Knight of the Garter. He was twice married. By Lady Charlotte Douglas-Hamilton he had four sons and four daughters. It was the heyday of the Gothic Revival and the Romantic Movement when everything that was medieval was venerated, when turreted and battlemented castles grew like mushrooms and sham ruins were built in the parks of country houses. So, in keeping with the times, the family name reverted from Seymour to the medieval St Maur, though the eldest son was still Lord Seymour. It was also a period in which plain Christian names were at a discount. Thus the Somersets christened three of their sons Adolphus, Archibald and Algernon.

The eldest son, invariably called Seymour, was the favourite grandchild of the old Duke of Hamilton and was criticised in his youth for indolence. However, he was a deep thinker and after spending five years abroad, including a lengthy visit to Russia, he returned home with his horizons broadened and a firm belief in the educational value of foreign travel. In June 1830, at the age of twenty-five, he married Jane Georgiana, youngest and most beautiful of the three granddaughters of Richard Brinsley Sheridan. The duchess had died three years earlier, but in those caste-conscious days there were some of Lord Seymour's relations, including the Douglas-Hamiltons, who thought marriage to a Sheridan a *mésalliance*. They had no premonition of the far more startling *mésalliance* to come in the next generation.

# 2
# *The Sheridans*

The Sheridans with their vivid Celtic imagination claimed descent from one Ostar O'Sheridan, said to have been a mighty chieftain in the eleventh century whose offspring married into almost every princely and noble house in Ireland. This is as unlikely as the claim of the Seymours to descend from King Solomon and the Queen of Sheba.

In sober fact the first Sheridan to emerge into historic daylight was the Revd Dennis, a Church of Ireland clergyman who lived during the first half of the seventeenth century. He profited from the decree issued by the Protector Somerset some eighty years earlier allowing priests of the Established Church to renounce celibacy. Taking advantage of this agreeable dispensation, he married a Scottish servant girl from Inverness-shire, whose father, Murdoch MacIain, was a shepherd of the Macpherson clan reputed to have slain the malign witch of Laggan. He had a living in the diocese of Kilmore, Co Cavan, bestowed on him by the scholarly Bishop Bedell whom Sheridan recompensed by helping to translate the Bible into Erse.

The Revd Dennis sired four sons of whom three won some distinction in their lifetime and the fourth by his descendants. The eldest, William, became Bishop of Kilmore, as his father's friend and benefactor had been. Though not an active Jacobite he refused to take an oath of allegiance to William of Orange. As a result he lost both his episcopal see and the family house at Quilca in Cavan. The second son, Patrick, was Bishop of Cloyne, near Cork. The third, Thomas, was an unwavering supporter of James II whom he accompanied into exile as his private secretary. Thomas's son became tutor to Bonnie Prince Charlie, went with him to Scotland in 1745 and after the Battle of Culloden escaped in a French man-of-war.

James was the fourth and youngest son. His principal, indeed only, claim to be remembered is that he produced a son, called

Thomas like his Jacobite uncle, who himself had an unusual career and was the grandfather of Richard Brinsley Sheridan. Born in 1687, the year before James II fled into exile, this younger Thomas was educated at Trinity College, Dublin, thanks to some avuncular assistance in paying the fees. He was a splendid character, witty, good-natured and brim-full of Irish blarney. In his chosen career as a schoolmaster he was too idle to be more than intermittently successful, but he made up for it in other ways.

Shortly after leaving Trinity College, he had the bright idea of marrying Elizabeth MacFadden, whose father, a Protestant of impeccable record, had acquired Quilca in recognition of his services to William of Orange after Thomas's uncle had been dispossessed on account of his Jacobite leanings. So the house and small property surrounding it returned to the Sheridans, Elizabeth being her father's heir.

Thomas moved to Dublin and established a select school for the sons of the gentry which, for a time, provided him with a steady income. In 1713 he met the Dean of St Patrick's Cathedral, Jonathan Swift. They became friends and then inseparable companions. The Dean would spend months at Quilca and it was there that he wrote part of *Gulliver's Travels*. He returned this hospitality by acting as temporary headmaster of Thomas Sheridan's school when Thomas was ill, and he persuaded the Lord Lieutenant of Ireland both to make Thomas one of his chaplains and to appoint him to a living in Co Cork.

Unfortunately, just before he was inducted to the living, Thomas preached in Cork a sermon on the text 'Sufficient unto the day is the evil thereof', which was one of his normally successful repertory of sermons. It happened to be the anniversary of Queen Anne's death and he may well have made some remarks from the pulpit which were thought unseemly for such a solemn occasion. When the episode was related to the Lord Lieutenant, with the comment that the preacher was suspected of being a Jacobite (as any friend of Swift might well be), his name was struck off the list of Viceregal chaplains and he lost his chance of the living. The Archdeacon of Cork thought this unfair and, in compensation, presented him with a manor near his home in Co Cavan which produced an annual income of £250. In the following year Thomas became a Doctor of Divinity.

His school lost its following, doubtless because of inattention by the headmaster, and after one more short and unsuccessful educational enterprise near his home, he settled himself at Swift's deanery in Dublin. Many years before he had promised to tell Swift if he ever showed signs of avarice. In fact Swift often did, and Sheridan, ill-advisedly true to his undertaking, made a list of examples. His host was furious and he was turned out of the Deanery. He died shortly afterwards, leaving a number of creditable translations from the classics (for he was no mean scholar) and a book, which was never published, of jests, witticisms and madrigals in keeping with his light-hearted approach to life. He also wrote a much-applauded treatise on the Art of Punning. His epitaph was the one he wrote himself: 'I am famous for giving the best advice and following the worst.'

By his long-suffering wife, Elizabeth, he had three sons, of whom the youngest was called Thomas after his father and was Swift's godson. He went to Westminster School as a King's scholar, but soon returned to Dublin because his family could not afford the additional cost of his living in London. Though short of funds his father was never short of friends, and these had enough influence at Trinity College to arrange for the boy to be 'chosen of the foundation' when he was sixteen. He was elected a scholar in the year his father died.

The elder Thomas, undeterred by his own limitations as a pedagogue, wanted his son to follow in his footsteps. The son had different ideas. As an undergraduate he had written a farce with the promising title of *Captain O'Blunder, or, The Brave Irishman*, and shortly afterwards he was so well received as Shakespeare's Richard III at the Theatre Royal in Dublin that he was invited to appear at Drury Lane in London. The stage, not schoolmastering, became his chosen career.

Back in Dublin from Drury Lane, he became manager of the Theatre Royal. It had a sordid reputation and he took steps to improve matters. This, in the best Irish tradition of improbability, led both to a riot and to true love. One evening in 1745, a drunken member of the audience from Galway, called Kelly, insulted the actresses in a coarse manner not uncommon at the Theatre Royal. He was publicly reprimanded by Thomas Sheridan. Kelly vowed vengeance, the audience took sides and a violent riot ensued. A young lady called Frances Chamberlaine was so impressed by Sheridan's courage and demeanour that she wrote some verses and a pamphlet in his honour. Touched by this, Sheridan sought her acquaintance, fell in love and married her.

Frances Chamberlaine was a lady who won distinction in her own right. Her father, a prebendary and archdeacon, disapproved of girls being taught to read and write, which he thought unnecessary accomplishments for women; but her elder brother, also in holy orders, disagreed and gave her surreptitious lessons. These were so successful that by the age of fifteen she had written a romance in two volumes which was published many years later.

Having married young Thomas Sheridan she gave birth to two daughters and two sons, of whom the second was christened Richard Brinsley. These preoccupations in no way hindered her career as a writer of plays and novels. Her novels won acclaim from such discriminating readers as Samuel Richardson, the author of *Clarissa*, and Charles James Fox; and David Garrick himself acted in one of her plays. Her best conceived novel, *The Memoirs of Miss Sidney Biddulph,* was greeted with enthusiasm and translated into German and French. A character in one of her less successful plays, called Mrs Twyfort, was the inspiration of a more notable personage invented by her younger son, Mrs Malaprop.

Thomas moved restlessly between London and Dublin, praised for his acting at Covent Garden, which was then a theatre rather than an opera house, and finally deciding to settle in England. He developed a passion for elocution, on which he lectured tirelessly, and his small house in Henrietta Street, near Covent Garden market, became the resort of eminent politicians and intellectuals. His brief period of glory as an actor led to his being given the Freedom of the City of Edinburgh. One of his friends was Dr Johnson, for whom he managed to procure, by Lord Bute's intervention, a pension of £300 a year. However, Samuel Johnson was less grateful than he should have been, for when Sheridan began to work on a dictionary of pronunciation, as a result of which he himself was given a small pension, the Doctor, presumably determined that dictionaries of any kind should be his personal monopoly, took umbrage. 'Why, sir,' he said to Boswell, 'Sherry is dull, naturally dull; but it must have taken him a great deal of pains to become what we now see him. Such an excess of stupidity is not in nature.' Clearly Sherry was not dull; but to incur Dr Johnson's wrath was unfortunate. His witty and frequently ungenerous comments were conscientiously immortalised by Boswell.

In 1764 Thomas and Frances Sheridan set off for Blois to economise or, as Thomas put it, to 'bid defiance to my merciless creditors'. His younger son, Richard, was at Harrow, but the rest of the family accompanied their parents. While they were there, Frances Sheridan died and her unhappy husband, retracing his steps to London, Bath and Dublin, took occasional parts on the stage, taught elocution at Bath and eked out a decreasingly prosperous living by giving public readings. When he died in 1788, his already renowned but seldom solvent son Richard paid all the expenses of his illness and funeral.

Thomas's elder son, Charles, was an undistinguished member of the Irish House of Commons for twenty-five years and an equally undistinguished author. At the end of his life he became absorbed in efforts to discover the secret of perpetual motion, receiving no support or encouragement; but he did have one glorious period of seven years as Secretary at War in Dublin, a post procured for him by his younger brother who, while professing fine liberal principles, was typical of his generation in seeing no connection between publicly denouncing governmental corruption and privately practising it in support of the family.

If Charles was a man of straw, his brother Dick was certainly not. He was born in Dublin in 1751, but at eight, after a year and a half at school, he left that city for London and never revisited it. At eleven he was sent to Harrow where he remained for six years. After some additional tutorial instruction, but no university education, despite the fact that both Oxford and Cambridge had 'incorporated' his father as a Master of Arts, he joined Thomas at Bath. There, in 1770, he met Elizabeth Ann, the outstandingly pretty daughter of a music teacher, Thomas Linley, who had previously given Richard's mother singing lessons. Eliza Linley, in addition to being lovely in person, had a fine voice and sang oratorios at Oxford. A Harrovian friend of Dick, with whom he collaborated in a number of early literary efforts, developed an unrequited passion for her, but when an incorrigible (and married) admirer called Major Mathews refused to leave her alone, it was to Sheridan that she turned in her distress.

She asked him to take her to France where she might seek refuge in a convent. He thought well of France, but less well of the convent. They fled to Dunkirk and Sheridan pointed out that unless she married him, she would undoubtedly return to England as apparently damaged goods. She was, in fact, nothing loth, and they found a Roman Catholic priest, used to such runaway matches, who performed the necessary ceremony in a village near Calais. Mr Linley then arrived on the scene in a rage and removed his daughter to Bath while Major Mathews, to escape whose attentions they had eloped, challenged Sheridan to a duel. Fortunately Sheridan had been well instructed in fencing: he disarmed the Major, forcing him to beg for his life and publish an apology. A few weeks later Mathews challenged him to another duel and in this one it was Sheridan who was quite unpleasantly wounded.

Both the fathers now intervened and Dick Sheridan was packed off to Waltham Abbey to study mathematics, science, French and Italian. He also read for the bar and was admitted to the Inner Temple. Meanwhile the high paternal temperatures began to fall and in April 1773 Dick and Eliza were able to marry again, with grudging parental consent and in accordance with respectable Anglican liturgy. Old Thomas Sheridan was scarcely reconciled: he felt his son was marrying beneath him. Sixty years later it was the turn of the Sheridans to be considered insufficiently grand.

The young couple took a house in London, in Orchard Street, and in 1774, when Dick was only twenty-three, rehearsals began at Covent Garden of a comedy he had written, *The Rivals*. It was an instant failure, but after some revision it was once again performed and achieved the success it has retained for well over two hundred years. Other plays followed in rapid succession, including *The Duenna*, and by the end of 1775 young Sheridan was a widely acclaimed playwright who became Garrick's successor as manager of Drury Lane Theatre shortly after his twenty-fourth birthday. A few years later he had, by borrowing and mortgages, become part-owner of Drury Lane. There, in 1777, he had his greatest triumph as author and producer of *The School for Scandal*, which came close to being banned by the Lord Chamberlain. It was followed in 1779 by *The Critic*.

Sheridan's contemporaries esteemed him as a politician no less than as a playwright, perhaps even more; but it is as a superb writer of comedy that he is remembered today. It may be appropriate to compare his literary achievement with that of Oscar Wilde a hundred years later, though they were much more than a century apart in taste, temperament and behaviour. There was never anything 'yillery-yallery' about Sheridan and the two men, equals in wit and stagecraft, would probably have found each other antipathetic; but they were masters of dialogue and outstanding writers of comedy.

While Sheridan was perfecting *The Rivals,* Eliza sang before King George III and Queen Charlotte at Buckingham House. She had already established her reputation as a concert singer of high quality. The King, who was no mean judge, told her father that he 'never in his life heard so fine a voice as his daughter's, nor one so well instructed'. Her good looks were universally acknowledged, Horace Walpole declaring her superior to all living beauties. Sir Joshua Reynolds painted her twice, one of his portraits depicting her as St Cecilia; and Gainsborough vied with him in presenting her lovely face and figure with all the inspiration he possessed. A full-length portrait by Gainsborough, in which she seems to flutter in the breeze and represent spring at its most exhilarating, now hangs in the National Gallery in Washington. Fanny Burney wrote: 'The elegance of Mrs Sheridan's beauty is unequalled by any I ever saw, except Mrs Crewe.' Mrs Crewe, a Greville by birth, was the wittier, the more intelligent and probably the less likeable of the two.

Eliza's intelligence did not match her beauty or her voice, but she was both loving and conscientious. She kept the accounts when her husband was manager of Drury Lane; she read manuscripts for him; she wrote quite good verses; and she worked zealously in Sheridan's cause when he became a politician. The society in which her husband and his associates indulged their whims was a permissive one, and Dick Sheridan was a compulsive libertine. It would have been surprising, therefore, if the dazzling Eliza had never strayed from the path of virtue. She was a faithful wife, resisting many would-be seducers, including the Duke of Clarence, the future William IV; but she did fall, just once. It was for that handsome idealist and future rebel, Lord Edward FitzGerald, one of the Duke of Leinster's nineteen children, who subsequently married a girl with whom Sheridan was in love, the gifted Pamela, illegitimate daughter of Philippe Egalité, Duc d' Orléans. By Lord Edward Eliza had a daughter, Mary, whom Sheridan welcomed into his family with unembarrassed affection, but who died a few months after her mother while still a child. She was buried in Eliza's tomb in the cloister of Wells Cathedral and both Sheridan and Lord Edward were distraught with grief.

Meanwhile success at Drury Lane bred success elsewhere. Dr Johnson had Sheridan elected to the Literary Club, Charles James Fox made friends with him, and Georgiana, Duchess of Devonshire, finding him witty and agreeable, introduced him to the Prince of Wales whose confidential adviser he soon became. In 1780 he was elected Whig Member of Parliament for Stafford, as an ardent supporter of Fox and with the assistance of an eloquent letter from the Duchess of Devonshire. He found it expedient to pay five guineas to each voter.

He had been twice blackballed for that Mecca of the Whigs, Brooks's Club in St James's Street, even though Fox proposed him. This was no doubt because some of the members thought a mere playwright and theatre manager unsuitable to join their number. Two months after his election to Parliament he was again proposed. It seemed likely that the same fate would befall him, but the Prince of Wales, still an acquaintance rather than the close friend he later became, saved the situation. He drove to Brooks's from Carlton House and, while the ballot was held, engaged the would-be blackballers in earnest conversation from which they could not escape without unthinkable discourtesy. Sheridan was elected. As a convivial claret drinker, witty conversationalist and lover of a wager, he was soon a popular member.

His wit included a capacity for writing spontaneous verses. His friend Lord Erskine, an active and intelligent Whig politician, though on this occasion perhaps too merry, infuriated Lady Erskine one evening by declaring that 'a wife was only a tin canister tied to one's tail'. Sheridan went to her rescue, seized pen and ink and wrote there and then:

> Lord Erskine at Woman presuming to rail
> Calls his wife a tin canister tied to his tail;
> And the fair Lady Ann, while the subject he carries on
> Seems hurt at his lordship's degrading comparison.

> But wherefore degrading? Considered aright
> A canister polished is useful and bright;
> Should dirt its original purity hide
> That's the fault of the puppy to whom it is tied.

Lord Erskine himself could be witty. He shared Sheridan's and the Prince of Wales's love for Mrs Crewe, the woman Fanny Burney thought Eliza Sheridan's only rival in beauty. Sheridan proved his affection by dedicating *The School for Scandal* to her. The Prince of Wales publicly toasted 'Buff and Blue and Mrs Crewe' – buff and blue being the Whig and also the Crewe colours. But when the Erskines and the Sheridans were vinously entertained at Crewe Hall, it is Lord Erskine whose farewell verse in the visitors' book deserves to be remembered:

> The French have taste in all they do
> Which we are quite without,
> For nature who to them gave *goût*
> To us gave only gout.

Instant verse was one of Sheridan's specialities. In May 1800 George III went to see a play at Drury Lane and as he entered the theatre a demented guardsman fired two shots at him. The King escaped harm and stayed to see the play. Meanwhile Sheridan, whose close association with the Prince of Wales did not diminish his widely shared affection for the King, wrote a special verse of the National Anthem. It was sung from the stage by the actors and actresses:

> From every latent foe
> And the assassin's blow
>   God Save the King.
> O'er him thine arm extend
> For Britain's sake defend
> Our father, prince and friend:
>   God Save the King.

Perhaps it was Sheridan's natural theatrical flair, as well as the lessons his father had given him in elocution, that made him one of the finest House of Commons speakers at a time when orators of the calibre of Pitt, Fox, Burke and Wilberforce were stars in an unusually bright parliamentary constellation. He opposed the war against the American colonies with such skill and vigour that Congress sought to make him a thank-offering of £20,000. Sorely as he must have been tempted (for his extravagance, generosity and addiction to wild bets left him, despite an annual income of £10,000 from Drury Lane, perpetually embarrassed financially), he had the good sense to decline the American offer. He had already been in trouble over those five-guinea rewards to supporters in his constituency.

In 1782 the Whigs under Lord Rockingham replaced Lord North – to the discomfiture of the King and to the delight of the Prince of Wales. Sheridan became Under-Secretary at the Foreign Office and a year later he was Secretary to the Treasury in the coalition led by Fox and Pitt and headed by Rockingham's successor, the Duke of Portland. The coalition lasted but a year, for George III decided to replace it by a more effective Government under William Pitt. However, during his brief period of office Sheridan addressed the House on Treasury matters twenty-six times and contrived to make even financial affairs entertaining.

In 1788 the King became insane. The Whigs saw their chance. Plans were concerted with the Prince of Wales, who was to be Regent, for a Whig Government in which Sheridan would be Treasurer of the Navy. Sheridan's affection for the Prince of Wales prompted him to join Fox in proposing that the Prince should become Regent without seeking the approval of Parliament, an ill-advised initiative unlikely to endear him to the House of Commons. Then the King unexpectedly recovered. The Whigs' dream of renewed office faded and the necessity for a Regency was postponed for twenty-two years.

Sheridan was one of the principal actors in the impeachment of Warren Hastings, which from first to last dragged on for over seven years and ended in Hastings's acquittal. He was not such a bitter protagonist as Edmund Burke, but he was as assiduous and as eloquent. Warren Hastings, the first Governor-General of India, had been an unrivalled administrator and had handled military affairs with cool efficiency. He had also earned large sums for the East India Company and comparatively little for himself. All the same he was responsible for a number of ruthless, unscrupulous measures, of which one was the shameful treatment of two Begums of Oudh from whom he had extracted huge sums by wholly reprehensible means. In prosecution of the various charges against Hastings, the case of the Begums was allotted to Sheridan.

In February 1787 he made a speech on the subject lasting nearly six hours. Macaulay gives a graphic account of events:

> The impression which it produced was such as has never been equalled. He sat down, not merely amidst cheering, but amidst the loud clapping of hands, in which the Lords below the bar and the strangers in the gallery joined. The excitement of the House was such that no other speaker could obtain a hearing; and the debate was adjourned. The impression made by this remarkable display of eloquence on severe and experienced critics, whose discernment we may suppose to have been quickened by emulation, was deep and permanent.

When some years later Lord Holland asked Charles James Fox what was the best speech he had ever heard in the Commons, Fox replied without hesitation that it was Sheridan's about the Begums of Oudh.

In the following year the trial of Hastings by the full House of Lords was officially opened in Westminster Hall with the utmost pomp and circumstance. The walls were hung with scarlet, the Princes of the Blood brought up the end of the long procession of fully robed peers, and Queen Charlotte was there with her daughters. So were the whole Diplomatic Corps, Sir Joshua Reynolds, Mrs Siddons and all the great Whig ladies headed by the Duchess of Devonshire. Eliza Sheridan had recently posed for Reynolds as St Cecilia, a picture which had been greatly admired. So Macaulay wrote: 'There too was she, the beautiful mother of a beautiful race, the Saint Cecilia whose delicate features, lighted up by love and music, art has rescued from the common decay.'

The accusers were in full dress. Even Fox, who never took any trouble with his appearance, was well turned out. Macaulay relates that there was 'an array of speakers such as perhaps had not appeared together since the great age of Athenian eloquence. There were Fox and Sheridan, the English Demosthenes and the English Hyperides'. Burke spoke so movingly that 'handkerchiefs were pulled out; smelling-bottles were handed round; hysterical sobs and screams were heard; and Mrs Sheridan was carried out in a fit'.

When Sheridan rose in Westminster Hall four months later, people paid £50 for a seat, the equivalent of at least £1,000 in the 1980s. He spoke on four separate days and on the last, exhausted by his effort, he sank back into Burke's arms. The trial was so drawn out that the public lost interest, though Sheridan stuck to his last as a manager of the impeachment. Warren Hastings was acquitted in 1795 by a majority of the slender number of peers who still attended the trial.

The rest of Sheridan's political career was far from inactive. He made an eloquent plea for the freedom of the press, he attacked the oppressive game laws, he was a leader of the opposition to union with Ireland, believing that his native land should retain its own bicameral Parliament. When the French Revolution came, he spoke for the right of the French to choose their own form of government, caustically condemning interference with the affairs of other countries. He was out of sympathy with Burke's vivid denunciation of the revolutionary excesses, but when the French became bellicose, and when the Royal Navy mutinied at Spithead and the Nore, his patriotic instincts took charge. He expressed strong opposition to Napoleon, called for volunteers to defend the country from invasion and even became Lieutenant Colonel of the St James Volunteer Corps, forerunners of the Second World War Home Guard.

Meanwhile he suffered domestic afflictions. The delectable Eliza succumbed to galloping consumption in 1792, leaving, in addition to Lord Edward FitzGerald's little daughter Mary, a seventeen-year-old son, Tom. Though Sheridan married again three years later, the full, exciting years were over. He had abandoned writing for the unpaid career of politician. Drury Lane, from which his only income derived, was falling down and had to be reconstructed at great cost. His creditors became pressing and when, in 1809, the newly restored theatre was burned to the ground, he was close to destitution. His faithful friend the Prince of Wales helped a little by appointing him Receiver of the Duchy of Cornwall with an income of £800 a year. Always cheerful, his wit constantly ready, the melancholia from which he sometimes suffered effectively disguised, he put a brave face on his difficulties. He remained attentive to his parliamentary duties and was rewarded briefly by appointment as Treasurer of the Navy and Privy Councillor in the 'Ministry of all the Talents' formed on Pitt's death in 1806. Fox died in the same year and Sheridan was disappointed not to be chosen Leader of the Opposition. He could have had a peerage, but that meant switching his party allegiance, which he thought shameful, and he said that 'he declined to hide his head in a coronet'.

Those whose words and witticisms win them applause seldom escape contamination by that leveller of successful men, vanity; and vanity quickly corrodes. One reason why Sheridan was not chosen to succeed Fox may be traced in quotations from the letters of those who loved him best. In December 1802 Fox wrote to Georgiana, Duchess of Devonshire:

> I long ago made a determination never to be out of humour with Sheridan . . . but I am concerned that he should scarcely ever now speak but for the purpose of shewing that he has wit, which nobody ever doubted, and increasing the doubts entertained, or rather taking away all doubt about his steadiness.

Two years later Georgiana Devonshire herself wrote that vanity was Sheridan's idol and

> to this idol he sacrifices friends, fortune, consistency; and as he is ever watching to catch applause somewhere, of course he is always veering with the winds that blow it. But as to pecuniary advantage he is *intacte* and places as much pride in refusing a place whilst he is wanting a dinner as other men do in shewing off the dinner which they have obtained by servility.

Sheridan had in Charles James Fox and the Duchess of Devonshire two devoted friends; so their candour must be taken as evidence that years of success had carried relentlessly forward the penalty which accompanies them.

In 1812 he could not find the five guineas a head required by the electors of Stafford and they accordingly returned his opponent. Those responsible for rebuilding Drury Lane, under the chairmanship of Samuel Whitbread, withheld part of the sum due to him and in 1813 he was arrested for debt, being temporarily incarcerated in what was known as 'a sponging-house' until Whitbread handed over the money. No longer a public figure, worried about the declining health of his son Tom, he even gave up drinking his favourite claret. He was beset by inexorable creditors, but as he lay dying a kind bailiff sat by his bedside, less with the object of distraining his goods than of warding off the flow of financially impatient callers. He was, in fact, well looked after, with three of London's best doctors in attendance and frequent consoling words from the Bishop of London. He died at his house in Savile Row in July 1816 and was given a funeral in Westminster Abbey even grander and better attended than those of Pitt and Fox.

Richard Brinsley Sheridan's only child by Elizabeth Linley was Tom. He was good-looking like his mother, a companion esteemed by his contemporaries and a poet of some quality. Unfortunately he inherited his mother's consumptive tendency and in early manhood his health became precarious. He procured the office of Colonial Treasurer at the Cape of Good Hope where the climate might with luck restore him to health. He went there in 1813, just when his father's afflictions were mounting, and he took with him his wife, Caroline, a child of Colonel James Callender by Lord Antrim's daughter, Lady Elizabeth McDonnell. Thus, Caroline, like her husband, had Irish blood in her veins. The Colonel, who married several times, and finally changed his name to Campbell, was little esteemed by his daughter. In writing to her sister she usually referred to him as 'The Ogre', or alternatively as 'Barabbas'.

Caroline was described as 'very pretty, very sensible, amiable and gentle; indeed so gentle that Tom insists upon it that her extreme quietness and tranquillity is a defect in her character. He accuses her of such an extreme apprehension of giving trouble that it amounts to an affectation'. This amiable and unassuming lady produced for Tom four sons and three daughters. Her daughters became known as The Three Graces. The celebrated Shakespearean actress Fanny Kemble wrote in the 1820s: 'Mrs. Sheridan, the mother of the Graces, is more beautiful than anybody but her daughters.'

Tom Sheridan grew steadily weaker and in 1817 he died at the Cape. Caroline sailed home with her eldest daughter, Helen, the two younger girls having been left in England in her sister's care. Safely home, she received from the Prince Regent a small pension and an apartment at Hampton Court. There she set her mind to the task of educating and launching in the world her gifted children. The Three Graces were Helen, aged eleven, Caroline, aged nine, and Jane Georgiana, born on Guy Fawkes Day in 1810 and thus aged seven when her mother returned to England.

# 3
# *The Queen of Beauty*

Straitened though Caroline Sheridan's circumstances were, she had the grace-and-favour apartment at Hampton Court, the goodwill of George IV, the Sheridan name and a host of attractive children. She wrote a novel called *Carwell, or Crime and Sorrow*, which had excellent sales and was followed by two more almost equally successful. All three are now equally forgotten. Moreover, before they were twenty-one her two elder daughters were making money from the publication of their songs and verses.

Accounts of physical beauty are often exaggerated, especially in retrospect; but with a mother whose looks were consistently praised, and a grandmother, Elizabeth Linley, whose exceptional loveliness can still be admired in her portraits by Gainsborough and Reynolds, it is not surprising that the three Sheridan girls stood out from their contemporaries. Their brothers were also thought remarkably handsome. In addition to their beauty, the girls had inherited from their grandfather artistic gifts and a ready wit. In the schoolroom at Hampton Court a series of tutors ensured they were tolerably well educated, learning French, Italian, dancing and the Odes of Horace. They were never short of Latin tags.

In 1833 Benjamin Disraeli wrote to his sister Sarah describing a dinner party given by George and Caroline Norton, the second daughter. It was to celebrate the birthday of Brinsley Sheridan, who, Caroline Norton told him, 'is the only respectable one of the family, and that is because he has a liver complaint'. Disraeli said that the sole woman present apart from Mrs Norton was 'her sister Mrs Blackwood, also very handsome and very Sheridanic'.

> She told me she was nothing. 'You see Georgy's the beauty and Carrie's the wit, and I ought to be the good one; but then I am not.' In the evening came the beauty, Lady St Maur, and anything so splendid I never gazed upon. Even the handsomest family in the world, which I think the Sheridans are, all looked

dull. Clusters of the darkest hair, the most brilliant complexion, a contour of face perfectly ideal.

Disraeli himself made an unusual impression. Helen Blackwood's description is worth quoting. 'He wore a black velvet coat lined with satin, purple trousers with a gold band running down the outside seam, a scarlet waistcoat, long lace ruffles falling down to the tips of his fingers, white gloves with several brilliant rings outside them, and long black ringlets rippling down upon his shoulders.' Dandies were still acceptable in society, but this one was thought to have gone to exceptional lengths.

Helen, who said she ought to be the good one, in fact was precisely that. She had a selfless nature, unblemished by pride in her looks or her talent. The eldest of the three sisters, she met a naval officer, Price Blackwood, at a ball when she was seventeen, fell head over heels in love and despite the objection of Blackwood's parents, Lord and Lady Dufferin, that both the bride and bridegroom would be penniless, they were married at St George's, Hanover Square, which was then the setting for all fashionable weddings. They went to Florence to economise and produced a son who was given the peculiar nickname Ghigo. As Helen's mother-in-law was called Mehetabel Hester, idiosyncrasy in the choice of names was evidently a family trait.

Through her sister Caroline, who married two years after her and was quickly established in political and intellectual society, Helen became a friend of the literary lions of the time, Samuel Rogers, the two bluestocking Misses Berry and Sydney Smith. That acrid Lord Chancellor, Brougham, fell under her spell, and Disraeli said many years later that she was 'his chief admiration'. Her husband's elder brothers died and in 1839 he succeeded his father as Lord Dufferin. Two years later he himself died from an inadvertent overprescription of morphia, and his widow thereafter devoted her life to the welfare of Ghigo. He prospered so well that he was in due course Governor-General of Canada, Viceroy of India, and Ambassador in St Petersburg, Constantinople, Rome and Paris.

Helen, or Nelly as her sisters called her, was unobtrusive, but she did not bury her talents. She wrote a play, which ran for a full year at the Haymarket Theatre, and some of the songs and verses she composed, in particular 'The Irish Emigrant', won popularity on both sides of the Atlantic. One of Nelly's early admirers, Lord Gifford, sighed vainly for her love all his adult life, and it was typical of her that when he was stricken with a mortal disease she married him so that he might die happy. She herself died shortly afterwards, barely sixty years old, and the future Viceroy built a tower at his Irish home, Clandeboye, to commemorate her. *Helen's Tower* is the title Harold Nicolson gave to the charming book he wrote about Nelly and her son.

Caroline, next in age, had a tempestuous life. Her verses, forgotten in the twentieth century, were much acclaimed in the nineteenth. They were sufficiently good, or at least sufficiently popular, to secure her an entry in the *Dictionary of National Biography* under the heading 'Poet'; and one in particular, *The Sorrows of Rosalie,* which she published when she was twenty-one, was received with immense public enthusiasm. She made a living by writing articles in numerous periodicals and she was the author of three indifferent novels. She was also a campaigner for social and economic reform, attacking the indefensible conditions of her time in pamphlets with titles such as 'A Voice from the Factories' and 'The Child of the Islands'.

Caroline made the mistake of marrying, when she was just nineteen, Lord Grantley's unprepossessing brother, George Norton, who scratched a living as Recorder of Guildford. Even the good-natured Nelly referred to him as 'my insufferable brother-in-law'. She bore him three sons, the youngest of whom was killed by a fall from his pony. It did not take her many years to rue her choice, even though George Norton did have a house in Storey's Gate where Caroline gathered the fashionable and the powerful in her salon.

She became an intimate friend – many believed mistress – of Lord Melbourne. Aspiring politicians courted her and in 1835 she acted as Melbourne's confidante and go-between in an endeavour to form a coalition with the Tories. She left George Norton in the following year, unable any longer to abide his uncouth behaviour. He thereupon brought an action for 'criminal conversation' against Melbourne in the Court of Common Pleas. He lost the case; but there was embarrassment in court when counsel, pointing to Caroline's children, referred to 'those little lambs'. Lord Melbourne had been William Lamb until he succeeded his father. It is strange to reflect that only a few months before the start of Queen Victoria's reign the Prime Minister could be involved as co-respondent without any apparent prejudice to his political career.

Some years later Caroline was forced to seek legal protection from the odious George, who had designs on her literary earnings and on the children. The pamphlet she then wrote on women's earnings, and on the custody of children when a home was broken, had a notable effect on subsequent legislation to establish women's rights. She also had to fight against a slander, developed by George Meredith in his novel *Diana of the Crossways*, which was based on Caroline and Melbourne and implied quite falsely that she had betrayed political secrets imparted to her.

Her stormy passage through life made her even better known in mid-Victorian society than her reputation as a poet and she was certainly the most notorious of the Sheridan sisters. In 1877, seeking repose at sunset, she married the rich and amiable Sir William Stirling-Maxwell of Keir; but she died only a few months after her entry into calmer waters.

With two such sisters, both married by the time she was seventeen, Georgy could in any case expect an exciting introduction to London Society; but so striking was her appearance and so ready her wit that no helping hand was necessary. In January 1829, aged eighteen, she wrote to her brother Brinsley who, liver complaint or no liver complaint, had gone to India: 'We have been to several balls here lately. Really Hampton Court is much gayer than I had imagined.' One of these balls was given by the Duke of Clarence, the future William IV, for the ten-year-old Queen of Portugal, whose wicked uncle, Dom Miguel, was scheming to usurp her throne while she danced at Cumberland Lodge 'in a pink gauze gown, with her hair turned up and flowers in it!' As for Georgy, she and Caroline 'had gold and green wreaths with scarlet berries in our hair, and I had a red velvet body, a Maria Stuart, which is the fashion now, and a white satin skirt'.

A year later she was bidden by Prince Leopold, afterwards King of the Belgians and Queen Victoria's trusted uncle, to stay at Clairmont. Describing the dinner party on the second night of her visit, she wrote:

> Lord Aberdeen took me in, and of course I went last as being of lowest rank. When I came into the dining-room, not knowing

the people sat as they liked, without attention to rank, I was surprised to see no place vacant but the chair next the Duke of Wellington, and thinking some of the great ladies had not come down, I hesitated to take it: upon which the Duke thinking, I suppose, this was timidity and awe at approaching his god-like self, beckoned at first to me with a most royal wave of the hand and then gave a resounding clap to the astonished chair (as if I was a column of infantry instead of a young lady), to which kindly invite I acceded with a grace peculiar to myself and no doubt pleasing to those around me!

Others more eligible than Wellington were smitten by the grace which she self-mockingly ascribed to herself. Three months after the party at Clairmont she wrote to Brinsley:

Your Georgy is going to be turned into a chaperone. Lord Seymour, the Duke of Somerset's son, asked me yesterday to marry him and I, being very civil and polite, said Yes. Joking apart I *am* going to marry him. He is very clever and good. The Duke, his father, has no objection and is very kind indeed. So are his sisters; but my acquaintances are rabid and frantic at my daring to do such a thing, and they turn round after first congratulating Mamma and say 'Good Heavens, is Lord Seymour mad? What a fool!' with other pleasing intimations of their good wishes towards me . . . the Duke of Somerset (she wrote in another letter) is the kindest old man you ever saw and is going to give us money to buy a house in town.

The Duke of Somerset was indeed a kind man (though not yet particularly old) and his courtesy was unfailing; but, as later became evident, there were murmurings in the Seymour family about the heir to such an eminent dukedom marrying a Sheridan whose ancestral reputation was not considered wholly respectable and whose Irish blood was inadequately blue, even though her mother, Caroline, was certainly not of humble origin.

The wedding took place in June 1830 at the house in Grosvenor Place belonging to Sir James Graham of Netherby, about to become First Lord of the Admiralty and one of the chief promoters of the great Reform Bill. Sir James's wife, whom the Sheridan sisters called Aunt Graham, was Caroline Sheridan's sister. Eleven years later he was Home Secretary when the Prince of Wales was born. In duty bound he was present at Buckingham Palace to ensure no changeling was substituted. On subsequent such occasions, up to and including the birth of Princess Margaret in 1930, it sufficed for the Home Secretary to be on the premises. But in 1841 it was thought expedient he should be in the room when the birth took place. So a screen was placed in a corner and behind it the embarrassed Sir James lurked. When the baby had been safely delivered he emerged, satisfied himself there was no warming-pan evident and looking at the newly born infant, said 'A fine boy, Ma'am'. A faint voice from the bed replied 'A fine *Prince* you mean, Sir James.'

This is how Nelly Blackwood described the wedding:

> A very merry wedding it was, only rather patriarchal as the shy bridegroom induced Georgia to beg there might be no one present but the members of the respective families. Ghigo assisted at the ceremony with his hair curled and was excessively admired. Georgia was dressed in plain white satin with no ornaments but a diamond brooch and earrings, beautiful blonde seduisantes and a magnificent blonde veil thrown over her head, so large that it nearly reached her feet. She was to have worn a tiara of diamonds and emeralds on her forehead, which her husband gave her, but unfortunately it was not finished in time. I think I never saw anything so perfectly beautiful as she looked and she was in excellent spirits. The dinner which was given by Uncle Graham on the occasion consisted only of the Duke and his two sons, my mother, and we three daughters, husbands etc., and my uncles and aunts and the clergyman. After dinner the rooms were lighted up, the back drawing-room arranged as a chapel for the occasion. Georgia put on her veil and as soon as the gentlemen came up from dinner, they were married and immediately set off for Wimbledon Park, (the Duke of Somerset's house) which is only five miles out of town. Then the fun began for us who were not shy, as the company began to arrive and a very pleasant party we had of about two hundred people.

Lord Seymour must indeed have been shy since he denied his bride any participation in the fun of her wedding party. What he in fact did, after a honeymoon at Wimbledon, was to whisk her off to Berry Pomeroy from which he conducted an election campaign resulting in his becoming a Member of Parliament. For Georgy there was some historic consolation; for she slept in Jane Seymour's bed.

George IV died a fortnight after the wedding. The new King had a large family of illegitimate children, the FitzClarences, and no legitimate ones at all. Georgy wrote from Berry Pomeroy to her brother Brinsley:

> William IV, formerly Duke of Clarence, is at present very popular and excessively pleased at being King. All the FitzClarences are great people now. I went to see Amelia, the youngest of them, the other day at Bushey, just before I left Wimbledon Park; and as I was quietly sitting with her in her dressing-room, a servant came to the door and said the King wished to see Lady Seymour. So down I went in a great tribulation, for I was not in proper mourning for the late King and if the Queen was there should be obliged to kneel and kiss her hand; but, however, he alone was standing with some FitzClarences before the front-door of his house, ready to ride with the Queen. He received me kindly, kissed me, and seemed in great spirits and quite delighted at hearing himself addressed as His Majesty.

Perhaps in kissing Lady Seymour His Majesty remembered the improper, but unsuccessful, advances he had made to her grandmother, Elizabeth Sheridan, many years before.

The Seymours were genuinely devoted to each other and remained so for more than fifty years. However, Lord Seymour's career as a Liberal politician, who was given a series of offices by Melbourne and was eventually a Cabinet Minister under Palmerston, led to frequent absences, and he was also unable to resist invitations from his friend Mr George Bentinck to go for long yachting trips in his large cutter yacht *The Dream*. Meanwhile Georgy, with evident ease, gave birth to a series of five children, starting with two girls and then producing in 1835 a son who was christened Ferdinand after the heir to the French throne, the Duc d'Orléans. Orléans died a few years later and bequeathed his sword to his godson.

Lord Seymour's letters, written when he was electioneering in the West Country, were frequent and affectionate. He won the love of all Georgy's brothers and sisters, Helen Blackwood saying that 'he is the kindest and dearest brother-in-law that ever was invented'. He was earnest as a politician. Disraeli noted: 'Lord Seymour. Great talent, which develops in a domestic circle, though otherwise shy-mannered.' He wrote a learned thesis called 'Reflexions on Truth and Intellectual Acuteness' and pondered heavily why 'men most given to reflection and to the exertion of their thoughts are often least capable of expressing them'. This may have been a subjective judgement, but at least he was capable of expressing his thoughts in letters to his wife.

While Georgy was in London after the birth of her second daughter, Seymour wrote: 'If it grows like you, I shall be more pleased with it than with a boy.' At Maiden Bradley she had collected a number of pets. He wrote thence to tell her that the chickens had gone unhappily to roost, the silver pheasant 'was tearing his tail in despair, and the little bantam cock was wringing his crooked claws in grief for your absence'. A few days later, however, he threatened: 'Remember that some of that writing paper I gave you should be sent very often to Bradley, or I will eat the bantam cock.' When she returned to the country, a typical ending of a letter to Seymour was: 'Carlos is a very obedient dog. The donkey has a large spavine in his back. The tortoise, I fear, is ill: his eyes are watery and his body shrivelled.' She also developed an interest in guinea pigs; but her feelings for them were different from those affecting the silver pheasant, the bantam cock, and the tortoise. She thought them delicious to eat and experimented with different methods of cooking them.

In 1834, when Parliament had risen, the Seymours ventured down the Rhine. They did not think highly of the food. Seymour, writing to his father, described a *table d'hôte* dinner on the island of Rolandsworth. It began at 'half after one'. It is interesting to note how expressions now believed to be Americanisms were then in common English use. Seymour spelt both honour and rancour without the 'u'. The dinner which began at half after one

> crawled on till four – a succession of oily dishes, puddings and meats, boars' heads and wonderful sauces. I saw a partridge and was pulling it towards myself to carve it, but the waiter snatched it from me because, he said, nothing must be carved on the table. Sixty strange German eyes stared at me as if it was a barbarous

greediness and unmannerly behaviour, but when they saw I only laughed, they despaired of me.

The Duke of Nassau ordered everything in his territory. At Schlangenbad the inn belonged to the Government and they were amazed that the price of every room was written over the door. They were still more amazed that the Duke also fixed the price of a bath. Because it was late in the season the bathing-house was locked and the key entrusted to the mayor. So Seymour was only able to 'dabble in a foot-tub, thankful that the Duke had, in his wisdom, left me at least this limited enjoyment of the water'.

In delving into contemporary German literature, Seymour was still more critical. The philosophers in particular incurred his displeasure.

> When a German feels philosophical, he pours out such curiously long sentences, and borrows so many new and heterogeneously compounded words, that it reminds me of that invaluable Scotch definition of metaphysics: when a man speaks, and nobody understands what he means, and when he himself does not understand what he means, then that is metaphysics.

Back in England, he was appointed a Lord of the Treasury in the spring of 1835 and, according to Disraeli, headed the Whig faction which sought a coalition; but he would have nothing to do with the Radicals. Seymour himself wrote that 'many of the Liberals are so angry that the old Tories have changed into Whigs that they would themselves change into Radicals'. However, these serious political manoeuvres were interrupted by family problems.

Without telling Seymour, Georgy abetted her brother Brinsley in an elopement and marriage at Gretna Green with the daughter and heiress of Sir Colquhoun Grant, who owned a handsome property at Frampton in Dorset. Sir Colquhoun, wrongly believing Seymour to have been privy to the conspiracy, challenged him to a duel beneath the windmill on Wimbledon Common. Seymour, by then informed of the truth by the penitent Georgy, decided it was better to accept the challenge than to incriminate his wife. Pistols were the weapon, seconds were chosen and the assailants met in what was one of the last duels fought on English soil. Sir Colquhoun fired and missed; Seymour discharged his pistol in the air. Honour was satisfied, Seymour explained that he had in fact known nothing of the matter, Sir Colquhoun relented, and in a few years Mr and Mrs Brinsley Sheridan became the proud owners of Frampton. Nine years later, when 'Uncle Graham' was Home Secretary, duelling was made illegal.

Georgy, increasingly known and admired, remained strictly faithful. Nor was she extravagant, though as this letter from Seymour shows she could be unorthodox:

> There is a hat come for you, a most curious contrivance, an acre of black beaver. It will be impossible to ride against the wind in it, but perhaps it is meant for your baby; it will make him look like a black mushroom. Francis [one of the servants] is in great distress how to pack it, in order to preserve its shape – if shape it can be called, which shape has none distinguishable. *Le Chapeau Monstre*, that is its name. It shall be sent as soon as a box is made large enough to hold it: I must then have one of the vans from Newmarket to carry it.

Georgy's sister, Caroline Norton, who arrived while Seymour was writing, started at the sight of the *Chapeau Monstre* but declared it was not in the least what had been ordered.

Child-bearing had no ill effect on Georgy's exquisite figure, which quickly reasserted itself, and at twenty-eight her face and fair complexion were unblemished. Thus in 1839 the forty knights selected by Lord Eglinton to take part in the great medieval tournament he was planning to hold at his castle in Ayrshire unanimously voted that she was to be the Queen of Beauty. Her duty would be to bestow garlands on those successful in the jousting. Lady Londonderry had been tipped as the probable choice, but Lady Seymour outshone her in every physical attribute.

Never since Tudor times, since the costly entertainments organised by Leicester and other noblemen to glorify Queen Elizabeth, was there at any rate on British soil an extravaganza to compare with the Eglinton Tournament. The Gothic Revival was already well launched. Rich and poor, the sophisticated and humble, in Britain, France, Germany and even in distant America, were one and all immersed in dreams of the Middle Ages, of knights in armour, damsels in distress, towering castles, halberds and arrow slits, heralds and minstrels. Horace Walpole's Strawberry Hill and Beckford's Fonthill had established an architectural counter-revolution. Sir Walter Scott enthralled a vast public with *Ivanhoe*, Tennyson moved countless hearts with his *Morte d'Arthur*, his *Idylls of the King* and his *Lady of Shalott*. The theme was to last another fifty years while Burne-Jones painted his pale medieval ladies bedecked with flowers and Wagner composed *The Ring*.

Lord Eglinton, a dashing young man of twenty-seven when his Tournament was held, spent much of his fortune on it. The remainder he devoted partly to racing, winning the Derby with a famous horse called Flying Dutchman and the St Leger three times, and partly, during two spells as Lord Lieutenant of Ireland, to maintaining the most costly viceregal court ever seen at Dublin Castle. His Ayrshire castle, built by his grandfather, was an enormous example of the Gothic Revival at its least beguiling.

The preparations for the Tournament aroused immense interest. Forty knights, clad in real armour, proposed to enter the lists, though the number had shrunk to fourteen on the actual day. Eglinton had made for himself a suit of gilded armour, engraved with leafy scrolls, the breastplate adorned with a pair of wyverns. The spectators, too, were encouraged to wear clothes of fourteenth and fifteenth-century design, and they arrived in their thousands from all over the country, some even travelling from the United States. In all it was estimated that 100,000 people crowded into the great park at Eglinton Castle to see the unique revival of medieval chivalry advertised for Wednesday, 28 August 1839.

There had been rehearsals in the south of England, the costliest clothes and suits of mail had been ordered, the rules of tilting had been sedulously studied, ancient regulations originally drawn up in the reign of Edward IV had been given to each knight; and at Eglinton a large tilting-ground, flanked by splendid pavilions and capacious stands, had been built in the park. A gigantic tent had been attached to the castle for a banquet to follow the Tournament.

The fourteen knights who finally summoned up courage to take part arrived with retinues of pages, esquires, heralds and other retainers. Lord Glenlyon, heir to the Duke of Atholl and known for the occasion as the Knight of the Gael, arrived with seventy of the Atholl Highlanders to pipe him to victory. Men-at-arms, musicians, trumpeters, banner bearers and heralds were gorgeously armed and accoutred. Lord and Lady Londonderry, designated King and Queen of the Tournament, were arrayed in velvet and ermine. His lordship wore his marquess's coronet; and her ladyship, determined to make up for not having been chosen Queen of Beauty, was weighed down with bands of solid gold encrusted with jewels across her bosom, and scores of diamonds, emeralds and carbuncles elsewhere on her body. Prince Louis Napoleon, the future Emperor of the French, came as the Knight Visitor with a suitably enthusiastic French retinue, though he was not invited to perform at the lists.

The wild Lord Waterford, twenty-eight years old and already famous for outrageous and dangerous pranks, was the Knight of the Dragon. He wore fluted armour of polished steel and had his horses, men-at-arms, grooms, pages, and esquires bedecked in blue and white. Lord Eglinton himself was Lord of the Tournament, his banner born by Seymour's brother, Lord Algernon, halberdiers in liveries of blue and gold attending him and his charger magnificently caparisoned. But it was the Queen of Beauty whom the crowds were longing to see when she rode to the lists on a white palfrey, a silk canopy born over her by attendants. Sixteen pretty girls in medieval dresses, with wreaths of flowers on their heads, were to escort her as well as pages and esquires.

It was lovely late summer weather in Ayrshire, mild and sunny, when the guests and participants, some ninety in all, arrived at the castle. The morning of the great day broke bright and clear as the crowds of spectators arrived to find places of vantage. However, some people did notice that the distant hills of Arran looked ominously close.

The dazzling procession was due to leave the castle at noon, but there were delays in marshalling the forty different groups it comprised. Last to be marshalled was the Queen of Beauty. She was dressed in a long velvet skirt, violet in colour and adorned in gold with fleur de lys and the huge wings of the Seymour coat of arms. Her jacket was of ermine and miniver and a crimson mantle was draped over her shoulders. She wore a diamond necklace and her raven locks were surmounted by a gold crown encrusted with pearls. Lord Seymour must have been obliged to delve deep into his pocket – or perhaps his good-natured father's.

As Georgy walked across the great octagonal hall to the door where her white palfrey and sixteen maids of honour awaited her, all who saw her caught their breath, for they had never seen anything so enchanting. Her upright carriage, the lily of the valley complexion, the roseate cheeks untouched by make-up, the dancing blue eyes and jet black hair made an indelible impression on all present. The crowds were evidently not going to be disappointed.

Alas, they were. The Queen of Beauty's arrival at the castle door was announced by a chamberlain. Her palfrey was led forward, her pages lifted her train, there was a long blast on a trumpet; and then forked lightning flashed in the heavens and there was a deafening clap of thunder. The sky grew black and the rain came down in torrents.

The knights and their retinue set forth, drenched and wretched, and Lord Londonderry rather spoiled the effect by riding under a large green umbrella. Lord Eglinton decreed, however, that the Queen of Beauty should drive to the lists in a carriage. There was a delay while one was fetched and then, behind closed windows, Georgy was driven off, scarcely visible to the soaked spectators. Instead of riding in full state round the tilting-ground she was obliged to clamber on to the dais by a back entrance to the main pavilion.

There disaster awaited her; for such was the deluge that the rain had penetrated the roof of the pavilion and her royal box was flooded. Water cascaded on her hair and shoulders until her brother Charles, clad in rainproof armour, came to the rescue with a crimson parasol. The tournament began, but not with the panache planned, for the ceremonious challenges and flinging down of gloves were omitted in the wet turmoil, as were the heralds' addresses to the contestants. Most of the knights failed to strike with their lances, merely galloping ineffectually along the barrier and past each other. Lord Glenlyon's heavily caparisoned charger stampeded through one of the tents. The Knight of the Golden Lion nearly fell off in the mud and dropped the lance to which he had loyally attached his wife's cambric handkerchief. Eglinton did contrive to shatter his spear on Waterford's shield, and there was a final combat on foot between warriors with two-handed swords.

The tournament had been in every sense a wash-out and in

addition, as Eglinton sadly informed his guests, the tent erected at the castle was waterlogged so that the medieval banquet and ball planned for the evening must be postponed. The disgruntled crowds trudged wearily out of the park. The sodden knights and guests at the castle returned to console themselves in the hip-baths set before the fires in their bedrooms and filled by heavy cans of hot water lugged painfully upstairs by the long-suffering servants.

Two days later Lord Eglinton tried again. This time the sky was cloudless, but the tilting ground was deep in mud and despite the valiant efforts of maids and valets, the brilliance of the costumes was dimmed. However, thousands of spectators returned and the Queen of Beauty rode as originally intended, ending the tournament by crowning Lord Eglinton, in his gilded armour, with a circlet of gold. The jousting was an improvement on the previous occasion and there was an exciting episode when Lord Waterford and Lord Alford, losing their tempers, fought in deadly earnest.

The postponed banquet, too, was held in the castle with every known medieval dish, including lampreys, swans, boars' heads and flagons of malmsey wine. Silver dishes held the meats and golden dishes the puddings, this expensive plate having been specially commissioned by Eglinton for 400 guests. Behind each knight stood a page holding his banner. Afterwards there was a ball at which 2,000 guests in medieval garb danced in the restored marquee hung with tapestries and lit by thousands of candles. Music was provided by the band of the 2nd Dragoon Guards, all disguised as minstrels. Georgy, splendid in diamonds and ermine, sat with Lord Eglinton under a canopy flanked by velvet curtains and surmounted by coronets and feathered plumes.

Two days later the guests departed, the knights leaving their banners and shields to be hung in the great octagonal hall of the castle, their names and titles inscribed in gothic lettering beneath. The Seymours for their part went to stay at Buchanan with the Duke and Duchess of Montrose, the latter having appeared at the Eglinton ball in ruby velvet and a diamond stomacher, fastened with emeralds, amethysts and sapphires to replace hooks and buttons. Thence Lord Seymour wrote to his father to announce that he had been promoted from the

Treasury to the Board of Control responsible for overseeing the East India Company's Government of India.

After visits to the Duke of Argyll at Inverary and to Lord Breadalbane, who lived in neo-Gothic splendour at Taymouth Castle, presiding over more than 400,000 acres of Campbell territory, Seymour deposited his wife and children with his brother Archibald in Leicestershire where they were to spend the winter and Georgy could hunt with the best packs of hounds. Meanwhile all over Europe and the United States the newspapers were filled with accounts of the Eglinton Tournament, of the glamour and the mud, of the last artificial flowering of the Age of Chivalry. For Georgy it was an apotheosis: never again would she figure so prominently in the public gaze. Nor, indeed, did she wish to do so.

# 4
## *Prelude to Tragedy*

In times still not far distant, when a cook was an essential requisite even for families with a modest income, there was nothing better calculated than kitchen imbroglios to take the sparkle from a diamond tiara and wither the most flourishing strawberry leaves in a ducal coronet. In 1840, fresh from the splendour of the Eglinton Tournament, the Queen of Beauty engaged in a tilting-match about a cook.

Already in her devoted husband's eyes she was not rated as the finest judge of that profession. Two years after her marriage she had engaged in London a cook she proposed to send down to Maiden Bradley. This was Lord Seymour's comment

> Dearest Georgy,
>
> We shall receive the cook with the greatest goodwill and I hope she will soon become acquainted with the pans and dishes in our kitchen. Certainly when I was in town she called most forcibly to my recollection the old proverb, 'God sends good meat, but the devil sends cooks'. I do not mean any insinuation against your aunt who sent her to us. She will, I fear, prove to be one of those sort of cooks who seem as if they had learnt their art in a hospital, who instead of soup make a sick broth, conceive no other idea of bread-sauce but a poultice, and when an omelette is ordered produce a cataplasm of eggs. Well, I will try all this on Archibald when he has had a long day's hunting and is in good appetite.
>
> Yours very affectionately,
> Seymour

In 1840 culinary affairs took a graver turn. Georgy sent this inoffensive inquiry to a Lady Shuckburgh, wife of a Northamptonshire baronet.

> Lady Seymour presents her compliments to Lady Shuckburgh and would be obliged to her for the character of Mary

Steadman, who states that she has lived 12 months and still is in Lady Shuckburgh's establishment. Can Mary Steadman cook plain dishes well, and make bread, and is she honest, sober, willing, cleanly and good tempered? Lady Seymour would also like to know the reason she leaves Lady Shuckburgh's house.

Lady Shuckburgh who, perhaps because her maternal grandfather was an entirely undistinguished earl, had a high opinion of her own dignity, answered as follows:

> Lady Shuckburgh presents her compliments to Lady Seymour. Her Ladyship's letter, dated October 28th, only reached her yesterday November 3rd. Lady Shuckburgh was unacquainted with the name of the kitchenmaid until mentioned by Lady Seymour, as it is her custom neither to apply for, nor give, characters to any of the under servants, this being always done by the housekeeper, Mrs Couch, and this was well known to the young woman. Therefore Lady Shuckburgh is surprised at her referring any lady to her for a character. Lady Shuckburgh keeping a professed cook as well as a housekeeper in her establishment, it is not very probable she herself should know anything of the abilities or merits of the under servants; she is therefore unable to reply to Lady Seymour's note. Lady Shuckburgh cannot imagine Mary Steadman to be capable of cooking anything except for the servants' hall table.

This was too much for Georgy who could not resist attaching to her reply a well-drawn and unflattering caricature of the Shuckburgh children being fed:

> Lady Seymour presents her compliments to Lady Shuckburgh and begs she will order her housekeeper Mrs Couch to send the girl's character, otherwise another young woman will be sought for elsewhere, as Lady Seymour's children cannot remain without their dinners because Lady Shuckburgh, keeping a professed cook and housekeeper, thinks a knowledge of the details of her establishment beneath her notice. Lady Seymour understands from Steadman that, in addition to her other talents, she was actually capable of cooking food for the little Shuckburghs to partake of when hungry.

Lady Shuckburgh, in high indignation, then dictated to her doubtless browbeaten housekeeper this final philippic.

Madam, Lady Shuckburgh has directed me to acquaint you that she declines answering your note, the vulgarity of which she thinks beneath her contempt, and although it may be characteristic of the Sheridans to be vulgar, coarse and witty, it is not that of a lady unless she chances to have been born in a garret and bred in a kitchen. Mary Steadman informs me that your Ladyship does not keep either a cook or a housekeeper, and that you only require a girl who can cook a mutton chop; if so, I apprehend that Mary Steadman, or any other scullion, will be found fully equal to the establishment of the Queen of Beauty. I am Madam

Your Ladyship's etc.<br>Elizabeth Couch

History does not relate whether or not Mary Steadman became a member of the domestic staff at Maiden Bradley.

The Seymours were still deeply in love, but his parliamentary career and her preference for country life meant periods of separation. Georgy, who was no mean artist, caught butterflies and painted them. She collected pets of every variety, a habit which later became so pronounced that when she was offered some silkworms one of her sons wrote that 'the whole house will become a worm infirmary'. She hunted in Leicestershire. The Austrian Baron Zedwitz, himself a master of hounds, described how at Melton Mowbray he saw Lady Seymour take a tremendous leap and followed her over 'in a great fright for shame at being left behind by a lady'.

Husband and wife travelled together abroad when duties in the House of Commons allowed: to Germany, to Paris and for one whole winter to Italy. On their way by carriage to Rome and Naples, they spent a day or two in Genoa where, Seymour reported to his father, 'Lady Seymour never moves without a piece of camphor in her hand, which is very necessary. I believe the sense of smell is obliterated among the Italians.'

The Victorians, though less formal in address than the eighteenth-century Georgians, were never familiar in the use of Christian names. That the eldest son should be called Seymour by his wife, his parents and his closest friends would not have been unusual even in the first half of the twentieth century; but in letters to his father he always wrote of his wife as Lady Seymour and when mentioning his stepmother (for the Duke had married again) he referred to her as 'the Duchess'. He invariably called the most intimate friends by their surnames.

The Hungry Forties, with their tragic implications for the Irish peasants, and with misery in England and Scotland due to widespread poverty and economic depression, did not cause grave inconvenience to the well-to-do. Those with liberal inclinations, like the Duke of Somerset and his son, did their best in Parliament to promote methods of alleviation, but they saw no reason to curtail their personal expenditure on yachting, hunting and shooting.

In the summer recess of 1843, the Seymours sailed off the west coast of Scotland, fishing in the rivers and shooting on the islands. During this Scottish tour they stayed with Lord and Lady Douro at Auchnacara near Fort William and made an expedition to Mull. 'We set out on ponies, with baggage tied to our saddles, and a very curious appearance we made, Lady Douro and Lady Seymour wrapped up in Mackintosh cloaks and plaid shawls.' They had ridden some miles when the heavens opened and they were drenched. The storm was such that they could not cross to Mull. They found no inn and were advised to turn back since their only hope of shelter was a manse in a village fourteen miles ahead, along a road so bad in places that they would be obliged to dismount and lead their ponies. However, 'the ladies were only intent on advancing and accordingly we went on' over the slope of a mountain, rough, steep and stony, eventually reaching the distant manse in torrents of rain.

> The clergyman was away, for he was gone to Australia. However, the women, his relations, and a clergyman who was his substitute, were as hospitable as possible. They killed chickens and boiled eggs and gave us all they could find. They were much astonished when they found it was Lord Douro and a party from Auchnacara who were rambling over the country in such a stormy night.

The storm did not abate on the following day, but the intrepid ladies insisted on setting sail for Mull with a reluctant boatman, and wet through from the seas which broke over the sailing boat they did finally reach the island.

The next autumn, 1844, Seymour, who had lost office as Under

Secretary at the Home Office when Peel became Prime Minister, persuaded Lord John Russell, leader of his party in the House of Commons, to give him leave of absence and set off on a long yachting trip in the Mediterranean. He left Georgy in Paris for the winter with her children, her mother and her sister Nelly Dufferin. Georgy spent hours improving her French while Ghigo, who was studying in Paris, found time to teach the children, even the youngest, Latin; and they all took part in an amateur performance of *The School for Scandal* at the British Embassy. 'I shall not', she wrote to Seymour, 'take them to the French theatres: the plots and jokes all seem to me as well to remain unheard by them.'

An old, rich and generally unpopular Russian Prince Labanoff fell for Georgy's charms (though not she for his). He was, she reported, a cousin of the Czar and very grumpy. 'But you may like him as he is *très instruit* and has just written a book which we shall all have to read and, I fear, is dull and profound.' The Prince lent her magnificent horses of sixteen hands with which she hunted deer at St Germain in company with the Orléans princes and some Arab sheikhs, whose white and purple burnouses were ill suited to damp forest rides. She was dismayed that the French *chasse à courre* involved no jumping; but she persisted, with the aged Russian prince providing the horses, in hunting wild boar at Fontainebleau and following the Duc de Nemours's staghounds. 'We ran for three hours in the wildest and most beautiful part of the forest – but nothing like fox-hunting.' She was given two stags' feet which she decided to dry and mount.

In more serious mood she went to the Académie Française to listen to a fine speech by Victor Hugo and meet Sainte-Beuve the famous literary critic. She also spent a day at the Chambre des Députés 'and came in for some good things, amongst others little Guizot in a great passion, flying his arms about like a windmill'.

Meanwhile, Lord Seymour had put to sea with his friend George Bentinck, M.P. for West Norfolk, who had a 100-ton cutter called *The Dream*. He was known in Royal Yacht Squadron circles as Big Ben on account of his size and his status at Westminster. On the way to Italy and Greece the yacht paused at Gibraltar, of which Seymour wrote:

> The town is full of bustle, and the variety of costume exceeds any place I have ever seen except, perhaps, Trieste. Spaniards,

Moors and African Jews in their national dresses crowd the streets, the trade, as you know, consisting chiefly of articles to be smuggled into Spain. The bay is enlivened by small vessels which are employed in the contraband traffic, and as long as they remain under the protection of the English batteries, the Spanish revenue cruisers can not touch them. This protection seems to be very effectual, for a short time since a cruiser in pursuit of a smuggler came within reach of the guns, and instantly a shot was fired with such effect that the cruiser went down before it could reach the Spanish port of Algeçiras. Boats were sent off to save the crew, but this certainly appears a rough mode of treating a friendly power.

The Spanish reasons for wishing to repossess Gibraltar seem less ill-founded than is sometimes supposed.

The principal activity of George Bentinck's guests in *The Dream* was to shoot woodcock and snipe in Corfu, Albania and the Ionian Islands, which were still British. In this pursuit they were remarkably successful, often killing up to 200 woodcock in a day and feasting off pâtés of woodcocks' brains. They were joined at Corfu by Prince George of Cambridge, whose father was the seventh of George III's nine sons. The Prince was a professional soldier, stationed at Corfu, who later became Duke of Cambridge and Commander-in-Chief of the British Army. Like his uncle, King William IV, he produced children out of wedlock rather than in it, and his offspring, called Fitzgeorge, matched the FitzClarences.

On this occasion sport was his prime objective and when *The Dream* party dined with Prince George at the citadel in Corfu the pâté of woodcocks' brains had required sixty birds. They were seven guns in all (a party, Georgy commented, 'which sounds very like St James' in the middle of Albania') and by Christmas these insatiable sportsmen had accounted for nearly 2,000 woodcock in addition to many snipe and duck, several enormous hawks and four deer. They confessed to having missed one or two wolves or jackals. With muzzle-loading shotguns the extent of the carnage was remarkable.

We no sooner land (Seymour wrote to Georgy from Albania) than everyone rushes off with his gun in different directions, and in a few minutes one is in a thicket, another in a swamp and others fording rivers or struggling through ravines. Yesterday I found Prince George in the midst of a wood, up to his middle in water and held fast by some inextricable brambles. . . .

A pertinent comment on shooting mania was made in a letter which Seymour wrote, shortly before this yachting holiday, from Hurn Court, Lord Malmesbury's house near Christchurch.

The late Lord Malmesbury was very fond of shooting, and for forty years he kept a journal of his shooting performances. In this he noted down every day he went out, every shot he fired and whether he killed or missed. The number of miles he probably walked in the forty years, according to his calculation, was above 36,000 and he shot above 38,000 creatures. A curious book this will be for the comments of future antiquarians, explaining to unborn generations the forgotten habits of English noblemen.

The party on *The Dream* behaved about as badly as the British normally do abroad.

We came the other day to a convent, a ruinous sort of tower where some monks lived. I wished to see the interior and accordingly we all rushed in to the building and clambered up a staircase into a wretched room, furnished only with wooden benches. On one of these an old monk lay asleep. He was startled at finding five or six men with guns taking possession of his apartment; and, indeed, our party *is* rather alarming – what with their costumes, beards and moustaches, it is a strange sight. Bentinck has got a most formidable beard and all the others dress as if they were acting banditti on the stage. The natives frequently run away at the sight of us, so that we go about as if the whole Morea belonged to us.

At Hydra they were taken for spies and were the inadvertent cause of a riot between the pro-French and pro-British parties in the town. At Athens they went to the National Assembly, where Seymour noted that six deputies were making speeches all at once and total parliamentary chaos had been established. But the time had come to return to his own legislative duties. The journey home, with stops at Malta and Lisbon, was a slow one, for they were frequently becalmed and it was the end of April (1845) before they reached England to find the political temperature rising, the Corn

Laws a subject of controversy and agitation for parliamentary reform fomented by the new Chartist movement.

Seymour's political career prospered. The Whigs returned to office in 1846. Three years later Lord John Russell, the new Prime Minister, appointed him Chief Commissioner of Woods and Forests, promoting him shortly afterwards to be First Commissioner of Works, with a seat in the Cabinet and a Privy Councillorship. In 1855 the borough of Totnes, so long a family perquisite, was disfranchised and at the same time the Whigs lost office. Seymour no longer had a seat. Disraeli, who had a high opinion of his qualities, wrote that he feared he would shortly be going to the Lords, which he much regretted 'as I always looked to the possibility of his taking a leading part in the reconstruction of parties'. Disraeli's premonition was correct. At the end of August 1855, while the Crimean War still raged, the liberal, intelligent and philanthropic Edward Adolphus died, and Lord Seymour succeeded as 12th Duke of Somerset. A few years later Palmerston became Prime Minister and Seymour joined the Cabinet as First Lord of the Admiralty, an office he held for seven years.

Meanwhile Georgy was principally occupied with the five children – three girls and two boys, born between 1831 and 1846. The girls grew up to their parents entire satisfaction and by the summer of 1865 they were all married.

The eldest, Lady Hermione, was the best-looking. She married Frederick, son of her great-uncle and aunt, Sir James and Lady Graham of Netherby. It was long a peculiarity of the Grahams to marry their close relations. Indeed many years later, when Lady Hermione's son, Sir Richard, died, one of his relations lost by that single death his first cousin, his uncle and his brother-in-law. This mildly incestuous tendency did not have any untoward effect on the family's looks or intelligence, and three of Lady Hermione's four daughters, Lady Verulam, the Duchess of Montrose and Lady Houghton, inherited much of their grandmother's renowned beauty. The fourth, Lady Wittenham, handsome but less strikingly so than her sisters, made a childless marriage with an immensely rich magnate who owned Covent Garden. Her nephews and nieces were brought up to be unmercenary. They were so afraid of being thought to have an eye on their aunt's fortune that they could seldom be induced even to call on her.

The second St Maur daughter, Lady Ulrica, married Lord Henry Thynne, the tall and imposing brother of Lord Bath. He had a successful career in the House of Commons, even becoming a Privy Councillor; but it was rumoured that he treated Lady Ulrica roughly, though she never complained, and he had strange hypnotic powers that earned him the nickname Svengali.

The youngest of the family, Lady Guendolen, was fifteen years younger than Lady Hermione and was the closest of the three girls to her parents, in particular to her father. She married when she was nineteen a rich baronet from the north, Sir John Ramsden, who was a Liberal Member of Parliament for over thirty years.

It is the elder son, the future Earl St Maur, born in 1835, whose actions were responsible for the events to be described in this story, and a whole chapter must be devoted to him. But he had a brother Edward, six years younger than himself, whose promise was great and whose unexpected demise changed the history of the Seymour family and brought grief to his father and mother that no passage of time erased.

The boys' father and grandfather were both educated at Eton and Christ Church, Oxford. A generation later, Eton, a stronghold of Tory landowners, was out of fashion with Whigs like the Somersets. Starting with Georgiana, Duchess of Devonshire, her sister Lady Bessborough, Lord Spencer, Lord Aberdeen and the Duke of Dorset, they switched their allegiance to Harrow which, though founded in Queen Elizabeth's reign, was until the second half of the eighteenth century a comparatively insignificant grammar school. But it was on a hill, and therefore considered healthy, and it was only nine miles from London.

Eton was not thought politically suitable and Harrow was said to be going through a bad phase. So Seymour finally decided to send his sons neither to a public school nor, remembering his own idleness at Christ Church, to a university. The elder, Ferdy, went for a time to a little-known preparatory school, but Edward was educated, and well educated, entirely at home. His father, however occupied with political affairs, took his younger son with him wherever he might be and never failed to give him personal instruction each morning; for Edward meant more to him than anybody in the world. The remaining lessons were left to competent tutors.

At eighteen, Edward, short but handsome, was better instructed, as his surviving letters prove, than most of his more conventionally educated contemporaries. His playmates were boys of social significance, including the Prince of Wales and Lord Carrington, and he was not so overworked as to be deprived of riding and shooting partridges at Maiden Bradley. Neither that nor the adoration of his parents and his sisters spoiled him; nor was he inclined to be a stay-at-home. On the contrary, he and his brother were adventurous and they were both determined to gain experience by travel, which was a time-consuming occupation in the mid-nineteenth century. As late as 1862 Ferdy, on his way from Nice to Genoa, had to cross the Col de Limone by sledge and mule, twice taking four hours to reach the summits.

> In coming down (he wrote) our mule got bogged in the snow and impelled by a desire to be actively useful, I plunged knee-deep in the snow and danced opposite the struggling animal. The live contents of the sledge tumbled out fearing we should go over the side of the hill – and the mule finally fell flat on his side. Full of English notions, I expected we should untrace him, but the driver with assistance fished up the mule by the tail by sheer force. . . .

Edward's precocity satisfied his parents' fondest hopes, and his interest in current politics, at home and abroad, left little doubt what his career would eventually be. His sensitivity was sharp. On reading of the vengeance taken by British troops during the Indian Mutiny, Edward, barely sixteen, wrote to Ferdy who was with the relief force besieging Lucknow:

> I really wish our officers might remember that if they owe no mercy to the Indians, they at least owe some respect to themselves. The press and public opinion jump from one extreme to another. They exhibit a kind of mixture between cant and cruelty, holding it up one day as our Christian duty to civilize and convert, the next as our divine mission to exterminate.

A few weeks later, when some of the more lurid accounts of the mutineers' atrocities were shown to be exaggerated, he wrote:

> I described to you the rabid attacks under which the public suffered, its gradual cure and how it found that half the things it

believed rested on no authority. Now some bright pates are trying to make out that the rebels are in the right and that it is all our fault. We must always be jumping from one extreme to the other.

At seventeen he was sent travelling with a tutor in northern Italy. When visiting a monastery he was shown a picture of St Francis preaching to the Turks and was astonished to be told by a monk, 'You understand that *le Grand Turque* is not a Catholic like us: he is a protestant.' That same year, after much drudgery, 'sweeping up the dusty floor of literature and gathering the dust into one's reading-pan', he took the preliminary Civil Service examination, passing with flying colours, though he protested that whereas he wanted to delve into the origin of matter and the formation of worlds, he was obliged to concentrate on practical studies. He felt like the ivy which, when it meant to curl round a romantic ruin, had been 'caught hold of and nailed up against a neat, comfortable white-washed cottage'.

At eighteen Edward went to spend a year as an attaché at the British Embassy in Vienna, followed by a year in a similar capacity at the Legation in Madrid. He found time to go to Venice and to set out on an arduous, solitary walking tour in the Dolomites. His descriptive letters to his father are evidence of his romantic nature and literary gifts.

> The day was fine though cloudy: wreaths of white mist curling round the hillsides as though all the fairies had fallen in love with the rough old mountains and were twisting their pretty white arms round their giant loves, an embrace you envied till your romance was damped by feeling it.

Between Vienna and Madrid he spent three months in the Carpathians, Bosnia, Serbia, Montenegro, Greece and finally the Middle East. He was not impressed by 'the Servians', as they were called in those days, writing to Ferdy in January 1861: 'The Servians are a despicable set of low slaves. Milosch, the late Prince, was a swine-herd, energetic, avaricious, cruel and poxy. He governed by the help of a tinker, a tailor, a shoemaker and a priest—his ministers.'

By the time Edward left Madrid, he was, at nineteen, exceptionally well-travelled for a youth of his age. He took a final examination and the Civil Service Commission commented on 'the marked proficiency which Lord Edward St Maur has displayed'. They rated his knowledge of German and Spanish as excellent and added that a report he had written on the Spanish situation was highly commended for its ability. The Chargé d'Affaires in Madrid wrote that 'a more promising young man it has never been my lot to come across'.

He was still too young to stand for Parliament, though this was undoubtedly his ultimate intention, and so when he returned home he spent some time writing a learned article on the Spanish Church and Exchequer which *The Fortnightly Review* published and which won, in a letter to Edward's mother, an unsolicited eulogy from the Speaker of the House of Commons.

Civil War had broken out in America. Edward persuaded his father, somewhat anxious, as a dignified member of the Cabinet, about the escapades in which his sons might take part, to let him cross the Atlantic. In New York he immersed himself in the politics of the northern States, writing percipient letters home about the opinions of Democrats and Republicans. Then, pausing for a few days on a slave estate in Maryland to see what slavery was like in practice, he set off for Washington.

It was June 1862, and the Southern Confederate forces were filled with enthusiasm and belief in victory. To a young man of twenty news-gathering in Washington seemed an unimaginative ploy. So he slipped across the Potomac and then the Rappahannock by night, slept on river banks and, on one occasion, in a marsh

> where the frogs were so large that their croaking sounded like the bellowing of bulls, and the fireflies skipped about among the tall rushes as if experiments were being conducted at some very extensive gasworks, not to mention the mosquitos who seemed to me as large as dragon-flies and bit voraciously *through* my clothes – in fact mosquitos is a tame expression, I ought rather to have said air-sharks.

He reached Richmond, Virginia, where he was courteously received and was the spectator of severe engagements in which, mindful of his father's position, he managed to restrain himself from taking a personal part. This was the description of the Confederates he sent to Ferdy.

> The Southern Army has been scrambled together and, considering that, it is wonderful how they get on. They march regardless of fours and do little in any kind of order. Withal they storm breastworks gallantly, a regiment losing two thirds of its number and never flinching. I was introduced to Jefferson Davis today, a spare, keen-looking man, very gentleman-like, even in dress which is a wonder here. The utter contempt for uniform of every description would please you – a general goes about in a straw-hat and any pair of trousers that happens to suit him. A large proportion of the army wear anything. Trousers and shirt is the prevailing uniform, but every man has a musket, a canteen and generally a blanket, and I have not yet seen a man with a bad pair of shoes.

While he was with them, the Confederate troops took, he learned, 10,000 prisoners, but he made careful notes of their shortages, in particular salt and saltpetre for gunpowder. They eventually returned him by flag of truce to the other side; and there the trouble began. The son of a duke, and an important duke at that, had no right to go to the Confederate States. At General McClellan's camp, the staff interrogated him sharply, gave vent to strong anti-British sentiments, and told him that he had acted in violation of both the President's and the Queen's proclamations. Arrest seemed probable and he had to journey hurriedly northwards to Canada whence he dispatched a long, informative letter to his father. 'I can assure you', he wrote, 'that the feeling of Venetians and Hungarians towards the Austrian soldiers is a mild and charitable sentiment compared with the feelings of a Southerner at the sight of a blue-coated Yankee.'

When he came home, *Blackwood's Magazine,* one of the most widely read publications, gladly accepted an article entitled 'Ten Days in Richmond'. He was now twenty-one, but in the autumn of 1862 no parliamentary seat was immediately on offer and a General Election did not seem imminent. So he joined Ferdy in Florence, explored Rome and Naples and then went home to enlarge his acquaintance and bring companionship to his family. The Duke, a Knight of the Garter in 1862 and much respected at the Admiralty (where he introduced reforms that included the restriction of flogging in the navy) took Edward with him in the Admiralty yacht *Enchantress* to inspect the fleet and dockyards at Malta, and in the Queen's yacht *Osborne* for an official visit to the north of France.

It was not sufficient for Edward. The diplomatic service did not attract him. 'Too much cutting little bits out of the papers, translating them and sending them to Lord John [Russell]; an occupation no doubt useful, but it seems to me this might be accomplished as well in London as in Vienna.' So he decided to see for himself the mysterious East, where Ferdy had spent eighteen months seven years before. He would go to India.

He stayed for the wedding of his sister Guendolen, five years his junior in age, during the summer of 1865. He paid a round of country house visits, enthralled by Dunrobin which, towering above the seashore and framed by wild purple hills, reminded him of the habitation of a princess in the fairy tales; but from a more austere party at Highclere, where he stayed with Lord Carnarvon, he complained to Guendolen that he was 'in a bevy of Deans and Dons, which made me feel like a black – I will not say sheep, but lamb, for you know I always feel like a lamb!'

Just after Edward set off for India, Palmerston died and he was tempted to return home in case there should be a General Election. Totnes no longer existed as an independent constituency, but perhaps Tiverton might select him. However, leaving messages that he should be alerted if any exciting proposition were made, he set sail from Marseilles and reached Bombay early in November 1865. Never short of introductions, as was indeed to be expected for a cherished son of the First Lord of the Admiralty, he found that the Governor of Bombay, Sir Bartle Frere, had left hospitable instructions for his reception together with an invitation to travel up country and join him on an official tour he was making.

On his way to Kohlapur, where the Governor was to attend the Rajah's durbar, he wrote this description of the Indian scene in a letter to his mother.

> If you imagine a succession of flat basins of land from twelve to twenty miles long, surrounded by high hills, many of which end at the top in a wall of rock so steep and so sudden as to look like the wall of one of those castles on the Rhine, ten thousand times

magnified. These natural fastnesses looking over the basin-land covered with crops of novel appearance and unpronounceable names, interspersed with trees strange to the European eye, some of which throw out roots from their top branches (I mean the banyan tribe), which hang like wooden stalactytes till they join the ground, and growing a fresh trunk make the tree spread cloister-like over the field. Others like the mango tree twisted and gnarled like oak, now of the old green where the leaves are still on, now the pinkish-red fading into light green where the new leaves are coming out. If you people the trees with red-beaked bright-green wingy parrots, that fly screeching after each other, and squirrels streaked yellow and brown, and if you put under them hump-backed cattle and hippopotamus-like buffaloes, wallowing in some muddy pool with their noses out of the water, near little thatched houses out and in of which are walking white-turbaned, dark faced Mahrattas, with silver and even gold bracelets round their unclad arms, and if you imagine the already described little stone temples cropping out among the huts and trees, and if you add to this two horses picketed under a tree or in a shed, and some very sleepy boys slowly answering repeated cries to bring me my fresh horses, you will have imagined as much of my travelling and of the country as is necessary.

After the long and formal durbar, Edward had had enough of stately occasions. He accepted an invitation from the Collector of North Canara in the south Deccan to see a wilder side of India and to shoot bison. Before setting out he wrote: 'And, darling Mother, as to your warning against exposure, my best answer is that I have been dining in white ties and on champagne and roast mutton ever since I commenced roughing it on my travels.' That might relieve maternal solicitude, but it was not the life Edward proposed to lead for the next week or so.

On 18 December he went into the jungle near a village called Lalgooly. The going was difficult. It was, he wrote at the end of the first day, like Scotland overgrown with tropical forest. It meant 'picking your way through grass high over your head and dodging among thorns and branches, trying to avoid the hollow, fallen canes of bamboo under your feet which sound like spring- guns if you are unlucky enough to tread on them'. To his disgust he missed a big bison at eighty yards and was far from content with a small stag as a substitute.

The following morning he set off at 5 a.m. with a local administrator and a native hunter. His companion went one way, Edward another. As he forced his way through the jungle, he came fact to face not, as he expected, with bison, but with two black Deccan bears. The Deccan bear is more like a hugh sloth than a bear, with short legs and claws as sharp as scythes. On its chest is a triangular yellow patch, the apex of which is the only target for a mortal shot. Edward fired at the larger bear, which rolled over, recovered itself and bolted. He followed the bloodstained track with the Indian hunter behind him, and in due course he came on the bear lying in some bamboos fifteen yards ahead of him.

The bear was far from dead. Had it risen on its hind legs, as it seems Deccan bears usually do, it would have presented a good target; but it charged on all fours. Edward hit it with both barrels of his rifle, but this failed to stop the charge. It seized him in its wounded fury and together they rolled down a steep hill in deadly embrace, Edward stabbing the bear with his hunting knife and inflicting a deep wound.

Four days later, despite all that two hastily summoned doctors could do, despite the amputation of a badly mauled leg, Edward died. He was just twenty-four. As delirium set in, he spoke of his lost hope and ambition: 'All this for a bear – and so I shall never govern this great Empire.' He had summoned up enough strength to write to his father and to dictate a letter to Ferdy. Perhaps he had one of those premonitions which sometimes enlighten the dying, for he ended the letter to his brother: 'Goodbye. Do marry, is the advice from your affectionate cripple, Edward St Maur.'

# 5
# *Disaster*

In the nineteenth century primogeniture, obsolescent in Europe as a result of the Code Napoléon, was the system of inheritance generally accepted in the British Isles and as often as not reinforced by entail. With modifications it still rules among landowners in Britain today.

It had clear advantages as far as landed property was concerned. Great estates could be efficiently managed; tenant farmers, unable to afford the purchase of land themselves, were supported by landlords who might defer, lower or even remit rents in times of agricultural depression; there was the means to keep fences, farm roads and buildings in good repair; and the large British farming units were, and still are, more economic and productive than those on the European continent where four or five generations of legally imposed family egalitarianism have reduced holdings to a few hectares or even less.

The disadvantages in the nineteenth century were personal. Younger sons received little to support them. As social status was important, they had to choose a career in the army, the navy or the Church (there were always family livings to bestow), because anything to do with trade and commerce was unthinkably vulgar, and the law and the Civil Service were middle-class preserves. Even the Diplomatic Service, though socially acceptable, required a candidate to have a guaranteed income as well as the ability to pass a stiff examination. Favoured younger sons might be just sufficiently endowed for a political career, unpaid though membership of the House of Commons then was. Some, such as William Pitt, Lord John Russell, Lord William Bentinck and Lord Randolph Churchill, won far greater distinction than their elder brothers. The Duke of Somerset would certainly have found the means to enable his favourite child, Edward, to enter and shine in politics.

Girls, of course, were in a different category altogether.

Sometimes the failure of the male line made them highly desirable heiresses. Otherwise they either married suitably or stayed at home as unpaid companion to their mothers.

The worst sufferers were, in many cases, precisely those supposed to benefit: the eldest sons. They lived on expectations, sometimes long deferred, and unlike their younger brothers they were discouraged from risking their valuable persons too near a field of battle. There were no death duties or onerous succession taxes to induce an early transfer of property. Jealousy might make parents hesitate to let the heir participate in managing the family estates or oversee the agents, and if young men sought to accommodate themselves to changing habits, methods and circumstances, they were labelled as irresponsible by an older generation intent on preserving traditions and fortunes just as they had inherited them. In addition there was often a nagging consciousness that much was expected of them: more than they felt able to deliver. Ferdy exemplified that malaise.

It is not surprising that unemployed heirs found dissipation a palliative and gilded indolence a vocation. If hampered by parental parsimony they knew that their expectations would satisfy the moneylenders. A seat in the House of Commons did nothing, in times when parliamentary sessions were mercifully short, to interfere with horse-racing, field sports and yachting or to inhibit long evenings at the card-tables and clandestine visits to Paris.

When it came to marriage, breeding was as important a consideration as in the racing stables. Girls of a lower class, or emanating from families said to have 'bad blood', had to be avoided. Arranged marriages were the order of the day although, as in the case of Ferdy's parents, love sometimes triumphed over heraldic quarterings. The domestic life of an eldest son tended to be a stock-breeding exercise rather than the intertwining of two mutually attracted human beings. This was normally accepted with resignation, and even sweetened by affection; but romance was seldom the companion of primogeniture.

In consequence, kings and queens, the foremost examples of primogeniture, were usually critical of their future successors, and great noblemen in Britain followed suit. This was the story of Queen Victoria and Albert Edward, Prince of Wales. It was also, with many variations, the story of the Duke and Duchess of Somerset and Ferdinand, Lord Seymour. If Albert Edward was less handsome than Ferdy, he not only had much greater expectations, but he was endowed with a firmer character and a doughtier constitution. The Prince of Wales was impatient but he survived forty adult years in waiting and many scandals. It is unlikely that Lord Seymour would have had either the patience or the resilience to support and outlast parental domination.

The bonds of natural affection between Ferdy and his parents were strained. Ferdy, on his incessant travels, did indeed write home frequently and conscientiously, and his father and mother, worried and irritated though they were by his apparently pointless activities, at first responded with little rancour. In due course, parental patience wore thin and his father's attitude was principally dictated by duty. His mother was genuinely attached to him, but many years later Ferdy's daughter and his sister Guendolen were so shocked by the vituperative language in some of the letters she wrote that they consigned them to the flames. One thing however, is clear: Ferdy was not distressed by his family's, and particularly his father's, obvious preference for Edward. On the contrary, Edward's future and Edward's prosperity were his prime interest, and though his character was scarred by many imperfections, jealousy was not among them.

His addiction to foreign travel started innocently enough, as did Edward's. They were positively encouraged by their father, mindful that his own education and development owed more to seeing the world than to Eton and Christ Church. Inheritor of his mother's good looks, Ferdy at twenty-one was judged by the Foreign Secretary to be an ideal choice to accompany Lord Granville, Queen Victoria's representative at the coronation in Moscow of the new Czar, Alexander II, just after the end of the Crimean War. Lord Clarendon wrote that his only request to Lord Granville was 'to take Lord Seymour with him. G's answer was that he should be most happy, as Lord S. was just the specimen of English aristocracy that he should like the Russians to see'.

His letters home did not vie with Edward's in interest or descriptive quality. He dutifully sent his father an account of a visit to Nishni Novgorod, of the Czar's entry into Moscow riding at the head of 200 A.D.C.s, of the massive golden carriages and the tedious presentations, and he noted the false tinsel in Russian magnificence.

In writing to his mother he described an official visit to the splendid white and yellow palace of Peterhof:

> We were (all except the ladies) conducted into a small room whose walls were literally covered with painted women's faces, all more or less ugly. These paintings were not framed but fixed in the wall and only separated by narrow gold beading. There were six men, blackies and brownies dressed in an eastern costume, with white turbans and red slippers and green gold-laced jackets, standing at the three doors, two at each.... Soon the Emperor appeared with Lord Granville, who introduced us all as his czarness walked down the line saying a few words to each. The Emperor was tall and well-made, but not remarkable in any way and rather brusque in his manner. He said to me and most of us that he remembered our mothers, but (he added) long ago. The Empress passed us, also saying a few words to each. She was not pretty and had a jade's look, putting one rather in mind of a Queen on the stage of some second rate theatre. In spite of some superb diamonds I thought her ill-dressed: three ladies of the Court who stood in the back-ground had the same little play-house appearance.... We sailed back to St Petersburg by moon light, Lord Granville taking on himself all responsiblity as our pilot was very unwilling to go (he was soon after our start carried downstairs drunk). This feat has rather astonished the Russians.

After his Russian excursion Ferdy was only home for two months before deciding on further travel. He set off for Persia, where the British were waging a minor punitive war against the Shah. At Bushire he procured employment as Assistant Political Secretary to General Sir James Outram, who made an unsuccessful effort to procure a commission for him so that he could join in the fighting. However, the Shah soon made peace and Ferdy journeyed on to Ceylon, Calcutta and Madras. While he was in Madras, in the summer of 1857, the Indian Mutiny assumed cataclysmic proportions with the hideous massacre of men, women and children at Cawnpore and the siege of the Residency at Lucknow. Ferdy hastened back to Calcutta so as to take a part in the affair and not only disregarded an unequivocal order from his father at the Admiralty that he should sail for home, but contrived to evade the watchful eye of the Governor General, Lord Canning, whom the

Duke and Duchess had begged to restrain him. The Somersets had no ambition to see their son crowned with military glory. Their son, however, had: with no formal commission he joined the army preparing for a rescue operation.

In the summer heat he marched hundreds of exhausting miles on foot and took part in the relief of Lucknow. Sir Colin Campbell, commanding the troops, mentioned him in dispatches as having displayed 'a most daring gallantry at a critical moment'. This was because on one occasion the men hesitated in an attack and Ferdy, drawing his sword, rushed to the front, having eventually to be ordered back from an exposed position by Sir Colin himself. In reply to a remonstrance from his mother for his failure to obey his father's injunction, he wrote: 'You know I wanted to enter the army in the Crimean War: had I done so, I should probably not be here now, as I only wished to serve a few years and never intended giving up all idea of entering parliament.' By the end of 1857 he had in fact given up all parliamentary ambition; but he did not tell his family, and he hoped that Edward would assume the legislative mantle he had been expected to wear.

Having burned a temple built by Nana Sahib, the butcher of Cawnpore, and carried off from it a gilded marble bull (which he dispatched as a gift to the British Museum), Ferdy went back to England after an absence of eighteen months. He did not receive the welcome to be expected by a long-absent son. So he joined the 4th Dragoon Guards and believing war between England and France to be imminent (a belief then widely shared in both countries), he also applied himself, most ineffectively, to organising a Volunteer Corps of Wiltshire men centred at Maiden Bradley. 'The Wiltshire Daisies', Edward irreverently called them.

Restless, impetuous, unsure of his own intentions, Ferdy stuck to no last. He resigned his commission after a few months, he did his best to hand the Wiltshire Daisies over to a reluctant Edward, and announcing to one of his sisters that the sound of the cannon in any part of the world was music to his ears, he went to observe the conflict between France and Austria in Northern Italy. He arrived in Vienna just too late, for peace was signed in July 1859.

A year later, without telling his parents, he journeyed to Sicily, Salerno and Naples where the sound of cannon was distinctly audible as Garibaldi, with his 1,000 red-shirted enthusiasts heavily reinforced, advanced against the King of Naples and the

Two Sicilies. The poor young king, Francis II, had only been on the throne for a year and was married to an attractive sister of the beautiful Empress of Austria. The majority of his subjects were loyal to their Bourbon sovereign, but Garibaldi and his followers were inspired by the vision of a united Italy and this vision was shared in Great Britain. Large sums of money were subscribed and 600 British volunteers joined Garibaldi's standard.

Ferdy, calling himself Captain Richard Sarsfield so as not to embarrass the First Lord of the Admiralty, joined the volunteers and was appointed Military Secretary to their commander, Colonel John Pearce. The Colonel was an excellent shot and killed a lot of the enemy with the rifle he had hitherto used for deerstalking. The 600 British volunteers were not a force of high quality. Indeed, as one Italian historian wrote, 'with the exception of their gallant Colonel and Lord Seymour, they were assuredly not very manageable fellows'. The British Minister in Naples was more explicit: he reported that they were consistently drunk and disorderly, and most of them, as one of their own number admitted, 'did not care a button for one side or the other, but wanted at all costs to have a lark'.

Ferdy showed courage and initiative. He took a gallant part in the battle to seize Capua on the River Volturno. But the Duke was deeply vexed by his escapade, whatever the pseudonym with which he disguised himself. Even his tolerant brother Edward was incensed. He wrote:

> What is your object in gadding about on excursions? It is one thing to see and learn and gain experience; another to poke oneself into a subordinate command for the pleasure of drilling and smelling powder. . . . You have often spoken to me of the duties of position: I am only a younger son, but do you think Captain Sarsfield will make a useful peer of England? What is your ultimate object? Will you sacrifice all county and hereafter country duties in order to smell powder?

Ferdy did not know what his ultimate object was. He had inherited not the brilliance of the Sheridans, but their instability. His uncle, Sir James Graham, did his best to soothe the angry Somersets by writing to Georgy: 'I am truly sorry that any act of Ferdy should annoy his father and give you so much pain and anxiety; but it is only an indiscretion, pardonable in a youth fond of military adventure.' They were perhaps a little mollified when the *Daily News* reported that 'Captain Sarsfield is the very soul of the regiment . . . kind to his soldiers, untiring in the performance of his duties. His courage, activity and zeal would do honour to the best officer of any army in Europe.'

As for Garibaldi, he was so delighted by the help, moral, military and financial, he received from Great Britain that he wrote this:

> England is a great and powerful nation, foremost in human progress, enemy of despotism, a friend of the oppressed; and if ever England should be so circumstanced as to require the help of an ally, cursed be the Italian who would not step forward with me in her defence.

Eighty years later Ferdy's daughter declared that Garibaldi's curse should be invoked against Benito Mussolini.

Whatever Garibaldi or the London *Daily News* might say, the Duke and Duchess were uneasy, unimpressed and worried about the future. They wanted their son to come home and take his responsibilities seriously. There was indeed good reason for him to do so. Edward told him: 'My father's affairs in the way of estates I believe are grossly mismanaged.' There were, Edward asserted, not forty thieves but four hundred. Their mother, who had been suffering from much illness, was now in good health. She had been acting with vigour and good sense,

> but her habits incapacitate her from business of a regular kind. However, the only stay of the family is in the mother. Otherwise the Festings* will become proprietors in fee simple and leave my father nothing but his library. If you were to become practical you could do much. At present they speculate ('they' means thieves and parasites generally too numerous to name) on your being the most inert of a very respectable line of King Logs.

Unlike some of their contemporaries the Somersets would probably have acquiesced if their son had wanted to take a leading part in managing the family estates. The Duke certainly would. But Ferdy was incorrigible. Home for a few months, he could not bear his family's clearly expressed displeasure and before long, disregarding every plea to settle down, he was off again abroad. This was partly because he had fallen desperately

---

*Mr Festing was the estate agent.

in love with a daughter of Lord Cowper who had the fortuitous advantage of being an unexceptionable choice by prevailing standards. However she, less impressed by his good looks than by his evident instability, rejected his advances.

In deepest dudgeon he set off for Dresden with the declared object of learning Russian, inappropriate though Dresden seemed for such an exercise. In the late summer of 1862 he announced his arrival there with a letter to his mother beginning 'Your affectionate rolling stone trundled in here this morning. . . '

Edward did not mince his words:

> In God's name what the Hell are you after? Forgive my language if strong, but if your actions generally puzzle me, this time I have cudgelled my brains in vain to find a motive – burying yourself in Dresden to learn Russian, and then talking of *Turkish*. Are you going in for a Panslavonic Empire or is it your intention to become a Mahommedan Luther?

He was not far off target, for Ferdy had begun to flirt with Islam and when out of his family's sight took to wearing Islamic clothes, beads and necklaces.

A month later young Edward, more influential with his brother than parents or sisters, tried again.

> I cannot help thinking that constant travelling, gadding about the world, if I may so say, without any very definite object, is nothing but a kind of intellectual dissipation which must end in intellectual sea-sickness and head-ache. . . . You are one who has wrapped himself in cerulean clouds of aspiration and thinks wishing is the highest action of the mind. To me a little *deed* appears more useful and more ennobling than a great *wish*.

The Duchess had said in a letter to Ferdy that Edward, rising twenty-two, was too young to enter Parliament. Ferdy disagreed, fearing that his brother's eagerness for a political career would be damped if he was asked to feed on hope deferred. His reply to his mother showed his deep concern for Edward and ended with this declaration of his own discontent:

> Age is not in other families insisted upon as it is in ours – I have already had enough of expectation and my home is anywhere but in England in consequence. Edward does not feel *now* what I

have felt, but he will do so, and I shall not wonder at the consequences.

My letter may sound unkind, but whatever is *hastened* must be so by your influence – I only wish to prevent your remaining in a dream, which must at last be broken by a disappointment. My health and spirits have passed away with my youth, and perhaps I write gloomily – but rest certain that it is better to let a man, however young, have a fair start than to *repress* him. Time may bring experience, but it deprives a man of that youthfulness of heart which alone makes friends, and of the energy and hope which lead most surely to success – and what is it worth? Experience is of little importance compared with good feeling and *sense*.

Your affectionate son<br>Seymour

As far as his brother was concerned Ferdy was right. Edward was fascinated by politics and had natural ability. If a seat had been found for him in the Commons, he would doubtless have been given office in Mr Gladstone's subsequent Liberal administrations; and in 1906, when Sir Henry Campbell-Bannerman swept into power with a huge Liberal majority, it is not fanciful to suppose that Edward, by then sixty-one and 13th Duke of Somerset, would have held one of the highest offices in a Government chronically short of Liberal peers.

Moreover, Ferdy himself did have some cause to shun the family circle. His two elder sisters were married, his father, immersed in the cares of office, showed no more than dutiful interest in him, and his mother, partly due to ill health, was increasingly given to tantrums and was growing year by year more imperious. She quarrelled with her sister Caroline Norton and they wrote each other letters professing affection but exuding spite.

These are extracts from a typical letter from Caroline, who smarted from the belief that Georgy had disapproved of her affairs with Lord Melbourne and others:

No one's life is quite revealed – even that of the most imprudent, – and no one's life is any very great mystery, because it is always plaited in with other lives, – and even the most reserved persons are then at the discretion of others. . . . You do not know my life, any more than I know yours, – nor how, in spite of all unfavourable circumstances, I retain not only the regard, but the esteem and best sort of admiration –admiration for conduct under real trials, – of friends with whom I have lived intimately.

I do not say I am unhappy now. I am happy now, – but trials and misfortunes I have had were enough for a lifetime, – and you would not have borne for eight months what I bore for eight years. . . .

I do believe that often it is only in manner that you seem arrogant, – but is it only I who think that?

After all, in that single sentence 'disappointed in you', lies the seed of all that I feel in your character. Are you so sure that you are able to judge, before you can be disappointed? I have always loved you. I forgave, even when I thought myself mortally injured; I was miserable at losing you.

I love you still, – so that to me it is a positive pleasure to be even with one of your children. My letter to you, which was written in doubt, was also written in love, –because you seemed at least to think yourself lonely and uncomfortable; – because you said in losing my Mother, you lost the only person you talked to. I do not count your 'having a good house &c' – but I do count that you have two sisters, and a brother, – or, if you will make me a cypher, – you have Helen and Brinny, and your children, – and that all those ties are happinesses which I tried to set against worries! . . .

God bless you. It is, as you say, vain to struggle where people do not understand each other.

Nelly Dufferin, the dove in an aquiline nest, did her best to smooth her sisters' constantly ruffled feathers. It seems that on the whole she found Caroline the more to blame and she could, on occasions, be startlingly frank.

Another thing you are always thinking of [she wrote] is the peculiarity of your position laying you open to insult. Do, Car, open your eyes (and shut your mouth) and see that this is not our old world, when we were all young, handsome women, much observed and talked of, and that you are no longer an idol of Vanity Fair surrounded by admirers and enviers, but an elderly and clever woman received in all Society, with a position of your own, a great literary reputation and a large circle of friends which would be still larger if you were not so apt to fancy slights where none are intended. Do leave Georgiana and her family alone unless your communications are made in the interests of peace and not for the purpose of irritating.

A month later Nelly wrote again:

In a very few years the end of strife and everything else will be at hand for us all. When that time comes neither you nor Georgy will look back upon the pain and humiliation you try to inflict upon each other with either triumph or pleasure.

Meanwhile both Nelly and Georgy waxed understandably indignant at an abusive letter Caroline wrote about their dead mother, Caroline Sheridan, whom they had both adored.

Unwilling to return to the family rows at home, Ferdy went from Dresden to Florence, nominally to learn Italian. He was joined by Edward, freshly back from the American Civil War. Edward picked up the language easily and fast; Ferdy's progress was slow and painful. The two brothers then moved to Rome whence Edward, after happy riding expeditions in the Campagna with an exceptionally attractive girl called Lady Diana Beauclerk, went home. He left Ferdy to be fêted by Roman society which would have found the elder son of an English duke to have charms whether he had them or not. In haughty mood Ferdy wrote to his sister Guendolen: 'I see that what I want is an entrance into the literature of the country rather than its Society. I want their opinions and not their company.' Disappointed by the Italians he journeyed on to Corfu, to Albania and to Byron's death-place, Missolonghi, announcing that he intended to study Eastern Europe.

Eventually, in May 1863, he came back to England and made another unavailing attempt to win the affections of Lord Cowper's unwilling daughter. His father, in an effort to anchor him, hit on a bright idea. He persuaded Queen Victoria and the Prime Minister, Lord Palmerston, to create him Earl St Maur. It was unseemly that his second title should be a mere barony, but dukes of lineage as ancient as Norfolk and Somerset thought the historic English degree of earl more distinguished for the courtesy title of their eldest son than the comparatively new-fangled one of marquess, derived from the French. At the same time he arranged to have Ferdy, who now admitted he had no inclination to stand for the House of Commons, summoned to the Lords in his father's barony of Seymour. This was an unusual but constitutionally admissible device, used as late as the Second World War when Lords Cranborne and Wolmer, two ministers with seats in the Commons, were summoned to the House of Lords in their fathers' second titles.

The Duke hoped that Ferdy, thenceforward known by courtesy as Earl St Maur and having a seat in Parliament, would take an interest in public affairs. Ferdy, alas, had no such ambition. He had little capacity for concentration, was growing year by year more introspective and adopted a grim and serious manner unmatched by serious achievement. He thought himself misunderstood and, by way of compensation, assumed poses and airs of mystery which so alienated his friends that there remained only sycophants and his genuinely affectionate brother. His daughter Ruth was doubtless thinking of what she had learned about her father when she wrote to her grandson many years later:

> Introspection is stultifying – one's own development, one's own thoughts and feelings – and it ends in gazing at a little dessicated something in a glass case. Then though one may still walk and eat, one is really dead without knowing it.

He made some effort to please his father and wearily attended sessions in the Lords, assuming a fleeting interest in matters that engaged none of his genuine enthusiasm. By the end of 1863 he had abandoned even that pretence and was off again – to Trieste, Croatia, Belgrade and Slovenia, dutifully but dully reporting to his family stays in country inns, varying in little but the degree of his distaste for them, and meetings with fellow travellers of scant interest. He displayed the English 'milord's' disdain for foreigners especially the poor Serbs whom Edward had also maligned: 'The Servians are worse than the Greeks in all but falsehood, and their lack of proficiency in this is due to their want of intelligence.'

He was home in December 1865, staying with one of his sisters, when the shattering news came of Edward's death from the embrace of the bear. He was inconsolable, for however much his younger brother might chide and criticise, he loved Edward more than anybody in the world. His mother wrote to him, immediately she received the news: 'Oh Ferdy, don't quit the country. I am keeping up for your sake. I know that of all the children this will be to you the heaviest.' The light went out of his father's eye; for Edward, the bright promise of the future, whom he himself had educated, meant everything to him, and it was with difficulty that Georgy persuaded him to remain a further six months in the Cabinet. The light went out of Ferdy's eyes too. He wrote some verses to be engraved on Edward's tomb in the distant Deccan. They were not great poetry, but two of the lines came from deep in a broken heart.

> His spirit lives: may mine through time and space
> Find till we meet no lasting resting place.

Nor did his spirit find a resting place. Edward's dying wish had been that he should marry. There was no shortage of eligible brides. There was Lady Diana Beauclerk, with whom Edward had ridden in the Campagna and whom Ferdy, too, found attractive; and doubtless there were many other young ladies for whom parents, more often than not arbiters of their daughters' destinies, would have found the handsome heir to a dukedom a highly desirable match. But uppermost in Ferdy's mind was the unattainable daughter of Lord Cowper to whom he wrote endless love letters on plain blue foolscap, but who in the spring of 1866 said firmly and finally 'No'.

Depressed and disconsolate, Ferdy went for a solitary walk in Hyde Park. He was disturbed from his melancholy reverie by the sound of sobbing. On a park bench, her face buried in her hands, sat a young girl weeping uncontrollably. He was by nature sympathetic and a damsel in such distress was not to be disregarded. He sat down beside her to ask what was amiss, and when she lifted her head he beheld a tear-stained visage of striking beauty. The eyes were dark, with a startled expression; the lips and cheeks were glowing and the well-shaped face was framed by locks of black hair.

In reply to gentle inquiries, he learned that she was just seventeen and her name was Rosina Swan. The eldest of a large and desperately poor family, she had been a kitchenmaid in Lady Bathurst's household. Lady Bathurst's cook was cruel to her and she had run away, determined never to return. She was penniless and in abject misery. Ferdy, affected by her story, led her to his bachelor establishment in Dover Street and told his housekeeper to feed, clothe and cherish her.

In his own wearisome, meaningless life he now had something to occupy him. His health was worrying him. Perhaps his formidable exertions in the Indian Mutiny, and later with Garibaldi's army, had taken their toll; perhaps a deep-seated weakness in his lungs was gaining a firmer hold. In writing to Guendolen after Edward's death, he said 'If I cannot write cheerfully it is due greatly to weakness from ill-health in past years from which I have not quite rallied.'

As a stimulating diversion, he set about educating Rosina. Her father was a labourer who lived at Higham, near Bury St Edmunds, the son of a bricklayer and unable to sign his name. Her mother, Mary Ann Baker, was a gipsy. Ferdy's family later made a point of meeting Mr and Mrs Swan and were struck by Mary Ann's dusky magnificence. The Swans' first child had been born in wedlock, with a few weeks to spare, and baptised Rosina Elizabeth. By the time she left home, probably at fourteen, the size of the family, increasing annually by one, was already in double figures.

It would be pleasant to add the story of the Swans to that of the Seymours and the Sheridans. Perhaps an ancestor followed Wat Tyler to London or joined the Pilgrimage of Grace. Perhaps a Swan fought at Creçy or Agincourt, at Blenheim or Quebec; and as for Rosina's maternal forbears, the history of the Romany people is a tantalising, insoluble mystery. In the case of the Swans and those whom they married, the mists of the past, thickened by illiteracy, are inpenetrable except by occasional entries in parish registers.

Unlike her father, Rosina had learned to read and write. Ferdy took pains to improve her literacy and he taught her to ride. Later on she mastered French in a matter of months. She was beautiful, good-natured and intelligent. He was her saviour: the handsome prince who had miraculously appeared on the scene in the nick of time to rescue her from the dragon of hopeless despair. She became his mistress.

There was no question of marriage. For all her qualities, a servant-girl, with a mixed and humble ancestry, could not in 1866 be contemplated as a future Duchess of Somerset even by Ferdy, who was becoming month by month less orthodox and was yet more prone to strike histrionic poses now that Edward's restraining influence was gone. Moreover, his mother was increasingly critical and captious. So the only thing to do was to go abroad again, taking Rosina with him.

They went first to Germany, and then by train across Europe to San Sebastian, Burgos, Cordova and Seville, coming to rest in Gibraltar where the Anglican bishop provided comfort and proved himself more intent on helping sheep that had strayed than in condemning immorality. From Gibraltar they sailed to Tangier, and while temporarily renting a house belonging to the British Consul, Ferdy bought a patch of rocky land, euphemistically described as a garden, for £13.

He set about building a house with thatched walls, and he answered insistent family demands for his return home by pleas that the English winter weather was injurious to his uncertain health. When a warm English summer arrived, he declared that the builders could not be trusted to complete his house without his personal supervision. Meanwhile he took Rosina riding through the Tangier countryside disguised as a slim, attractive boy. In Tangier of all places this was injudicious. Scandalous rumours led the British Consul to warn Ferdy, who now called himself Captain Gray, that his association with this 'boy' was being misunderstood. So Rosina stayed in the thatched shack and contacts with neighbours and the British community were avoided. By the spring of 1867 she was pregnant. Ferdy had promised to return home that summer and in almost all his letters to his mother he gave a date, subsequently blaming the slowness and incompetence of the Moorish builders for changing it. To please Rosina he had one of her many brothers, Nathan, shipped out to Tangier and apprenticed to an English sheep-farmer.

On 21 October 1867 Rosina gave birth to a daughter in the rickety cottage at Tangier. A month later, determined not to desert his mistress and child, Ferdy told his mother that the weather in England must now assuredly be too bad for him to return; but he illogically promised to leave for England in January. He did so, bringing the so-called Mrs Gray and the baby with him and pausing in Gibraltar to seek comfort from the sympathetic bishop who agreed to act as guardian to Rosina and the child if anything should befall him. He also brought to England a Moorish boy, whom he continued to employ as a servant in England and who ended by marrying an Italian widow. The proud Duchess, Georgy, was sufficiently charitable in after years to maintain the widow's crippled Italian child at Bulstrode under the care of the head gardener's wife.

In the summer of 1868 Ferdy installed his family in a house at Brighton, making occasional journeys to his Dover Street apartment in London, but he insisted that the Brighton air was of such importance to his health that he must refrain from visits to Stover or Bulstrode. The child was baptised Ruth Mary (though she believed to her dying day that she had never been baptised at all) and when Rosina again became pregnant Ferdy bought a cottage for her at Redhill. She began to show signs of consumption, but Ferdy, preoccupied with his own health, failed to recognise the symptoms.

In March 1869 he did at last go to Bulstrode and it may have been then that he brought himself to confess the whole story to his father and mother. Whenever he did so, the immediate explosion of wrath and despair, especially by his mother, must have verged on the thermo-nuclear. In June he told his two elder sisters. Once the shock had subsided, his family resolved to accept what was irreversible and to concentrate their attention on Ferdy's declining health. He confessed to increasing attacks of breathlessness and a growing lassitude, which he tried to conquer by brisk solitary walks. At the beginning of August, leaving Rosina at Redhill with her daughter of almost two and a son, Harold, four months old, he again went to Bulstrode. On making a few passes with a rapier (for his histrionic poses had become a habit) he was seized with what he told the doctor, summoned from Windsor, was 'extreme oppression, spasm and panting'. He lost strength and colour and the doctor realised that both his chest and circulation were showing weakness.

The Duchess, more alarmed than her son, decided he must see a London specialist. Those she wished to consult were all on holiday and so she went to see a Fellow of the Royal Society, Dr Charles Williams. Ferdy had another attack at the end of September and his mother took him to his house in Dover Street where Dr Williams found him 'fatigued, weak and with an unsteady pulse'. The following morning he fell out of bed while trying to ring the bell, and lay on the floor finding it difficult to breathe. His sister, Lady Ulrica Thynne, arrived by chance from Maiden Bradley and she and her mother spent the day at Dover Street while his condition quickly deteriorated. Dr Williams was convinced that there was a tumour in his lung and he decided, without (so she said) consulting the Duchess, that his windpipe must be opened by an operation of tracheotomy. Surgeons were summoned and in a dark ground-floor room (for on arrival at Dover Street he had been too breathless to walk upstairs) the operation was performed. Little more than an hour later, Ferdy, thirty-four years old, died in the presence of his mother and sister.

Rosina, alone at Redhill with her two children, knew nothing of the sudden tragedy; nor, sheltering at Stover from his beloved wife's importunities, did the Duke of Somerset.

# 6
# *The Aftermath*

Georgiana Somerset, still witty, still preserving traces of her famous beauty, had grown imperious, truculent and hard to please; but her immediate response to the death of her son was a generous one. In his last hours he begged her to care for Rosina and the children, and early the next morning she had herself driven to Rosina's cottage at Redhill to break the news of the unexpected tragedy. She had loved Ferdy whatever their disagreements and her violent, disapproving letters to him. Now, despite her own wretchedness, she concentrated on bringing Rosina what comfort she could and solemnly pledging to take care of all her wants. She saw her new grandchildren for the first time and found them entrancing, especially the little dark Ruth, rising two years old.

The next day Georgiana's eldest daughter, Lady Hermione Graham, who had taken the first train south from Cumberland when a telegram told her of Ferdy's death, also went to Redhill bringing a locket containing some of Ferdy's hair and such gifts as she hoped would be useful for Rosina and pleasing to the children. The Duchess and all three of her daughters took an instant liking to Rosina whose gipsy good looks, simplicity and native intelligence they found irresistible. The Duke gave no signs of disapproval. On the contrary he encouraged his wife to occupy herself with the children, and she told Lady Hermione that she must indeed exert herself on their behalf – 'otherwise I should not care to live.'

The attitude of the Grahams was entirely commendable. Caroline Sheridan's sister Fanny, 'Aunt Graham' to her nephews and nieces, was high-principled and was held to be even better looking than Caroline, though it was generally admitted to be a near-run thing. At the Eglinton Tournament, attired in green and loaded with pearls, she had been almost as much admired as her niece, the Queen of Beauty. Among this delectable lady's children were two who matched their mother in looks but not in morals.

One of them was Sir Frederick Graham, devoted to his lovely wife (and cousin) Lady Hermione St Maur who, like her mother and sisters, never strayed from the matrimonial bed. This did not inhibit Sir Frederick from siring twelve bastards within a short range of his home, Netherby Hall. There may well have been more, for it was his habit to go for long rides and dismount in order to chuck under the chin any pretty girl he encountered. The combination of his good looks and his *droit de seigneur* was evidently most effective. Perhaps the Graham blood flows still more broadly by the banks of the River Esk and in the neighbourhood of Carlisle; but twelve bastards was the semi-official count, a figure for which the author, who is Sir Frederick's great-grandson (but in defiance of Graham tradition only married his fifth cousin), is glad to settle.

The other devotee of Venus was Sir Frederick's sister Mabel, Countess of Feversham, known in the family by the absurd name of Aunt Moppy. As immoral as she was beautiful, she was the mother of the four Ladies Duncombe, whose youthful glory stunned Society at home and abroad. It is almost certain that one of the four actually was Lord Feversham's child, and some authorities have asserted there were two.

The Grahams, for all their sexual vagaries, had large and generous hearts, none more so than Aunt Graham's younger, more staid and somewhat less beautiful daughter Nelly, married to General Charles Baring of Nubia House at Cowes. Lady Feversham and Mrs Baring sought out Rosina, never for a moment patronised her and were as impressed as their St Maur cousins by the radiance of her gentle, unassuming nature. Distressed as all these ladies were by the early death of the two St Maur sons, they could scarcely fail, sentimental Victorians that they were, to be emotionally thrilled by the contemporary re-enactment, with a few carnal variations, of the story of King Cophetua and the Beggar Maid.

After one of her visits to Rosina, Mrs Charles Baring wrote this to her cousin Georgy:

> I am so glad the doctor has found something to check her cough at night. I am very glad she thought me 'nice', for I was so pleased with her. I think her *very* handsome and her eyes are the most

beautiful *dark* eyes I have ever seen; and they have a peculiar *startled* look which adds to their beauty. I don't think she looks older than her age, merely so very, very ill and wan.

The Sheridans, including Ghigo (by then Lord Dufferin) and Georgy's brother Brinsley, were also sympathetic. Nelly Dufferin had died two years previously, but Caroline Norton, though still estranged from her sister, wrote to Ghigo that her heart ached 'for Georgia's folorn-ness – poor miserable mother'. But the St Maurs, or at least some of them, took a different line. The noses of the Duke's brothers, Lords Archibald and Algernon, went high in the air, and the most sanctimonious was their spinster sister, Lady Henrietta.

Georgy had confided in another sister-in-law, Charlotte Blount, whom she liked but always addressed with formality as Lady Charlotte, because the Duke refused to recognise Mr Blount, formerly agent at Bulstrode, since he thought it presumptuous of him to marry his sister. In writing to her Georgy let fly about a letter from Lady Henrietta, which

> is the more unpardonable as it is not the hasty production consequent on receiving some information that shocked her, though in no case has this old maid any justification for such insolent interference, or giving me unasked her opinion in censure on any conduct of mine or my son's. Her letter is written with the most deliberate conceit – neatly – pains taken with her iron pen from her iron heart.... It is the sinful, selfish conceit of women like Henrietta (themselves untempted) that drives them to obtrude their Pharisee notions on others far superior in all things to them. As to the children, she does not seem to consider them in the question at all, so I told her the English law did not permit them to be drowned like puppies though vastly more convenient for her views.... Let her try and understand God's mysteries before she pretends to be His expounder. I wrote to you, who I know have felt for us, because I thought, perhaps very naturally from you, this toad (who lives on her stone feeding on the idea of her own perfection, and hermetically sealing herself from the outer world and all knowledge) might have heard what I explained to you.
> 
> Ever truly yours,
> J. G. Somerset

Her second reaction to Ferdy's death was not praiseworthy. Convinced that Dr Williams had been rough in handling his dying patient, an accusation the doctor hotly denied, that he had been slow in coming when urgently summoned and that he had not consulted her before the tracheotomy operation was performed, she circulated to all her friends and relations a defamatory account of Dr Williams's lack of professional skill. There may have been a grain of truth in some of her allegations, but they were undoubtedly libellous and the doctor sued. The case went to court amidst much publicity, and an apology had to be offered with full withdrawal of the charges. This was so skilfully presented by her counsel, and the poor Duke won so much sympathy by insisting that his honoured name be coupled with his wife as defendant, that damages were assessed at only five guineas. Dr Williams then published a turgid book containing his account of the whole unhappy affair and seeking to justify himself in the eyes of his medical colleagues.

The Somersets did a great deal for Rosina. They built her a small house on the edge of the park at Bulstrode. They provided a cook, a Swiss nursery-maid and a French companion who warded off threats from a scheming Swan sister attempting to blackmail her. They took a house for her at Teignmouth, so that she and the children might be nearby when they were at Stover, and another in London. After eighteen months, Rosina, who spent much of her time in one or other of the Somerset houses (where, despite the material kindness lavished on her, she was expected to take her meals in the housekeeper's room), decided that as Ruth had become the idol of her grandparents she should go to live with them. A year later she also surrendered her son, Harold, for she became engaged to François Tournier, the brother of her French companion. He was the son of a Bordeaux wine merchant and himself a French master at Cheam preparatory school. Fortunately he was a Huguenot, for the Duchess objected to Roman Catholics and would neither employ them nor even allow one beneath her roof.

Rosina married M. Tournier in September 1872, and went with him to Bordeaux, the Duchess taking the children to see her off at Charing Cross Station and remaining outside in her carriage while they accompanied their mother on to the platform, one clutching a rose and the other a small bouquet for her. It was the last they remembered of Rosina, for the cough which kept her awake at night was the mark of a consumption that was already galloping. The Duchess explained to Lady Charlotte Blount:

> The poor young thing is pleased with her new doctor and the cessation of blistering, but he holds out no promise of recovery, only retarding the process of the disease and alleviation of suffering. She is a very good woman, thoroughly upright and honest in mind.

She arranged to see the girl's parents, of whom she approved, though it appeared that the numerous brothers and sisters had mostly turned out badly. After some months Rosina, having given birth to a Tournier daughter, who died as an infant, came back to England mortally ill. Her condition worsened, according to the Duchess, because she sat on the wet sands after a long hot walk. She was barely twenty-three when she died. A year later her illiterate father also died of consumption in his cottage near Bury St Edmunds.

Thus it was that Ruth and Harold, aged six and four, legally Swan but St Maur by informal adoption, became the cherished wards of the Duke and Duchess of Somerset. They lived in state at Bulstrode and Stover, and at Somerset House in Park Lane after the Dowager Duchess, the Duke's stepmother, died. There were forty servants, postillions, splendid carriages, dairies, stillroom and laundry maids, and all the trappings of a still thriving nobility.

Appearances were fully maintained, but the sun had set. Gloom pervaded Bulstrode and Stover where Ferdy's and Edward's rooms stayed empty, with the curtains drawn. That gloom was further inspissated by changes in society as a whole. The light furniture, bright chintzes and plain but pleasant architecture, which still prevailed in the first decade of Queen Victoria's reign, were replaced by massive mahogany, heavy curtains hung on brass rings and neo-Gothic red brick mansions. The Prince of Wales gathered round him a garish group of friends, and there was no shortage of young bloods dedicated to dissipation; but many more absorbed the dull, worthy sobriety which spread downwards from Osborne and Windsor. Gaiety had to be muted; strict morality, if not necessarily practised, was universally preached; and a sabbatarian melancholy gripped the upper and middle classes.

Lower down the social scale poverty became more pronounced

as the urban proletariat expanded. Despite Lord Shaftesbury, Factory Acts and incipient trade unions, hard-faced managers and supervisors ground the faces of the poor in years of economic prosperity no less than in those of adversity. England's 'dark satanic mills' were still a feature of the landscape and a scandalously high proportion of working-class families were tubercular, ill-clad and undernourished. Neither Georgy nor her naturally benevolent husband had any conception of the misery behind the façade of national prosperity, for among the upper classes ignorance of the state of their fellow countrymen was as widespread as it was deplorable.

It was some time before the two children became aware of their mixed fortunes. On the one hand they were scions of the house of Seymour and of the famous name of Sheridan. On the other, their grandparents were a village labourer and a gipsy. More immediately important for them, though the truth was hidden during their childhood, they were bastards. If at the end of the twentieth century bastardy has shed much of its stigma, in the nineteenth it still carried, for all classes of society, a dreaded shame. As Harold grew up he hoped to go to Eton and join the Brigade of Guards. Neither Eton nor the Brigade of Guards were disposed to accept bastards, even ducal ones. It was less obviously painful for Ruth, surrounded by loving relations; but she, too, felt the slur. When there was a garden party at Marlborough House for children as well as adults, the Duchess went in, but the illegitimate Ruth had to stay outside in the carriage.

The seeds of conflict had been sown at birth, sharp conflict between the genes of the humble Swans and the proud Seymours. They were marked with an indelible stain which Ruth's brother, Harold, tried to eradicate by futile efforts to convince himself and others that Ferdy and Rosina had been secretly married somewhere in Devonshire. Ruth poured the coldest of water on this fantasy, but though more realistic than Harold, and a great deal more sensible, she was possessed by rebellious instincts that were quelled neither by the kindness of her father's family nor by the gratifying admiration which, as the years went by, her good looks and quick wit excited. Generous, unassuming Rosina had felt no rancour; the Somersets showed an understanding untypical of their generation; but nothing would quench the fire of resentment which for all her life lay smouldering, largely unrecognised by Ruth herself.

The Somersets were unfailingly kind to their grandchildren, and the Duke liked to take Ruth for long and mainly silent drives. These included a call at Hughenden where she was presented to Disraeli. Writing to Lady Bradford he commented that the Duke

> is very fond of driving about from Bulstrode and was once much in the habit of paying these morning visits here, but they ceased when I became Minister. He is a lettered man and otherwise clever, but he has got deaf since earlier visits and I find that a good ear is almost as important as information and abilities.

It was the deafness that accounted for the silences during his drives with Ruth.

As Ruth recorded in a letter to her cousin Brinsley Ford, written some fifty years later, living with an increasingly eccentric grandmother, whose health was deteriorating, held little joy. She always expressed herself forcefully and allowance must be made for her addiction to the dramatic. All the same, the following extract gives what must in the main be a truthful account of life at Bulstrode and Stover in the 1870s and early 1880s when her patient and benevolent grandfather, devoted to Georgy though he always remained, absented himself whenever there was an opportunity.

> When Granny took us on she was already rather diseased and mentally affected. The death of her sons had begun the mischief and diabetes finished it. On rare occasions she could still say something amusing, and she kept a few friends who were genuinely fond of her. . . But she saw hardly anyone outside the family. She was absolutely devoted to us, yet she made our lives a Hell, as she had my father's, who found home unbearable and left it (I saw some quite unpardonable letters from her amongst my father's things. I burnt them at once, as he should have done). Her insane suspicion of every one, her terrible untidiness and unpunctuality, the Irish-cabin sort of room she lived in; old deal boxes piled on top of one another, boxes that were unpacked, packed, and repacked every time we moved (that is about four times a year), elaborate lists made of every rag and paper that went in, and *another* list made when they came out!

Granpa, poor man, used to go on to Stover or Bulstrode leaving her to follow, then *all* linen was put away and we had to eat our food off dirty sheets of newspaper for *weeks!* Most of the servants, of course, went on with Granpa; then when she came, all were accused of stealing or cheating.

To Harold and me she was kind, but we dreaded her fits of rage when she became *literally* black in the face, and we were not only worn out by her impossible mode of life, but we were so desperately sorry for the servants, many of whom we liked. When the schoolroom maid was told to make me some (hideous) garment, cut out of newspaper by Granny first (as a pattern!), I had actually to measure off a couple of yards of cotton óff a reel and wind it round a twist of paper for fear the girl should use sewing cotton on her own clothes. When she needed more she had to ask. I need hardly add that the result of this dressmaking was such that children jeered at me in the street when I went out and I could have cried – and often did. *No* decent governess would stay with us because of Granny and we had a succession of devilish *horrors* who made my life a misery and who were as ignorant as ill-tempered. – Dear old Giese, the last one, had no knowledge, but a kind heart, and she remained out of pity; and also as Granny was by then much confined to her room, her manias were less distracting. I can remember sitting on a deal box and seriously contemplating suicide. . . When Granpa, who had really been devotèd to Granny all his life, came in to see her there was never any chair for him to sit on in her sitting room. He had to stand. *Every* chair littered with rags, papers, chicken food or something being 'counted' – so they did not associate much in their later years. He, poor man, was well-nigh dead to the world after the death of his idolised younger son and took an interest in nothing but politics and shooting pheasants and *me* – indeed but for him I think I should have become an idiot. During our long silent drives he *did* sometimes say some remarkable things, and he was very fond of me, 'My little dear', but found it difficult to protect my sensitive and overgrown person from Granny's detestable customs and orders.

Then there were the eggs! Eggs to be counted, turned, marked with a date, kept in sawdust, listed and given out to the kitchen for fear one more should be used on the servants' puddings

— and the jam and the soap (to be cut and doled out) and the stores. Of course competent servants would not stay, and there was a constant scolding and sacking. Then there was all the dirty washing to count at her feet as she lay in her chair. This was really abominable. Butler, under-butler, groom of chambers, 1st, 2nd and 3rd footman, Odd man, His Grace's valet, Her Grace's valet, and more maids than I can count, and all the filthy kitchen cloths as well as sheets towels etc... *all* to be listed... and this every week (no wonder I never had any proper education!)

Your grandmother, Guendolen Ramsden, used to tell me all these nightmare experiences were what *she* also had to endure! She also told me that on the rare occasions when my father came home he used to try and incite her to rebellion and to say that she just would *not* do these things. But she was far too gentle, and also, like us, afraid of those black rages. I *did* rebel once, in London, and told Granpa what I felt about it. He went to Granny and did what he could. I expect things were better for a time after that, — but it was all just black *misery,* all the more tragic inasmuch as she really loved me and thought a lot of us both.

Perhaps if I'd known her before the death of her sons I could write differently — and yet not so *very* differently because what Aunt Guen told me all took place when she still had them. One thing I can thank her for: that she took me to every play going (Sarah Bernhardt, Dame aux Camélias and all!) from the age of 5, and I get great pleasure out of the stage to this day. I always put in a matinee every time I go to London and I enjoy reading plays. We always went in a box with Granny (a hateful one-sided way of seeing, but still one heard *and* saw). I can also be grateful to both grandparents for *never* having questioned my reading. I could pick on any book I liked and read what I chose. I had usually no time but, by fits and starts, I got in a certain amount and all was grist to my mill. One can discriminate later on. At any rate one comes across 'minds', and the way minds work, which saves one's own from a diet of counting and washing eggs, and listening to servants peccadilloes. I'm sure great and prolonged unhappiness, and grey dullness, and squalid surrounds, (for squalid is the word, inspite of an army of servants and a ducal household!) stultify mental powers; and the wonder is that, though this all damaged my poor brother's character (he was 3½ months when our father died, after which our poor little beautiful mother had little say in the matter till she also died a few years later) and to a great extent mine, the wonder, as I say, is that we both lived to do quite a lot!

What Ruth did not realise, though her cousin Ghigo Dufferin did, was that her grandmother, whose faculties were indeed gradually deteriorating, was intent on securing the future of her illegitimate grandchildren. It did not occur to Georgy that any of the Somerset possessions would ever be bestowed on them, but she hoped by skimping and cheeseparing in the household accounts to set aside enough money to provide at least a pittance. After her death, Lord Dufferin wrote that the Duke was astonished to find how much she had in fact saved for Ruth and Harold.

The Duke, dejected, indeed almost atrophied, by the death of his sons and silently exasperated by his wife's growing idiosyncrasies, absorbed himself in work of a kind to divert his attention from past sorrows and present irritations. He still attended the House of Lords, speaking on matters about which he felt deeply, but he resolutely declined Mr Gladstone's invitation to join his Government in 1869, having already, three years previously, given no encouragement to suggestions that he was the man to lead a coalition Government to promote a new Reform Bill. Instead he devoted five years to the study of the impact of scientific discovery on traditional Christian belief. Ruth was unjust in suggesting that his sole interest was in politics and pheasants.

The result of this study, involving research in the works of German, Greek and Hebrew scholars, was a book entitled *Christian Theology and Modern Scepticism*. It affected the thought and opinions of his granddaughter, Ruth, so that this well-written, deeply considered and, at the time of its publication, controversial treatise is relevant to this story.

He questioned the historic truth of parts of the Bible. This was labelled by many as a blasphemous outrage, especially as he did not exclude the Gospels themselves. He noted the discrepancy between St Paul's teaching in the Epistles and that in the Acts of the Apostles. He tore in shreds the Roman Catholic doctrine of the Assumption, doubted the Virgin Birth and expatiated on the cleavage between St Peter, who believed Christianity was for the Jews alone, and St Paul, who preached to the Gentiles. There were those who called him 'the atheist duke'; but he was a regular churchgoer and he ended his book by stressing his attachment to one unassailable fortress, faith in God. He declared it an error to suppose scepticism was necessarily irreligious.

In later years Ruth read and re-read this book. Some passages had a lasting influence on her. One of her grandfather's more dubious contentions, which appealed to her feminist instincts, was that even the gender of nouns affected religious convictions. Thus the word spirit is neuter in Greek, feminine in Hebrew and masculine in Latin. 'It may be reasonably doubted', wrote the Duke, 'whether if the Latin term had been female, the Three Persons of the Trinity would have occupied their present positions in the religious thought of Christians.' He held, too, that the Christian religion was distorted by the incongruous combination of the Mosaic Law and Greek philosophy; and he asked the worrying question whether as scientific knowledge increased faith would lose its empire over the mind. 'Is faith left as the heritage of the uneducated?'

By its very nature, faith has never become the exclusive property of the uneducated, however convinced eighteenth and nineteenth century rationalists were that it would do so. But these reflections were grist to the mill of the Duke's innately rebellious and unorthodox granddaughter. It is tempting to believe that the submerged gipsy influence of her mother was more dominant in her genes than that of the Anglo-Saxon Swans, the Norman Seymours or the Celtic Sheridans. Her brother Harold, long of face and fine of feature, was a Seymour in appearance. In Ruth, gipsy colouring blended with the aristocratic features and intelligence of her father's ancestors and the impetuous, unbridled nature of the Sheridans. There were a number of strong ingredients in the mixture: they generated a dynamic and in some respects split personality.

There were few neighbours with children thought suitable as playmates. For companions of her own age she depended on her cousins Hermione Ramsden and Ruth Thynne. There were visits to Frampton in Dorset, the property which Georgy's brother, Brinsley Sheridan, had acquired after his Gretna Green elopement with the heiress. There, on one occasion, Ruth embarrassed her grandmother by boxing the Queen of Holland's ears. She was very small and she was standing on a sofa to speak to the Queen who said something with a guttural accent that Ruth misunderstood and did not like. So she boxed the royal ears. The Queen was an understanding lady. She asked what Ruth thought she had said and then turned to the horrified Duchess insisting that the child must not be scolded, for if she had in fact said what Ruth thought, then she would have deserved to have her ears boxed. A few days later she sent Ruth a beautiful doll with many different costumes. There was no doubt that the child had a sturdily independent mind, but under successive governesses, some disagreeable and some plainly incompetent, time dragged slowly by.

Wimblédon Park was sold and the Somersets rotated between Bulstrode, Stover and London. Somerset House, large, tall and of no great architectural merit, stood at the corner of Park Lane and Oxford Street, close to Marble Arch. It was fronted by a garden flanked by lilacs, with a great tree in the centre of the lawn; and it was backed by a courtyard in which the carriages could turn and by stables stretching far down Oxford Street. There the horses' straw was changed every morning by the grooms who had to embroider the edges with a pattern of plaited red and blue wool.

Until her death in 1880 the old Dowager Duchess of Somerset lived there, but the Duke, caring little for his stepmother, seldom called upon her. When she died, he was astonished to find she had filled the house with hundreds of pairs of shoes which were stacked in every cupboard. They were removed and Georgy was given a free hand to redecorate. She did so, according to her granddaughter, in execrable taste. She told Ruth, perhaps with a touch of Irish imagination, that in days gone by the roof of the house had been the spot chosen by the socially distinguished to view the more lurid executions at Tyburn. Those had ended a hundred years earlier, but it was only in the year Ruth herself was born that murderers ceased to be hanged in public.

In due course Lady Hermione Graham inherited the house, but her Casanovan husband died two years after she did so and she wisely moved to the less expensive purlieu of Pont Street. A cinema was built on the site of the stables and a block of flats replaced the house and garden. Today all traces of the old house have vanished and there remains only one Somerset House, the governmental palace that reaches from the Strand to the Embankment.

Georgy, despite her slovenly habits at home, invariably travelled from London to Bulstrode in a carriage with four horses and postilions in blue coats, white top hats and high boots, the horses being changed at Isleworth. Before they left Park Lane a crowd would collect, for she was always late starting. The splendid equipage would stand waiting for sometimes as much as an hour, and when she finally arrived at the carriage door, it would be to the accompaniment of sharp questions to her maid: 'Have you packed my little clock? Where are my Java sparrows?' and to Ruth, 'Have you got my little pillow?' As illness and old age took firmer control, she developed illusions. Highwaymen, like pirates and Jacobites, had long been relegated to the pages of romantic novels, but when travelling in her carriage she took to arming herself with a large carving knife in case some highwayman should emerge from a side-road.

The Duke by contrast, perhaps deliberately by contrast, became increasingly careless of appearances, even though his valet provided the time-honoured services and before he went out a footman would wash such coins as he might wish to put in his pocket and bring them to him on a silver salver. Despite these attentions he looked dishevelled and on one occasion a passer-by tipped him in the belief that he was a crossing sweeper. He wrote another book, less deeply thought out than his *Christian Theology and Modern Scepticism*, which he called *Monarchy and Democracy*. It caused a mild stir in an age when the powers of the sovereign, even in a parliamentary democracy, were still of unquestioned importance, especially in foreign affairs, official appointments and matters affecting the armed forces of the Crown.

He seldom went to Maiden Bradley now, for Lord Henry Thynne and Lady Ulrica were living there. Lord Henry had grown increasingly boorish, driving his elder son first to drink and finally to suicide, and so behaving that another left the country and settled in Buenos Aires. Lady Ulrica's nephews and nieces ceased even to call him Uncle.

At the end of 1884, when Ruth was just seventeen and on the verge of 'coming out', her grandmother died at Somerset House. Harold St Maur, more generous than Ruth in his memories of her, wrote that her native Sheridan wit persisted to the end and that her entertaining conversation kept the family constantly amused. No doubt her uncouth domestic habits affected him less than his sister. She was not so malicious in conversation as in the letters she wrote and she had never been other than a thoughtful and affectionate grandmother.

The Duke, by then over eighty, found Ruth his main consolation. She went with him to Bulstrode and Stover, read aloud to him and patiently played chess during the long evenings. In late November 1885 she had an uncanny experience. She was at Stover, sleeping in the large room which had been her grandmother's so as to be close at hand. This is her account of what happened:

> A sudden jerk woke me in the middle of the night and I sat up, finding the room all light. Then close to me, by the side of my bed, men carried a coffin covered with violets. They carried it along the side of my bed and through the communicating door into Grandpa's room. It all seemed natural and I felt no fear. Indeed I slept again and told my old governess about it in the morning. Two or three days after, Grandpa had a cold in his head – he often had them – but because of this vision I sent for my aunts who all three came.
>
> Grandpa was not really ill. He sat in an arm-chair in a sitting room next to his bedroom and I read to him. It was a horrid day, all heavy rain and an icy wind. He said: 'What a beautiful day it is, isn't it?' My instinct made me say 'Yes, a fine day', and I went on reading. He leant forward, looked up at something with astonishment and fell back dead. When Grandpa's body was laid out, it was on the bed I had been sleeping in the night of my vision, and the men did carry his coffin, covered with violets, along the side of the bed exactly as I had seen it.

That was Ruth's story. She had a vivid imagination and she sensed things, as the gipsies do; but she was a scrupulously truthful woman to whom invention was entirely alien. What she did not know was that when her grandfather suddenly gazed at something he evidently thought beautiful, unconscious of the driving rain and the icy wind, it was twenty years from the day his beloved Edward came face to face with the bear.

In his will he left Somerset House to Lady Hermione, Bulstrode to Lady Guendolen and his estates in Lincolnshire, Cambridgeshire and Norfolk to Lady Ulrica as well as all the books and linen at

Maiden Bradley. To Harold he left in trust Stover and all its contents, including the valuable Hamilton pictures, and his land at Newton Abbot. To Ruth, the light of his old age, went the princely sum of £80,000, which was a fortune in 1885; and he appointed Ladies Ulrica and Guendolen guardians of his grandchildren.

His successor in the dukedom, Lord Archibald, inherited Maiden Bradley, partly denuded, but still surrounded by 15,000 fertile acres, and Berry Pomeroy with another 5,000. The new Duke, a crusty bachelor, was in the words of Ghigo Dufferin, by then Viceroy of India, 'a perverse ill-conditioned creature' who had contributed nothing to his county or his country. He had as much vitriol as blood in his veins. His elder brother had long ceased to respect him. Lord Archibald's indignation at the disposal of the family properties, and in particular of the Hamilton pictures, knew no bounds, and he unfairly laid the blame on Georgy. He left, framed and hanging on a wall at Maiden Bradley, a testimony of hate for his intelligent and distinguished brother. It ended thus:

> To gratify the low-born, greedy beggar woman he would marry in opposition to his father, the 12th Duke has seized and made away with the land, the pictures, the miniatures, the plates, the prints, the linen and the books. He was unable to make away with the title and he has left his successors his Will: His Will remains, and must remain, a lasting monument of infamy.
>
> Archibald Seymour, 13th Duke of Somerset

These sentiments were shared, though less vociferously, by Lord Algernon, who succeeded the curmudgeonly Archibald six years later, and by his elder son, another Algernon, who invented disagreeable and untruthful stories about Rosina. When this younger Algernon, the 15th Duke, died, the title and what was left of the estates went to the amiable and unembittered descendants of Lord Francis Seymour, Dean of Wells and fourth son of that Sir Edward who was playing chess at a wayside inn in 1750 when the innkeeper told him he had become Duke of Somerset.

# 7
# Gilded Youth

Fond though she was of her grandfather, Ruth rejoiced at her release from the routine of governess-controlled existence in his various houses, from the nightly games of chess and from the loneliness. She was now placed in the care of her youngest and favourite aunt, Lady Guendolen Ramsden, who understood her impetuous nature well. Lady Guendolen had been a frequent visitor to Bulstrode, always bringing her daughter Hermione, known as Mymee and exactly the same age as Ruth.

The two children were devoted to each other, and though Ruth grew up beautiful in appearance and original in mind, while poor Mymee, though intelligent, was plain and shy, they remained intimate all their lives. Lady Guendolen wrote from Bulstrode when they were small children:

> The Governess says that in Uxbridge the other day they created quite a sensation. The dark, dark Ruth with fiery eyes and the fair Mymee with her melancholy, dreamy eyes — for they look dreamy compared with Ruth. She says they kiss each other in the carriage till they both fall asleep in her arms.

As Ruth grew older, she was impatient for her Aunt Guen's visits.

> Oh, you wicked, *wicked* Aunt [she wrote from Somerset House shortly after her grandmother's death]. Do my eyes deceive me? Did I really read that you were thinking of not coming here till *Friday* . . . but it's no good going on scolding; you are a confirmed sinner and have and will always put off and put off coming till you'll probably not come at all. . . . And when at last I *do* get hold of you, I'll not let you slip away from me again in that eel-like manner. I will have and hold you tight and you shall stay with us all the year round. . . .

Mymee knew that her mother loved Ruth more than her own children.

So it was with unalloyed happiness that Ruth went to live with the Ramsdens who had a house in Upper Brook Street, suitable for launching young ladies into Society, a castle in Inverness-shire and Byram near Pontefract (pronounced in those day 'Pomfret', as it had been in Shakespeare's time). Byram, engulfed in the smoky fog of industrial Yorkshire and the acrid tang that accompanied it, marched with Fryston where Ruth's cousin Sibyl Houghton lived with her husband and small children. Sib, as they called her, was Lady Guendolen's favourite niece and though nine years older than Ruth she was one of her closest friends. According to Ruth, Sibyl's mother Lady Hermione Graham 'took one's breath away when she came into a room. She was the same type as Jenny Churchill, only still more resplendent and far more dignified.' Sibyl, too, was lovely to behold and photographs of her and her no less beautiful sisters, Lady Verulam and the Duchess of Montrose, were sold in all the fashionable Sloane Street and Knightsbridge stationers in spite of Lady Hermione's interdiction of such vulgar publicity. Sold alongside them were those of their equally splendid cousins, 'Aunt Moppy's' four Duncombe daughters, the survivor of whom, Lady D'Abernon, could still make passers-by turn admiring heads in the 1930s when she was over seventy. Elizabeth Linley and the two Callender sisters, Mrs Tom Sheridan and Lady Graham, had between them endowed a race of Greek goddesses.

There was another cousin, Ruth Thynne, Fair Ruth. Originally a constant friend and companion, she developed her Somerset grandmother's untidy and unpunctual habits, failed to answer Dark Ruth's letters and gradually grew apart from her. When in due course she married George Pitt-Rivers and produced a son called Joe, the rift became more pronounced, for Joe not only treated a succession of wives badly but joined the British Union of Fascists and became Sir Oswald Mosley's right-hand man. This, to Dark Ruth, was an act of ignominy beyond forgiveness.

There was yet another cousin, Lady Helen Blackwood, daughter of Ghigo Dufferin, the Viceroy of India. In a letter to Ruth she complained that life in Calcutta was stuffy and stultifying. Ruth at once advised her to liven things up by tobogganing down the stairs of Government House on a tea-tray. Nelly Blackwood replied:

I'm sure it would be great fun, and I should do it with pleasure at Bulstrode, but here there are too many impediments. In the first place I should have to send for the tea-tray to the household A.D.C. through the A.D.C.-in-waiting. Then I should have to get the tea-tray carried upstairs by two or three gorgeous individuals whose sole duty in life is to carry up belongings from place to place, for in this country you are hardly allowed to carry your own person about, much less your person's belongings. Then, arrived at the starting point, I should find a seven foot Life Guardsman on duty who might think it his business to interfere with my little voyage and *agrèment*; and finally, after meeting the Military Secretary on the second floor, I should inevitably toboggan into another Life Guardsman standing at attention on account of my august presence, even though that august presence was seated on a tea-tray...

Nelly Blackwood also described an Indian visit by the Duke and Duchess of Connaught, during which His doubtless astonished Royal Highness was entertained by a peculiar tiger hunt.

When he arrived at the place after a march through the jungle, he found a grand-stand erected and a band playing God Save the Queen. Then, when he'd taken his position in a gilt arm-chair a very tipsy tiger was introduced upon the scene, at which he fired and missed, whereupon the band again played God Save the Queen ... someone put an end to the absurd scene by shooting the beast who was much too sleepy with drugs to be scared by Royal Dukes or national anthems.

The process of 'coming out' was one that Ruth and Mymee Ramsden viewed with mixed feelings. Neither of them had first-hand knowledge of the poverty and indeed starvation suffered by the British working classes in the industrial depression of the 1880s. Neither of them knew that a third of the young men volunteering for the army were found to be physically unfit because of undernourishment. But they were voracious readers, of tracts and pamphlets as well as of books, and unlike the majority of their parents' generation they had developed a social conscience.

Ruth said to Mymee: 'Let us go to Aunt Guen and tell her we think it our duty to give up London balls and parties and to work in the East End instead.' When it came to the point, their courage failed them, but they did spend hours writing 'An Appeal Addressed to Girls in Society' (which was never published), urging their contemporaries to rebel against a system the sole objective of which seemed to be success in the marriage market. Although closely chaperoned, and not even allowed to walk down Upper Brook Street without a maid marching at a discreet distance behind them, they did subscribe to progressive magazines, entered into illicit correspondence with the producers, visited the new Salvation Army hostel and even made a surreptitious tour of the East End of London and the new 'People's Palace' in Stepney.

However, coming out could not be avoided. First they spent a foggy winter at Byram, alleviated by ambitious amateur theatricals, quarrels with the local clergyman, the company of Sibyl Houghton from Fryston, and a fancy-dress ball at Huddersfield where Ruth, dressed as a Turkish lady, flirted outrageously with the subsequently notorious Horatio Bottomley. Then the Ramsden family and Ruth made their way to London. The first call of duty, after driving round London in a brougham to leave cards, was to choose a dress in which Mymee could be taken to a Drawing Room at Buckingham Palace, be presented to Queen Victoria and kiss her hand. Ruth, on account of the bar sinister, could not be presented at Court.

Then came the 1887 Season. It began in February, but there was an interlude in the spring when they went to Bulstrode. There Ruth and Mymee witnessed a strange irruption from the Stock Exchange. Evidently stockbrokers in the 1880s bore little resemblance to those of the 1980s. This is Mymee's account:

> The Miss Thornhills and their brother arrived bringing six stockbrokers to sing at a concert which Mama gave for the labourers and their wives and children. The stockbrokers interested us greatly. They were all of them well-to-do men who went about singing for charity, but they had hardly ever been in the country or even seen it before, their only idea of a holiday being the seaside. They were as amused and surprised at everything they saw at Bulstrode as though they were from Mars. When they passed the little shop on Stoke Common, they burst out laughing because they had never seen such a shop before!

For Ruth an endowment of £80,000, striking good looks, a ready if sometimes mordant wit and an unorthodox approach to life which contrasted sharply with that of the majority of well-brought-up young ladies, combined to provide a passport to popularity with young men. As her literary but plain cousin wistfully recorded, proposals rained on her. The parents of those who proposed tended to be less enthusiastic; for her illegitimacy was known, all kinds of rumours circulated and it was said with something approaching horror that her mother was a gipsy. She had been much taken with the charms of the son of the Ramsdens' agent at Byram, but Lady Guendolen successfully diverted her and before many weeks of the London Season had passed she fell deeply and permanently in love with Frederick Cavendish-Bentinck.

She met him at every ball and soon had eyes for none other. She pitied Princess May of Teck, the future Queen Mary, with all her heart 'because she was shabbily dressed in the fashion of the year before. The Duke of Teck was always in debt and we used to think that his daughter must mind very much being so shabby.' She was less charitable about the future King Edward VII. After Lady Sykes's ball on July 14, to which she went with Sibyl Houghton and Nelly Blackwood (temporarily released from Calcutta for 'coming out' purposes), she scribbled in her diary: 'I was introduced to the Prince. Fat oaf.' Ruth was neither then nor at any time in her life a respecter of persons. But then a month previously Freddy Cavendish-Bentinck had proposed, and she had said yes. So for the time being neither princes nor paupers were of any account.

Many of the happiest marriages thrive on contrast. Freddy was shy, so prone to embarrassment that, according to Mymee, 'he used to rush into the room and straight across it, upsetting every article of furniture that happened to be in the way'. Ruth, downright and outspoken, was the reverse of shy. Freddy was worldly and cynically tolerant. Ruth was deeply emotional and incapable of cynicism. She was also intolerant of people of whom she disapproved and of views she disliked. Freddy was a Conservative. Ruth did not even claim to be a Liberal, like the St Maurs and her Graham cousins: already in 1887 she was an avowed Socialist.

Freddy's father, the Right Honourable George Augustus Frederick, was the son of Lord Frederick Bentinck, and his mother was a daughter of Lord Lonsdale. On this account it was natural, by the standards of those days, that he should be the Member of Parliament for the Lonsdale family seat at Whitehaven. He inherited a trust from his cousin, Lord Henry Bentinck, and had a reasonably successful parliamentary career, holding two offices in Disraeli's Government. This may have been because Disraeli's own start in politics was much advanced by his association with Lord George Bentinck and he felt under an obligation to the family; for this younger George, amiable and good-natured, was carefree, self-indulgent and a gambler. He owned Brownsea Island off Poole and a large house in Grafton Street. Though respectably married and the father of four children by his lawful wife, he had a least one illegitimate family hidden away. He welcomed Ruth with unfeigned delight and she, for her part, found him wholly lovable.

Her future mother-in-law was born Prudence Penelope Leslie, so named after her grandmother, the Duke of Wellington's aunt. At her wedding with George Bentinck the eighty-year-old Wellington gave her away. She was a strong-minded woman. When George was in Disraeli's Government, she was once called upon to give a large official dinner party. Protesting that the Office of Works had not provided for the cost of flowers, she had the table arranged with a row of earthenware gallypots down the middle, each containing a bunch of groundsel. In London Society she was nicknamed Britannia. She prevailed upon the painter G. F. Watts, who owed much of his success to her mother-in-law, Lady Frederick, to paint two majestic portraits of her, one of which, with the infant Freddy on her lap, is now in the Tate Gallery.

Prudence, or Britannia, took an entirely different view of Ruth from her husband. She was horrified that her son should marry a bastard and she was scandalised by the nineteen-year-old girl's openly expressed radical views. Ruth felt equal antipathy to her mother-in-law.

The wedding was fixed for 8 August 1887, in the Henry VII Chapel of Westminster Abbey. On the afternoon before, Sibyl Houghton called at Upper Brook Street to see the bride. She was shortly going on a visit to India with her husband. Ruth thought her uncharacteristically gloomy and was dismayed when she said: 'I have come to say good-bye and with this sort of good-bye one never knows for how long it may be.' Sibyl had dreamed that she was standing beside a coffin in an Indian temple and the coffin was her own. Now she told Ruth she would never get to

India and she asked her to tell her four small children what she had been like and, when they grew up, to talk to them about her.

As there was nothing the matter with her I tried to laugh it off as an absurd fancy, but she stuck to it. Then I began to feel it too, and when she kissed me and left, I nearly ran after her on the stairs, but I stopped as it seemed as if I, too, believed it.

Sibyl Houghton never did go to India, nor did Ruth see her after her wedding day; for six weeks later she caught scarlet fever from her children and died. Ruth, as instructed, always took an interest in Sibyl's children and became their lifelong friend.

After the wedding Ruth and Freddy spent the first part of their honeymoon at Clandon Park, lent to them by Lord and Lady Onslow whose daughter Guendolen (subsequently Lady Iveagh) was a bridesmaid. Thence they set off for Brownsea Island which Freddy's father had bestowed on him with £10,000 a year. Their arrival on the island was idyllic, the fishermen cheering, the small port bedecked with flags and bunting, bouquets presented, an illuminated address ready by a grizzled inhabitant, a band playing and a beribboned pony removed from the shafts so that the people could drag the bride and bridegroom to their home under a series of decorated arches. When the castle cannon stopped firing, Ruth and Freddy made their way alone to the other side of the island and sat hand in hand to watch a glorious sunset. She wrote to her Aunt Guendolen: 'The sun is bigger here than anywhere else, and the fir trees were so dark against the gold sky and sea that one couldn't talk – and then in the evening the people lit huge bonfires and sent up fireworks and rockets.'

Dinner was less appealing. 'The cook sent up glue instead of bread sauce, a filthy compound of chopped cabbage and bad custard under the name of *Omelette aux fines herbes*. Imagine F.'s wrath and fury!' There was a lovely sailing boat, the *Ruth*, which Freddy had had specially built, and life on Brownsea Island seemed set fair, especially when Ruth, who found the small villa they inhabited rather cramping, persuaded her easygoing father-in-law to restore and redecorate at great expense the castle on the island. Meanwhile Freddy, who had started his career as a barrister but had recently been appointed Secretary to the Royal Commission on Education, commuted to London, spending seven hours a day in the train.

The exigencies of the Royal Commission were not so severe as to prevent foreign travel. As an extension of their honeymoon they set forth in September for Austria and climbed precipitous mountains in sleet, slush and snow, in pursuit of chamois. Among their companions were Count and Countess Vetsera whose names echoed throughout Europe and America two years later. After one especially rough and cold day, Ruth came down the mountain to the inn to find a letter with the news of Sibyl Houghton's death. She was too distressed to leave her room, and remembering that strange farewell on the eve of her wedding she cried all night long.

In the spring of 1889 they were invited on a Mediterranean cruise in a yacht called *Lancashire Witch*. Their host, Frank James, was taken ill just before they sailed, so his guests went without him in this large auxiliary schooner which, as Ruth learned with awe, cost £1,000 a day. After seeing Malta, Corfu, many Aegean islands and Constantinople, they anchored off Mount Athos, that republic of some thirty Orthodox monasteries in which no woman, or even female animal, is allowed to set foot, though insects of both sexes abound. Two of Ruth's fellow guests on the yacht, having spent a hot day tramping round the Athos peninsula with Freddy, wanted to dress her up as a man and take her ashore with them. She refused and they told her she would be dull alone on board.

'Shall I?' said I, 'we'll see.' So I saw them set off, but to miss such excitement is not my line and when we got near the monastery of Iveron, I repaired to the Captain and announced my firm and unalterable intention of landing. He had a fit and said *no* woman *could* land there. 'All right.' I said, 'then I'll go down the coast anyway, but set my foot on this land I shall and will.' So, poor man, he had to man the boat and go with me. I even insisted on taking my little maid. The heat was intense when we landed and we'd hardly set our feet on the shore when two Turkish officers with guns and swords were seen flying towards us. They jabbered and chattered and groaned whilst my imperturbable self played the smiling idiot, picking flowers. The men understood only Turkish, but with many gesticulations I explained that the Captain was desirous of seeing the monastery. All Turks are corrupt and so seeing a chance of 'backsheesh', the men gesticulated that if *we* went back the

Captain might go and see it. I nodded approval, told the Captain to go and as soon as they turned the corner of a rock, I resumed my walk. After a time I met the Captain returning and he informed me he had met a monk able to speak English... He was a working monk and got £2 a year pay. I should think he saved a lot of that as he only wore a hair shirt which I am sure was never changed.

The Captain presented the monk. Ruth described him as 'the most disgusting looking criminal you could possibly set eyes on and he hadn't spoken English for thirty years.' All the same, twenty-one years old, tall, exceedingly beautiful, with a slim figure and dressed in a navy-blue yachting coat and skirt, she must have appeared to him a vision from some other world; and she probably vamped him too. So he led her up a steep hill to a summer house and on the way she was able to peer over the walls into the monastery of Iveron itself. She was followed by a whole cortège of monks, some angrily telling their beads, others clearly charmed by her appearance.

They came crowding out of every hole to have a look at me. Two or three grandees also came out and after exorcising me with two fingers led the way on. The summer house was perched on a great rock exposed to any sea breeze there might be and with a great sun painted on it. Here they spread out some lovely carpets for us and then the head of the monastery came, a curious old white headed man, like a picture, white hair down to his waist and eyes that looked through you at something beyond.

There was much bowing and many incomprehensible compliments until the arrival of a monastic doctor who spoke good German and could translate the exchange of civilities.

In the meantime shoals of monks had hurried to the spot and I saw countless heads pressing in, growing bolder, so that first one and then more came in till the place was crowded, and outside a sea of heads being frizzled in the sun and all staring at us. Then trays were brought in of a strong spirit made of aniseed, *oh* so strong, in little glasses, and large glasses of water and pots of red jelly. Each of us with many bows took a little of the spirit (I should have died if I had taken more than a drop).

Then more bows and speeches, then a spoonful of jelly . . . then Turkish coffee. . .

Ruth, undaunted, invited them all to accompany her on board the yacht, but first the obviously infatuated German-speaking doctor took her for a walk in forbidden territory, along arbours and avenues, past springs flowing into marble basins and into a Byzantine chapel where she was presented with some incense for use at home. A procession of monks then led her down to the yacht's launch.

Towards evening I prepared a collation for them – coffee, macaroons, preserved fruits, chocolates, etc. and imagine the astonishment of the three men on returning when they found me, *me*, who wouldn't land, who was to be dull, who could do nothing, *me* entertaining all the heads of the monastery, with hundreds of monks walking all over the ship; and oh rapture, the Turkish Governor himself rode down to the shore on an embroidered velvet saddle, and in full fig, to pay me a visit. He spoke a little French and ended by presenting me with his own buttonhole, saying I was the most beautiful and charming person in the world and giving me a pot of preserved lemons. . . .

Then the second most important Archbishop in Russia, who was visiting Mount Athos, came on board, to the growing astonishment of the other guests on the yacht. The whole monastic body showed itself loth to leave and so Ruth arranged for the yacht's crew to give a concert, singing and playing musical instruments. Finally the Archbishop and the monks left, taking handfuls of chocolates tied up in handkerchiefs. They expressed their thanks with a boatload of presents, wholemeal bread, jars of wine and all kinds of vegetables; and the ship's company of the *Lancashire Witch* sent ashore all the chocolates they had on board, for it seemed that the monks of Mount Athos had an insatiable desire for chocolates.

Ruth is not the only woman ever to have succeeded in invading that monastic male preserve, but her rivals have been few in number and the reception given her must surely be unique. The sole explanation she herself could offer was that they believed her to be a boy dressed in petticoats, especially as they had watched her, shortly after dawn, firing with a rifle at floating bottles which they judged to be a purely masculine diversion.

Back at home troubles began. While the castle at Brownsea Island was being repaired, Ruth and Freddy moved into a part of the Grafton Street house, separate from the apartments of Freddy's father and mother. Relations with her mother-in-law did not improve. Ruth, as befitted a rich young woman (however egalitarian her professed views), had a carriage with a pair of high-stepping horses, a butler, footman, lady's maid and full staff of servants. Prudence Penelope made her daughter-in-law's life as wretched as she could by bursting into her rooms when she was entertaining friends and being rude to them, and by persistently sending Ruth's footman on her errands (though she had three of her own).

> Of course my darling old pa-in-law soon saw how matters stood and persuaded her to go to fashionable watering places abroad till Brownsea Castle was ready. He used to hide from his wife in Grafton Street, slink upstairs and pretend he was out. But he petted me, his 'diabolezza', and gave me expensive presents.

With his illicit family in mind he used also to talk to Ruth of 'the scorpions of remorse'.

The expensive presents soon had to stop and, indeed, to be sold; for when old George Cavendish-Bentinck, who had speculated heavily in the hope of supporting his lavish way of life, suddenly died in his bath, he was found to be bankrupt. Lord Henry Bentinck's bequest was untouchably in trust, and Freddy and Ruth were faced with huge debts. Brownsea Island had to be sold, as did a fine pearl and diamond brooch and Georgiana Somerset's valuable old lace. Freddy's brother and two sisters had all found rich partners in marriage and they contributed to the salvage operation. Provision had to be made for George's secret lady friend and her illegitimate offspring, who were suitably endowed and shipped off to Canada. Matters improved when a fairy godmother alighted among the wreckage and pointed her magic wand most opportunely in Freddy's direction. She was Lady Howard de Walden.

Lucy Howard de Walden was a daughter of the 4th Duke of Portland, whose four sons all remained bachelors. When the last of them died in 1879, and the Dukedom went away to a cousin, she inherited the vast family estate in Marylebone, stretching from Portland Place to Marylebone High Street, from Wigmore Street and Cavendish Square northwards to Marylebone Road. She was old enough to remember the arrival of the news of victory at Waterloo, and she had a soft spot for her young cousin Freddy. Lady Howard de Walden provided him with a house in Mansfield Street and, as money was now short, she employed him to supervise her London property. After some years Freddy moved to another of her houses, 78 Harley Street, thus becoming one of the rare non-medical inhabitants of that famous street.

If Lady Howard de Walden was a fairy godmother to Freddy and Ruth, it was not a part she always played; for though enormously rich she was notoriously mean. On the death of her husband, a former diplomat of some distinction, she decided that a solemn funeral was an unnecessary extravagance and had him buried in a pauper's grave. As she herself lay dying she told her faithful maid that she was bequeathing her her stays because she had always had such a dreadful figure. All the same, Freddy and Ruth had good reason to be grateful to her.

Meanwhile Ruth was having children, an occupation which did not hinder her from making friends of diverse kinds and ages and accompanying Freddy on frequent country house visits. They went to stay with the Lonsdales at Lowther, the Hillingdons at Wildernesse, the Sykes's at Sledmere, the Strathmores at Glamis and every Christmas to Freddy's rich and amusing sister Venetia, who had married Mr Arthur James and lived among pictures and furniture of great value at Coton near Rugby. She was generous when large issues were at stake and mean in small matters. Lady Elizabeth Bowes-Lyon, the future Queen Elizabeth, was her goddaughter.

Visits to Glamis continued over many years, because Lady Strathmore was a cousin whom Freddy adored, as did all who knew her. Apart from the ghosts, who sometimes insisted on throwing the bedroom door open in the middle of the night, the chief attraction at Glamis was Lady Strathmore herself. Once, in the late 1920s, when Ruth was having tea with her, her granddaughter, the three-year-old Princess Elizabeth of York, bounded into the room saying: 'You can't think how naughty I've been. Oh, *so* naughty, you don't know.' 'Well then tell me,' said Lady Strathmore, 'and I *shall* know.' 'No,' said Princess Elizabeth; and that was that.

Ruth was widely admired, but she could be acid. 'What do you think', she wrote, 'of a young man who compared me to a hard frost blighting a beautiful pink nectarine – *he* being the nectarine?' Her friends ranged from the bellicose political admiral Lord Charles Beresford and General Sir Redvers Buller to Freddy's cousin, Lady Ottoline Morrell, a central figure in the literary world, and Count Edward Gleichen, a naturalised cousin of Queen Victoria who had won himself a reputation on African battlefields.

By no means all Ruth's male admirers were middle-aged 'sugar-daddies' entranced by her good looks and quickness of mind. It would have been strange indeed if they had not included some, whether young or middle-aged, whose intentions were not wholly platonic. When they bored, embarrassed or irritated her she could indeed be the hard frost blighting a nectarine. Chastity was among her virtues, but patience was not. However, she dealt kindly with some of her suitors. One of the most ardent was Arthur O'Neill, heir of the most famous family in Ulster and later the first Member of Parliament to be killed in action in the First World War. He was nearly ten years younger than Ruth and there is no suggestion that he tried to tempt her to infidelity. In any case nothing would have induced her to be disloyal to Freddy. All the same Arthur O'Neill was deeply in love with her and she was fond of him. So she solved her problem and his by arranging a match with a girl to whom she was devoted, Lady Annabel Crewe-Milnes, the eldest daughter of her deeply mourned cousin Sibyl Houghton. She was by nature outspoken rather than subtle, but at least on this occasion she employed subtlety to advantage.

Her friends included many Fabian socialists, of whom more anon, and a number of foreigners. One of the more surprising was Marie Vetsera, the seventeen-year-old girl later found dead with Crown Prince Rudolph at Mayerling. She was a frequent visitor at Grafton Street during the months she spent in London. Ruth was always convinced there was no death pact at Mayerling, for she believed that Marie's mother, Baroness Vetsera, whom Ruth knew from her honeymoon journey to the Austrian Alps, was aiming for a morganatic match if Rudolph obtained an annulment of the marriage to his unloved Belgian Crown Princess. She said that Marie, as she knew her, was just a simple beautiful child with no guile. Whether Rudolph, seeing no way out of the situation he was in, killed Marie and then himself, or whether both were murdered, is likely to remain a subject of historical dispute and popular interest, in Hollywood no less than in Vienna.

Though financial circumstances were more strained than hitherto, there were means sufficient to rent an Elizabethan manor, with a garden of high quality, at Corfe Castle in Dorset. Nor was there need to economise on foreign travel. However, the outbreak of the Boer War cast a temporary blight. Ruth was a pro-Boer, which she maintained was not at all unusual among her friends; but her brother Harold was in the Army, and though there were things about him of which she disapproved, and she had been grieved when his financial embarrassment obliged his trustees to sell the great collection of Hamilton pictures at Stover, she had a sisterly and protective affection for him. If he was fighting the Boers, she could hardly support the other side and she became Chairman of the City Division of the Soldiers' and Sailors' Families Association. She visited the works at Erith where the famous Maxim guns were made. She evidently had the same effect at Erith as at Mount Athos, for they mounted a gun specially for her and she fired off belts of ammunition.

She had two sons and a daughter safely in the nursery, and there was another daughter to come. She had lost one baby, George, at Brownsea Island where he contracted typhoid from drinking the castle water unboiled. The specialist from Bournemouth thought it was anaemia and treated the child accordingly. Ruth always considered he had murdered her son. 'I was a fool of twenty-five and so still thought doctors knew things.' To the end of her days she remained deeply suspicious of the medical profession.

The war over and Harold safely home, the lavish Edwardian era began, an era in which vulgar opulence and the dedicated pursuit of pleasure by a large section of the upper classes was accompanied by dark political clouds at home and abroad, clouds which many, but not Ruth, chose to ignore.

However, she and Freddy did not forgo the joys of foreign travel. They went to Anatolia.

> The whole of this trip has been an unqualified success. No tourists can go to Anatolia really, and we travelled like princes in a beautiful country under the wing of the Ottoman Bank, all the officials of which were kindness itself; and also a Turkish friend of mine gave me a letter to the Governor of the Province

who is a very mighty emperor and who was perpetually telegraphing to the various parts of his dominion about our welfare, and the police used to come grovelling at the Infidels' feet asking us to say a good word for them! The only drawbacks were that the barns we had to sleep in were alive with bugs and the food was so really impossible (and I am not a very particular nor a large eater) that it was practically starvation. Even the bread was *inhuman*.

There were, moreover, some daunting voyages by sea. They went to Brusa in

> an overcrowded boat with Kurds and Levantines. No sitting room, so I took what seemed a lady's cabin below to place my things. It had no door, only a curtain; and first I found a Turk rinsing his mouth out with many nauseating noises in my basin, and, second, I found a Levantine eating his luncheon on my berth, spitting orange pips and gnawing chicken bones. After that I returned to the saloon where Armenians and Kurds were examining their feet, picking their toes, combing their beards and making themselves generally at home.

This was followed by the boat from Smyrna to Athens,

> also a filthy boat carrying five thousand live chickens from Varna and ninety Russian peasants going with their families steerage to Panama to dig the canal and leave their bones there. I was aware of hot whiffs of the most appalling stenches coming to me alternatively from the chickens and the Russians, though I am bound to add the Russians sang lovely eastern songs at night.

In 1904 Ruth and her children, including the youngest, Bill, aged six, had a lucky escape. The whole family were in Morocco and Freddy had set off on a pig-sticking expedition, leaving his wife and children encamped in tents 'on a richly beflowered plain not far off miles of the most glorious beach and the Atlantic'. In the middle of the night there was the sound of the galloping horses of an army detachment. They had been sent from Tangier by the British Minister and the Moroccan Governor, for the bandit Raisuli was approaching. They wanted to take the whole family back to Tangier at once. Ruth refused. The children's ponies would fall over the rocks in the dark. They would leave at daybreak, not sooner. The soldiers, terrified of the ruthless Raisuli, lit camp fires.

All the fine draped figures were standing near them with the high red-peaked saddles on the white horses – very pretty. I dressed and told the elder children to dress ready and then go to sleep again, and I ordered everyone on no account to wake Bill... Having made my preparations I went to sleep again – really slept soundly from 3.00 to 5.30 to the soldiers' terror and disgust (I never saw men so frightened as were the Sultan's soldiers), and in spite of the fact that the heavy dew had wetted my thin habit and soaked my feet, I woke to a glorious sight. The streaky dawn showed behind the sharp outline of the great black mountain, against which rich, velvety blackness the terrified soldiers had set fire to every bush and shrub as a sort of protection. These big bonfires all round us, with sparks like devil's butterflies floating up, and all the picturesque groups of soldiers and horses lit up in this lurid light. *Lovely*. We than had breakfast prepared by our cooks' trembling hands while we were pursued by the soldiers imploring us to go.

Lovely it may have been, but it was also dangerous. Although Ruth recorded that Bill was in high spirits, loving the Moors and 'quite ready to follow Raisuli or anyone else – also delighted with the caracoling soldiers', they were lucky to reach Tangier without being intercepted by the bandits. So were Freddy and his pig-sticking companions who, receiving a separate warning, had forded a fast-flowing river, galloped at breakneck speed and made in five hours a journey which normally took two days. Safely back in Tangier, Bill remembered seeing wretched figures slinking along under close surveillance and being told that they were slaves. Far more ghoulish were the severed heads impaled on the gate at the entrance to the Kasbah.

No generation fails to misunderstand the preceding one. We judge our predecessors by standards established in different circumstances. It did not, at the beginning of the twentieth century, seem illogical to live a gilded life with many servants, carriages and large houses while at the same time feeling deeply for those who were deprived. Once her family was complete Ruth pursued aims quite different from those of *la jeunesse dorée*. Freddy liked shooting, and so she accompanied him to large country houses, and she entertained friends and relations in their house at Corfe. They both enjoyed travelling and made many visits to Venice, Spain and Austria. However, Ruth had more serious purposes, in keeping with her advanced social and political views. It was to these that she now directed her abundant energy.

# 8
## *The Socialist*

Even before she married, Ruth, together with her scarcely less radical cousin Mymee, attended meetings of the Associated Workers' League, sure that it was the duty of the leisured classes to meet their less fortunate fellow citizens as friends and, above all, not to be condescending Ladies Bountiful. Marriage to a husband of easy-going Conservative opinions made no difference to her views.

She wrote light-heartedly to her Aunt Guendolen.

> *The Souls* are played out. I shall start *The Fools*. All great men have been fools. The very name of my little society, The Fools' Fellowship, would ensure courage in the members, courage in their own opinions. Unconventionality constitutes Fooldom. Yes, we shall be called the Fools, but I will have only Fools who have born fruits to testify to their folly. I will have no frumps in the Fellowship, no faint-hearted Fools, and they shall have a paper called Food for Fools or The Feast of Fools, or the Fools' Fiddler or the Fools' Firebrand or the Fools' Factotum, wherein each shall set forth his particular folly and question the public as to why they commit it. A Fool must look at things from the opposite side to the great P.O (public opinion, not bedroom utensil) and must be a fluent Fool too or the P.O. wont listen but will stuff up its gigantic ears and hug itself in its worn out wisdom. . . . Great wits to madness sure are near allied and thin partitions do their walls divide. Every great phase in the world's history has been inaugurated by a fool. Only think, some have been Fools in their life-time and geniuses after their death. A Fool must believe in his particular vision – never rest till he can believe in it to an extent that he will undertake what others would never talk of attempting. . .

Thus wrote Ruth at twenty-three, but beneath the Falstaffian humour there was serious intent. Much influenced, like so many others, by the writings and personality of William Morris, she embraced Socialism with total sincerity. Yet she saw nothing illogical in continuing to live in comparative affluence and in retaining friends with dramatically opposed convictions, though she declared that

> Conservatives never read or listen to anything they do not agree with, which means a mould forming on your sense of values and stagnation of reasoning power. If you avoid looking at anything you do not understand you must end by imagining you understand everything.

Some of Ruth's early expressions of her Socialist faith were inclined to be contradictory. Thus while she was still living spaciously in the newly restored castle on Brownsea Island, she told Mymee:

> a crowd of stinkards [sic] landed to-day in the Telegraph; they having asked leave to bring them and entreated them on printed handbills to behave themselves and cause no annoyance to the islanders. Adams wisely locked the garden and conservatory, but he quite forgot the house and whilst I was having tea, what do I behold but *crowds* trooping up the front stairs. I for one never dare enter anyone's house without knocking and I am sure it will take years of Socialism to make people understand the laws of privacy – laws of property utterly destroy all people's finer notions. We had to beg of them to retire or they'd have been in all the bedrooms and nurseries in no time, and they *must* have known it was the front staircase. . .

However that may be, compassion for the under-privileged and a deep discontent with the existing system, social still more than political, were the forces that moved her. 'So much that surrounded me all my days has not been worth preserving', she wrote many years later, an opinion based on what she witnessed personally in those Edwardian years. She had no nostalgia for the grandeur of Somerset House, Bulstrode and Stover. In Ruth Rosina Swan's blood was as strong or stronger than that of the St Maurs.

She slaved for weeks on end with Beatrice Webb on the reform of the Poor Law, which separated old married couples and planted lonely husbands and wives in workhouses where only one sex or the other could be admitted. She attended trade union meetings and collected subscriptions; she took charge of a girls' club in the East End of London; she preached to girls' societies from Nonconformist pulpits; she did all she could to back up the women who went on strike at Bryant and May to improve their wretched wages for a long unhealthy day's work of adding phosphorous heads to matches. Later, as her enthusiasm for women's suffrage drove her inexorably on, she stayed for days on end with working-class families in Newcastle, Sunderland, Bolton and Preston. In the Byker at Newcastle she saw the slums at their worst, unsurpassed even by London and Glasgow, and because she herself was natural and unembarrassed in her approach to the slum dwellers, they in their turn accepted her quite naturally. She found there what she described as strange and humorous courage, touching family devotion, unfailing willingness to take trouble, generosity to still poorer neighbours and amazing endurance. She had never lacked either courage or curiosity: while the railway bridge over the Forth was being built she had herself pulled up in a cage to the level where the men were working in a high wind which swung the cage from side to side in long sweeps.

In 1911 there were upheavals in the labour world. Ruth helped Ben Tillett organise a dockers' strike and she then set her mind to helping the women of South London, mainly Bermondsey, who went on strike against starvation wages. She wrote an account of the struggle in *The Englishwoman*, a monthly magazine well produced and widely circulated.

> The dock strike, the carters' strike and others had left every cupboard bare (not but what that is the chronic condition of many) and credit impossible to obtain. No matter, out they came, pouring out of their several factories, pale, hot, determined.

She worked with the National Federation of Women Workers to state grievances, form deputations, interview employers, see that processions were orderly and enrol the striking women in trade unions. There was a generous public response to the women's appeal for financial help, and Ruth was a leader among those who distributed loaves of bread to the often starving families of Bermondsey.

Mix in the crowds (she wrote) and become unpleasantly aware that many millions of your fellow countrywomen wear clothes that are not second hand but tenth hand. Listen to their account of woes endured, as they recite them in an English your educated ear will find it hard to follow... Squalor, neglect and destitution shriek to you from every gaping blouse and greasy ragged skirt. Frowsy heads; soleless boots out of which shameless toes obtrude themselves; stained ulsters worn in the heat of a tropical summer in order to prevent their mothers pawning them during their absence.

One day, while she handed out the loaves of bread, she heard a woman wearing a man's old torn cap say with resignation: 'Oh well, there's a better time coming.' 'We shan't see it', replied another woman, aged far beyond her years, shapeless, dull of eye and sparse of hair. Suddenly, said Ruth, the first woman stiffened her flabby form and cried with eyes flashing: 'But by Gawd our children shall!'

It was, said Ruth, the spirit we should either be with or against. Which should it be? The women of Bermondsey won their demands, and in due course their children did see a better time. Ruth, who had played a considerable part in the winning of the strike, never tired of paraphrasing Hamlet to the effect that 'One should not treat people according to their deserts, but according to one's own worth and dignity'. She was not smug or self-satisfied, though she had reason to be proud of her activities. But they did not win approval at the Duke of Portland's Welbeck Abbey where Freddy still went to stay with his cousin, the Duke, but was only welcome without his wife.

Ruth was invited to write a number of articles in *The Socialist Review*, and when, in 1911, the House of Lords threw out Lloyd George's budget, she wrote a virulent attack in the *Labour Leader* on their claim to be carrying out their duties and obligations.

Duties! Your duties are to the mighty millions who own this House. Obligations! Your obligations are to those you call 'the mob' in their own country and 'British subjects' when it suits you elsewhere. Responsibilities! I've seen the way you remember them: Go! Look at the future parents of our race in their dingy schools, their unhealthy houses, their squalid streets, their second hand rags. *Your* Responsibilities: you are too late – you have none left.

This, too, was ill received at Welbeck.

In addition to her relations and her circle of social friends, she became intimate with some of the Fabians and leaders of the newly organised Independent Labour Party. She took the chair at one of Keir Hardie's meetings when she had a temperature of 102° and she formed a lasting admiration and friendship for one whom she described as 'this most perfect knight'. She loved his quiet oratory and his self-taught mastery of the English language; and she approved his determination never to attack individuals, whatever the provocation, but to denounce only policies, inequalities and miscarriages of justice. She saw nothing strange in being on close terms with both Keir Hardie and King Edward VII's friend, Mrs George Keppel.

Then there were Sidney and Beatrice Webb, with whom she stayed frequently and corresponded incessantly. She did not share all their austere convictions, but she did share their serious Fabian dedication to political progress, as well as Sidney Webb's love of Bach. She was inclined to agree with Beatrice Webb that this world must be the lunatic asylum of our planetary system. 'Hardly anybody ever thinks', Sidney said to her, 'they just let their mind wander round any subject that concerns them for the moment.' The pauperisation of the old and helpless was an evil with which Beatrice wrestled resolutely and in the end successfully. That, and the all-pervading horror of the overcrowded slums, were causes in which Ruth fought with all her might alongside the Webbs. It meant much committee work. On that subject she wrote:

> In a committee, when all the members agree readily to some proposal, I know that not one of them really cares what is done. Whereas when everyone argues and suggests a different course of action, then I know that all are keen and we shall get something done before long. Every human being views the world through a different window. All one can hope for is that one's window is not curtained by prejudice and intolerance.

Cunningham Graham, the writer, painter, Socialist and original Scottish Nationalist was among her Left-wing associates. She was not always impressed by him as a painter: 'There are only two good sketches in Cunningham Graham's charity sale: Aunt Eleanor and the French prostitute.' Highest on her list were George Bernard Shaw and his much-loved, if sometimes deceived, wife Charlotte. They exchanged visits and he encouraged Ruth to write to him, usually replying by postcard.

When in September 1912 the agitators for women's suffrage were imprisoned, G.B.S. could be crushing: 'As to all this dreary old nonsense about political prisoners having special privileges, I simply forbid you ever to insult my intelligence by mentioning it. So there!' Ruth answered by inviting him to stay the weekend in her house at Corfe. Bernard Shaw replied as follows:

> Do not tantalize a poor author. A run down to Corfe Castle and back is just what I need; and a talk to you (chiefly about myself, of course) is just what I should like; but I am rehearsing two productions, one every morning and one every afternoon, and may not miss a day as the bills are up and the dates impending. Not until the 21st Oct. shall I get a moment's respite from producing and be able to take up my pen again. For men must drudge and women must have diamonds and motor-cars. (But do not quote this remark to Charlotte, who pays her way and a good deal of mine too.) I will attend to Miss Evans if I have time; but I really cannot spend every day rescuing prisoners. By the way suppose Mrs Leigh promptly burns another theatre, what then? G.B.S.

However, he did succeed in rescuing some prisoners as this postcard, presumably referring to a male supporter of Women's Suffrage, shows:

> 'I did,' said Shaw,
> 'With my Caxton Hall jaw
> *I* got him out.'

The friendship lasted fifty years. In 1946 Ruth wrote to her grandson:

> I went to see dear old G.B.S. yesterday. Very frail and thin and white. He can just hobble into the room on two sticks and maintains it was not his fault that he fell, but that his swivel chair turned round abruptly and shot him out! Mentally he is alert and amusing as ever.

She wrote one of the celebrated Fabian Tracts. It was called *The Point of Honour* and was an imaginary correspondence between two politically opposed friends about aristocracy and Socialism. As she was both an aristocrat by upbringing and environment and a socialist by conviction, she was well placed to compose the argument.

All things carry within them the seeds of their own dissolution and aristocracy is no exception to this rule. I maintain that no-one, saturated as we were in the spirit of a once proud race, could fail to grow up into an uncompromising Socialist the moment he applied his tenets to modern conditions – unless some powerful influence counteracted his early training.

She asserted that aristocrats believed life for others should be one of hard work and enjoyment should be reserved for themselves; and she maintained, with greater injustice, that the unpaid services performed by the upper classes as magistrates and on county councils were usually undertaken to prevent any progressive measures being introduced and to guard their own interests. She was apt to generalise.

It used to be all but axiomatic that Socialists were pacifists and that, from 1917 onwards, they were blind idolaters of the Soviet Union, unwilling and unable to admit any correlation of Communism and Fascism. Ruth was no exception to either rule. On foreign policy, although after the First World War she had a son in the Foreign Office, she tended to be naively critical, to accept half-truths and to believe rumours that were false or exaggerated. Occasionally her deep-seated, but often carefully disguised, patriotism declared itself. Thus in 1950, when the egregious Dr Mossadeq seized the Anglo-Persian Oil Company's property, she let fly and under a well-drawn sketch of Britannia, with shield and trident, she wrote: 'Why should we grovel? I feel quite absurdly British.'

Allowances are always being made for the Russians, whether by Socialist intellectuals for the bloody excesses of the Leninist revolution, whether by President Roosevelt and the American State Department at the Tehran and Yalta conferences, or whether by Ruth Cavendish-Bentinck at the time of the Soviet aggression against Finland and the ruthless seizure of eastern Europe after 1945. She even sent her grandson, Joseph Hoare, the words and music of the Internationale while he was still at his preparatory school. She had imbibed all that had been written about the injustices of the Czarist regime –

> the teaming millions in that enormous land, all far lower than any animals; and even those who were rich and highly placed socially were every bit as disgusting as the hungriest and dirtiest starvelings. What hypocrisy it is now to denounce Bolshevists, Communists, etc. who are trying to make people realise the dignity of a human being.

If they were trying to do so, they were using dubious devices, but for Ruth they could seldom do wrong. Like her friends Sidney and Beatrice Webb, who were pathetically deceived about the genuineness of Soviet trade unionism, like the majority of Labour Members of Parliament, she watched what she believed to be a noble experiment through the rosiest-coloured lenses.

On 23 August 1939 a shocked world learned of the signature of the Molotov-Ribbentrop pact. It was a short-sighted act of Russian folly which meant that Poland's fate was sealed, that Hitler's eastern frontier was secure and that a second world war was a certainty. Not the least shocked were the genuinely idealist Left wing, even members of the British Communist party; for God had made a pact with Mammon, and the Nazis, their supreme bogeys, were now the allies of Soviet Communism. Joan Hoare and her son Joseph were staying with Ruth and Freddy in Harley Street. Joseph records that he sat at breakfast with his mother and his grandfather – his mother, who was strongly Right wing, eagerly awaiting the opportunity for an onslaught. Ruth swept into the dining room, her face black as thunder; but the kindly and ever tolerant Freddy looked at Joan and put his finger to his lips. Illusions must not be shattered too brutally. Not a word was said on the matter pervading all men's thoughts on that sunny August morning.

It needed more than the doom-laden Nazi-Communist pact to shatter Ruth's illusions. After the initial shock had subsided and the war was proceeding on its long course, she asserted that Stalin was right to have executed all his leading generals: they had been plotting with the enemy. The old Bolsheviks, tried and shot one after another, had been traitors to the Communist cause. She declared Stalin's speeches to be those of a great statesman. She was hospitably received at the Soviet Embassy in London where 'my friend the Ambassadress' showed her lovely photographs of the Crimea. When the war was over she really did think that the new People's Democracies, established under the guns of Soviet tanks while the leaders of the liberal and peasant parties lay in prison awaiting execution, were bright harbingers of a better world. An avid reader of the *New Statesman* she was just as intolerant as was its editor of any suggestion that the People's Democracies might be a little short of democracy and more than a little subject to Soviet strategic designs.

Her pacifism was devout, but it was nagged by a patriotism which she failed to subdue. When the pacifists, including her friend Keir Hardie, were bowled over by the raging surf of 1914, she was primarily concerned, quite naturally, with the fate of her elder son, called Ferdy after his St Maur grandfather. He was a subaltern in the 60th Rifles and he was dangerously wounded in the retreat from Mons. However, before that happened, she found time to write to her cousin Mymee, who was in Norway, that all that had happened made her feel

> the imperative necessity of doing away with a governing class, secret understandings and compacts in all countries. Militarism is quite aware that progress and enlightenment are its bitterest enemies and will conquer in the end.

In another letter, written four days after the outbreak of war, she gave vent to her feminist obsessions:

> This Armageddon is the obvious result of a *male* world which has so far enthroned Property (not life and health), Force and Armaments (not knowledge and beauty) and false values leading to huge military despotisms and the adoration of flag wagging and drum tapping by all school boys. Well, we must just see this through and having swept away *all* the old, leave a clearing for our children to rebuild on better foundations.

She directed her energies to organising women factory workers, making speeches to them 'all over the place' and busying herself with their welfare, in collaboration with the Women's Trade Union League and other comparable bodies, 'all the same organisations that we used during the strikes'. To them she offered and gave her services.

She agreed whole-heartedly with Bernard Shaw who said of the national elation displayed in every town and village: 'There was only one virtue – pugnacity; only one vice – pacifism. That is an essential condition of war.' She was rightly disturbed, as were many others, by the mindless campaign against all things German, a campaign which led to the hounding from the Admiralty of Prince Louis of Battenberg, as able and dedicated a sailor as the Royal Navy possessed, and of Lord Haldane from political life because of his learned study of the philosopher Hegel.

Remonstrances met with accusations of pro-Germanism and

> the impact of death and destruction tore off the masks of education, art, science and religion from our ignorance and barbarism and left us glorying in the licence suddenly accorded to our vilest passions and most abject terrors... The Christian priest joining in the war dance without even throwing off his cassock, and the respectable school governors expelling a German professor with insult and declaring that no English child should ever again be taught the language of Goethe... It was natural that German militarism and dynastic ambition should be painted as European dangers (as in fact they are), but when it came to denunciation of German chemistry, German poetry and music, German literature and philosophy, even German engineering, as malignant abominations, it became clear that the utterers of such ravings had never really understood the arts and sciences they professed and were profaning, and were only degenerate descendants of the men of the 17th and 18th centuries who, recognising no national frontiers in the great realm of the human mind, kept the European comity of that realm loftily above the rancours of the battle-field.

When Ruth felt strongly on a subject her pen galloped.

The depression and unemployement of the 1930s recharged her combatant batteries as she read the articles about that all too familiar slum housing she had known before the war and thought out means to encourage the Hunger Marchers and support the trade unions. When the Second World War approached, her pacifism and her anger both multiplied, though when it came to the point she accepted the discomforts, the shortages, the blackout and the bombing with incessant care for her ageing husband and little for herself. She had resented the waste of wealth and human effort on armaments, and once the desperate plunge was taken she wrote to her grandson, Joseph Hoare:

> If all our present discomforts were for the sake of something *con*structive, one would be quite pleased. Unfortunately everything one does, or goes without, goes to the work of *de*struction. Also it is infuriating to see how many silly people think our sole aim must be to return to the worn-out system that brought all this upon us. Of course one might as well ask the sun, or the earth, to move widdershins (a good old English word meaning the reverse way round)...

As in the previous war the movement of opinion distressed her. Already after seven and a half months of war (she wrote in April 1940)

> many people thought hitherto to be ordinary, kindly, sensible beings exult in cruelties, triumph over advantages gained by any means, however unworthy, and generally come out as precisely the same stuff as the Germans they denounce.

This was a slander on the British of 1940 who had been guilty of few, if any, knavish tricks; but there was greater wisdom in what she wrote a year later.

> How can we desire to live in a world where all activity and every effort is concentrated on furthering the work of destruction? A human creature wants to make, raise, organise and build. When this instinct is crushed a moving corpse results and a vicious, unreasoning one at that. It is death in life.

As the years go by, the fires of youth glow dimmer. The agnostic goes to Mattins, the revolutionary takes his seat in the House of Lords and the Radical votes Conservative. With Ruth it was precisely the opposite: the older she became, the more rebellious was her spirit.

> When we boast of democracy, we should pause and consider that if we had been a *real* democracy, we should have had no slums and no unemployed nor would our shipyards have been ruined for the sake of profits by competing interests. Naturally

every business wants to do all it can for its shareholders, and if the workers suffer, well.. !

She stood up for Stalin and Molotov. She took the Left-wing view in all international matters (except, for some reason, Persian oil), hotly opposing 'misguided interference' in the Korean War, the temporary exile of Seretse Khama, the military action against the Mau-Mau terrorists, and above all nuclear weapons. She was too old to march to Aldermaston with Bertrand Russell, Canon Collins and the members of the Campaign for Nuclear Disarmament, but she viewed the development of atomic bombs as the ultimate horror. 'Well,' she said, 'the way to love one's fellow creatures, singly and collectively, is not to expect too much of them. We most of us really love animals because we expect nothing from them.' Almost everybody has a favourite Chinese proverb. Ruth's was: 'We cannot prevent the birds of sorrow from flying over our heads, but we can prevent them from nesting in our hair.'

As with all iconoclasts, and Ruth was certainly a social iconoclast, pessimism infiltrates the minds even of those who believe their recipes are the key to a golden future. So, as the shadows lengthened she felt bound to repeat one of the favourite sayings of her grandmother, Georgiana Somerset: 'I hope for the best but I expect the worst.'

# 9
## *The Suffragist*

Since time began the conviction that a woman's place is in the home was held, in every country, by the majority of men and women alike. The German saying that Church, Kitchen and Children were the appropriate occupations for wives and daughters was only disputed in Asia and Africa where women, then as now, toiled in the fields while the men sat watching in the shade. Only men could own property, only men could fight to defend the country: therefore only men could have a say in the choice of Government. Besides, it was widely accepted, though it might be discourteous to say so publicly, that women had neither the intelligence nor the knowledge, nor the senses of responsibility and proportion requisite to make wise use of the ballot-box. By 1900 New Zealand alone had given parliamentary votes to women. It was not till 1920 that the United States did so, and the French ladies had to await the liberation of their country from the Germans in 1944.

In Britain Mr Gladstone adamantly refused to listen to pleas for women's suffrage made by such influential Liberals as John Stuart Mill and John Bright. Queen Victoria saw nothing illogical in herself playing a large part in governing the country but hotly opposing votes for women. In this attitude many women, probably the majority, satisfied with their role as wives and mothers, supported their sovereign. Most Conservatives were opposed; so were most Liberals; and so were a high proportion of the new Independent Labour Party, for working men had a deeply traditional view of a woman's place in the scheme of things. The outstanding exception in the Labour ranks was Ruth's friend and *beau idéal*, Keir Hardie; and he was later supported by the God-fearing George Lansbury and the devout Nonconformist, Philip Snowden, who with his energetic and outspoken wife, Ethel, built an eloquent platform for women's suffrage. It was indeed the Socialists who provided the backbone.

Bernard Shaw wrote to Ruth: 'I have always believed the two movements to be bound up with each other.'

Even before the turn of the century, Ruth, still living affluently on Brownsea Island and enjoying an agreeable life of travel and entertainment, began reflecting seriously on what she called in her letters to Mymee, 'The Thing'. That 'Thing' was the cause of women's parliamentary suffrage, for she was infuriated by the mere suggestion that her sex were less qualified than men to choose their country's Government, and her antagonism was aroused by the arguments, which indeed seem ludicrous in the clearer light of later years, used by those who were opposed. It was as well that Ruth never came nearer to Queen Victoria than when, at last deemed respectable, she was presented at Court on her marriage.

The family record in the struggle for women's rights was laudable. Ruth's great-aunt, Caroline Norton, had launched and won the campaign to give women undisputed right of access to their children when they were estranged from their husbands; and Caroline, as well as Ruth's grandfather, the Duke of Somerset, were eloquent in the cause of married women's property rights. By the last quarter of the nineteenth century women's suffrage meetings, never violent or unduly militant, were attended by highly respectable people – including Lady Guendolen Ramsden.

There were soon two influential women's suffrage organisations, the potentially militant Women's Social and Political Union, led by Emmeline Pankhurst, and the National Union of Women's Suffrage Societies, dedicated to achieve its aim by peaceful persuasion and commanded by Mrs Henry Fawcett. The militant members were known as suffragettes by the public and the more peacefully inclined as suffragists. They could count on a growing body of male supporters.

In 1905 there was a General Election meeting in Manchester addressed by the Liberal statesman Sir Edward Grey. Two suffragettes, Mrs Pankhurst's daughter Christabel and Annie Kenney, twenty-two-year-old representative of thousands of Lancashire cotton weavers, rose to ask Grey what the Liberal Party would do about votes for women if they won the election. Perhaps they were deliberately provocative; but whatever their demeanour, they did not deserve to be grabbed by stewards and thrown headlong down the stairs from the gallery of the hall. Picking themselves up they proceeded to hold a meeting in the street outside and were arrested for causing an obstruction. In court next day they refused to pay a fine and were accordingly sent to prison. That, of course, was good public relations for the movement. It was at this stage that Ruth flung herself energetically into the fray.

As the years passed and successive private member's bills in support of the women were rejected by the House of Commons, the enraged suffragettes took to violence, destroying property and chaining themselves to railings. The police arrested them; they went on hunger strike and were forcibly fed, often with unnecessary brutality. Several nearly died and a few actually did. By a disgraceful Act of Parliament popularly known as Cat and Mouse, those women who were seriously ill in consequence of forcible feeding were allowed out of prison to recover their health and then recalled for further imprisonment. 'The mice', said Ruth, 'are tending to disappear.'

Ruth walked up and down outside the Houses of Parliament with billboards strapped to her, front and back. Addressing a meeting at Knightsbridge she arranged for Annie Kenney, who had been imprisoned and forcibly fed with great physical damage, to be carried in on a stretcher in her nightgown. This was a deliberate act of defiance, for Annie Kenney's licence under Cat and Mouse had expired and she was due back in prison, even though her treatment had left her unable to walk. 'She has given all, as so many have, in a cause Grey, Haldane, Lloyd George profess to believe in, but do nothing for – and they can look on!'

The normal quiet of 78 Harley Street was disturbed by the noisy presence of the movement's leaders, Mrs Fawcett, Mrs Drummond, Lady Sybil Smith and others. Lady Sybil's husband and Freddy stood poised to bail them out if, as was hourly expected, they should be arrested; but the husbands made no grave remonstrance. Freddy contented himself with speaking cynically to his children of 'those splendid women, your mother's friends'. It may be thought Ruth gave inadequate recognition to her family's forbearance when she wrote some years later: 'I have always thought there should be an unknown warrior's tomb for women. There is no life-long martydom a woman wont endure, as a matter of course, for those she loves.'

She discovered that she was a ready and eloquent speaker and she stumped the country from north to south and east to west pleading for the cause. The police forbade her to address an audience in Hyde Park, but she did so for over an hour, speaking to a huge and enthusiastic crowd before which she flaunted the O.H.M.S. envelope forbidding her to speak. That same day she set off for Hampstead Heath and repeated the performance. She invaded the north, staying for six days with the family of a moulder employed at Armstrong's works who bicycled to the factory every morning at 5.30 a.m. For the first time in her life, over forty years old, she made her own bed. She lobbied town councillors at Morpeth, Jarrow, Whitley Bay and Newcastle, and whether or not they lived up to the promises they gave her, they were evidently conquered by her fiery eloquence and magnificent appearance. She won the support of the town councils in Bristol, Reading and Margate.

She stormed Glasgow where she addressed a public meeting in the poorest area. Her scribbled account of that meeting, sent to Mymee in Norway, reads as follows:

> Whirled from the station, dog tired, to most awful part of the city. Seething mass of gutter humanity. Evil, godless, animal faces; distorted, stunted bodies. Stench unspeakable (foggy, still night). Crowd enormous. Was put with my back to iron rail of men's public lavatory for safety, *in case* the animal crowd, full of drunks, closed in. No police, but faith is greater than posses of police. Gradually the evil faces lighted up. The obscene shouts ceased. The pressing in was from interest. The dull eyes shone – poor creatures, all they need is love. They yelped encouragement and friendly shouts arose. Then came a general desire to shake hands, to touch me – almost did some of the poor old women want to kiss the hem of my coat – most embarrassing . . .

Doubtless in addition to votes for women, she had said much else that her audience found edifyingly revolutionary.

She took part with thirty other women in a march organised by Mrs Drummond, the General as they called her, from Edinburgh to London via Newcastle. They covered fifteen miles a day, wet or fine, and every day at noon and in the evening they addressed the crowds about women's suffrage. Ruth alleged that the *Daily Mail* hired or instigated young hooligans to throw stones and pieces of burning wood at them, a probably libellous allegation. Anyhow, after a month on the march they arrived footsore but triumphant to a heroines' welcome at Chelsea Town Hall.

Back from the crowded meetings and the long journeys Ruth found no respite. 'All women live to grease the wheels of other people's work as well as do their own', she proclaimed with feminine fervour, and she applied herself to organise various women's suffrage organisations, becoming Chairman (she would have objected strongly to the hideous modern concept of a Chairperson) of the twelve-strong United Suffragist executive. She wrote articles for the papers and letters to editors. When it seemed on the cards that Parliament would debate a new Reform Bill granting universal adult suffrage to persons over twenty-one, abolishing all property qualifications, but omitting women on the strange legal argument that the word 'person' signified a male and not a female, her wrath was righteous indeed. She composed and had printed a telling pamphlet entitled 'Heads I Win, Tails You Lose' which contained a parody of a speech on the subject by Mr Asquith.

Amidst all these preoccupations she found time in 1909 to found the Cavendish-Bentinck Library containing a thousand or so books on every topic concerning women or likely to be of interest to them. One objective was to provide information for those who although still refused a vote at parliamentary elections were permitted by Act of Parliament, as early as 1896, to vote in local elections. Ruth spent a large sum in purchasing the books, which included a section of rare volumes printed in the sixteenth and seventeenth centuries. The Library found premises in Marsham Street and was eventually incorporated in the larger Women's Service Library of which it now forms a valuable part. It was an achievement of which she was justifiably proud and she continued to present books to the Library for the rest of her life. It remains to this day a lasting monument to her industry and idealism.

There was a strange, almost uncanny, coincidence on the day the Library was formally converted into a Society with its own constitution. The presiding lawyer proposed that Ruth should hand over ownership by the symbolic gesture of opening a volume and presenting it. The Secretary of the Library Committee went upstairs, chose a book at random and brought it to Ruth. It was a volume of a long and dreary life of C.J.Holyoake, founder of a Society of Secularists and the last man to be sent to prison for atheism. She had never heard of him and she wondered how such a book, which she had not herself bought, had come to be included in the Library. She opened it at a page where Holyoake was describing a Garibaldi Fund Committee and the first sentence to meet her eyes was 'One member of the Committee was a pale and handsome young man who gave the name of Captain Sarsfield. He was Lord Seymour, son of the Duchess of Somerset.'

More often than not the zeal of ardent reformers grows excessive and their pronouncements monotonous. They end by boring their audiences by repetition and even, perhaps, themselves. However, the women who fought for votes never lost their ardour or allowed their energies to flag. No cause in the present century, apart from war and, it may be, nuclear disarmament, has kindled such inflammable material or inspired more selfless dedication. At a distance of many decades it is a little difficult to grasp the depth of feeling and understand the fervour generated. However, what Freddy Cavendish-Bentinck said jestingly was in sober fact true. They were indeed 'splendid women'; and when war came they downed their placards, with votes unwon, and applied their fighting spirit to winning an even more momentous victory. Ruth, to the fore, worked hard for the welfare and fair treatment of women munitions workers, helping to remedy grievances and improve conditions.

In 1918 the long-postponed reward came, although it was only a partial reward. There was a Speaker's Conference to propose the terms of a new reform bill, and the resulting Representation of the People Act gave parliamentary votes to married women, women householders and university graduates provided they were over thirty. Shortly afterwards, a Bill was enacted enabling women to be elected to the House of Commons, though the House of Lords kept its doors firmly closed against them till the 1960s. Finally, in 1928, came the so-called 'Flappers' Vote' which reduced the voting age for women to twenty-one and put them, at long last, on a par with men. The hunger strikes, the public meetings, the long marches and the voluminous flow of pamphlets, letters and articles had paid off. No doubt women would, in due course, have been given the vote in any case; but there was much satisfaction in a victory won through turmoil and against vigorous opposition.

# 10
# The Philosopher

Ruth's restlessly dynamic personality and the intensity of her feelings, combined with an insatiable pen, induced her to commit her thoughts to an immense amount of paper. She was unselfconscious and cared nothing for what the world thought of her; but she did feel impelled to express her views to her friends and latterly to notebooks in which she jotted down the questions she asked herself and the conclusions she reached. She was an extrovert who seldom looked inwards and was interested more in humanity and its future than in personal problems except in so far as they affected those she loved.

Her friends and confidants were startlingly dissimilar. To balance the Webbs and Bernard Shaw, there were the Duke of Argyll, a clever Anglo-Catholic eccentric who was an expert on ancient Celtic inscriptions and Erse scrolls; there were Lords Newton and Clinton; there was Mrs George Keppel and there were passing friendships with such men as Lawrence of Arabia. Politicians, of all colours, were generally avoided; they had proved their frailty over women's suffrage and they had a tendency (all too gentle in the 1930s, as events proved) to spend on armaments money which Ruth thought should be used for peaceful construction.

Are we to blame those born rich and influential if, though conscience-stricken by the poor and powerless, they cling to their own privileges? Should they be castigated like the young man in the New Testament who 'went sorrowfully away, for he had great possessions'? It is a hard moralist, or perhaps a romantic one, who answers 'Yes', while those who answer 'No' merely condone persistence in a way of life to which they have always been accustomed. Francis of Assisi said 'Yes'; but he was a saint. The majority who say 'No' seem less reprehensible than former revolutionaries who in the aftermath of success turn greedily towards the fleshpots. If Left-wing aristocrats who unashamedly preserve their social status and inherited possessions may lay themselves open to criticism and even to ridicule, they are venial by comparison with those emerging from the other end of the spectrum who, having themselves known poverty and deprivation, close at least one eye to misery and distress while they journey triumphantly on towards the pot of gold where the rainbow ends. Their names are emblazoned on the record of every country in the twentieth century.

There is no good reason, therefore, to cast stones at Ruth Cavendish-Bentinck for living comfortably and retaining friends in affluent, privileged society. In fact, as time went by and money became scarcer, she led an abstemious life without complaint, caring for her husband's comfort and not her own. 'Some there are', she wrote, 'who do not possess things: their things possess them.' She loved what she thought beautiful, but she was possessive neither of things nor or people.

Capable of snubbing people, sometimes almost viciously, and not a complete stranger to that strong temper she had described in writing of her Somerset grandmother, she was not spiteful.

> You might as well remember (she wrote to her grandson, Joseph Hoare, early in the Second World War) that spite never bore good fruit and that an embittered spirit never bettered anything. What is the root of evil is lack of happiness and laughter – and all this nationalism, which is a myth and a mischievous one. To be overwhelmed by fear or by hatred, or by indignation, to be swamped by *any* emotion is a weakness. It consumes mental energy, it is enervating and it renders one useless.

Though she reacted strongly, in words, to those who disagreed with her or aroused her wrath, she did so within the strict limits of permissible language, and while she revelled in verbal strife, she abhorred any form of physical violence. In 1911, at a time when capital punishment was generally accepted as just and necessary, Ruth had written a powerful article in *The Socialist Review* attacking 'legalised murder', as she called it, denouncing it as a relic of barbarism detrimental to the moral development of the country. She insisted that violence by the State induced violence by the individual and she argued, in terms which might have been used two generations later, against the belief that the death penalty was a deterrent. Social conditions were a principal cause of crime: 'to a great extent we manufacture our own criminals and then, panic-stricken, we seek to revenge ourselves on that for which we are responsible.' There is nothing in this that strikes the people of the 1980s as unusual or original; but in 1911 it was *avant garde* indeed.

Few of Ruth's letters failed to mention the plays she had seen, for they were her foremost pleasure. Indeed she wrote one herself in the early 1920s portraying such characters as Queen Victoria and Mary Kingsley, and it was produced in a London theatre. She read voraciously, she missed no exhibitions of pictures and furniture at museums and galleries, and she loved orchestral music, singing and ballet. It was indeed a triumph to teach Sidney Webb to love Bach, as his obsession with political and social work frustrated most of those anxious to promote his cultural welfare. She drew well and loved pictures, but she was quite unable to understand modern art. She even failed to see the merit of Augustus John – 'The horror he did of dear Ottoline Bentinck made me wish to murder him' - and she declared that Lord Athlone would succeed in claiming heavy damages for 'the libellous canvas', purporting to be a portrait of him, that John exhibited at the Academy. In all matters relating to the Arts, and in many others as well, she kept closely in touch with Lady Guendolen's grandson, Brinsley Ford, who had inherited a fine collection of pictures to which he made judiciously selected additions, and whom Ruth considered one of her most treasured relations.

Nothing aroused her ire more than anti-Semitism.

> In trade the Jews are well known to keep their word far better than most Christians. All the Jews I've ever known, Asher, Meyerstein, Natty Rothschild, Guggenheim, Marcus Samuel, were such fine individuals and one could only wish there were more Christians like them.

So when the Hitlerian persecution sent thousands of refugees scurrying abroad, Ruth gladly gave shelter to two Jewish girls of humble origin from Wiesbaden. They earned their living by swelling unnecessarily her domestic staff in Harley Street. As war approached they sobbed with terror at the thought of what might be happening to their parents left at home. Ruth wanted them to have a sitting-room of their own, away from her elderly English servants who disliked all foreigners on principle. So she offered them a large room in the basement which was never used. The English servants at one objected that the room was by rights theirs, that the girls would move the furniture, and probably damage it, and that they would not clean it in the way it always had been cleaned. 'Possession and territory', Ruth reflected sadly, 'mean more than human happiness.'

'Churchgoers and bibliolaters', she declared acidly and with that touch of arrogance normal in the anti-religious, 'create God in their own image and worship the reflection of their own miserable selves.' She was not a Christian. But she did believe in a Life Force, a phrase which Bernard Shaw used and implanted in her mind. Like many who cannot accept institutional religion, but have a strong spiritual element in their nature, she began by denying the validity of faith and by attempting to comprehend intellectually what must in essence be intellectually incomprehensible. She was generous-minded and always compassionate, but the Christian virtue of humility was not one of hers. The committed Christian tries to be humble and often fails; the pagan, such as Ruth, seldom tries. As time went by she developed her own religious theory and became totally convinced by it.

The Life Force, both Bernard Shaw and Ruth believed, was something you could not command: it possessed you. Finite minds were unable to grasp the mystery of which they were a part.

> Beauty in form or colour, and our ability to be aware of and admire beauty at all, is a form of worship of the Unknowable; and indeed it is the only manifestation of Universal Law which we poor insects are capable of understanding. Beauty can be felt, not explained, like a pain.

It is, she repeated again and again, the man who makes the religion and not the religion the man, and if he be a good man it will be a good religion whatever label he chooses to hang on it. The individual might have to submit his secular will to a Socialist State; but in matters relating to the spirit it was his individuality alone that counted. Among Ruth's papers was a verse by Mary Cholmondeley which expressed her feelings:

> Still as of old
> Man by himself is priced.
> For thirty pieces Judas sold
> Himself, not Christ.

These often undigested thoughts crystallised in a kind of pantheism, in which a version of the transmigration of souls was incorporated.

> I never understand how anyone who thinks we were just born from nothing can expect to go on and be immortal. If we *were* nothing we shall go back to nothing. As we are such wonderful beings, rooted in some soil from which we draw all our growth and spiritual strength, it is to me obvious that we are dust specks of the Divine Law – in fact part of 'It' and therefore indestructible. We were, are and shall be, and, moreover, as all things seem to move in their appointed orbit, from stars and constellations down to things infinitessimal, we probably also have an orbit in which we move. Perhaps the old narrow notions of meeting again have some truth (discard the harp!) and as individual specks of It (whatever we call God) we may come across the same ones again in our orbit, though not in the same appearance or relationship. Possibly that is why we feel drawn to some individuals more than others.

In another letter she wrote:

> A wave rises out of the ocean, rushes on, then sinks back to rise again and again, always part of the sea itself. But on homecoming give me a Nissen hut with someone to love and none of your cold and draughty Temples – though I'd love buildings to admire and hold festivals in and merry-make (so long as such a building does not entail a Priest). *Du reste* I'm eastern enough to say, with the Arab, the dogs do bark but the Caravan passes on – and so will even the present idiot world.

Ruth was revolted by the element of fear in religion, by the manmade bogey created from expectations of hell-fire, aided by insecurity, waste of wealth and concentration on armaments.

Individuals remain essentially the same, loveable and admirable. All they require is space to live, a feeling of security and the removal of the Bogey. If there must be a Bogey, at any rate go up and look at it, and talk to it, and very likely you'll find it's only a hollowed turnip with a candle-end inside.

She was fascinated by ghosts, though she firmly disbelieved in the supernatural. It must have been her gipsy ancestry which made her more conscious than most people of odd and apparently inexplicable experiences; but she was sure there was a scientific explanation. Activities long past had impressed their image on a place and those with sensitive antennae could on occasion recapture them.

She had had an uncanny dream or vision before her grandfather died, and she remembered Sibyl Houghton's conviction of approaching death. These were premonitions to which her explanation could have no relevance but she collected and noted down the 'strange happenings' of which others told her. She herself, while the guest of the Duke of Argyll at Inveraray, walked up a glen and heard the marching steps and voices of a whole regiment on the other side of a burn; and staying with Lord and Lady Strathmore at St Paul's Walden she rose from her bed one night because of a commotion outside her window and the sound of a strong wind. Looking out she saw men with lanterns and heard voices and the movement of horses. The house had once been, she was told on the following morning, the last staging post of coaches on their way to London.

When the Second World War exploded on civilians as well as the armed forces, Ruth and Freddy moved from London to his sister Venetia's house in Warwickshire. It was cold and deserted. 'I have been plucking and skinning and cutting up rooks – a nasty job but very necessary.' They moved from there to a rectory house near Salisbury. She wrote to Joseph Hoare: 'Granpa says that *my* being in a Rectory will fill the place with sulphur fumes and it will all go up in flames. I say that for once it will house a *really* religious person.'

Time moved slowly, for Freddy was in his mid-eighties and much as Ruth longed to be in the capital, active and useful, her affection for her husband came before all else. Month by month she set down her thoughts on the permanent features of a changing world. In June 1940, with the Battle of Britain about to start, she wrote:

> In spite of their cruelties and stupidities, why is it that only the human animal will unhesitatingly give up its life for an idea, a cause, when the other animals, who in many ways appear so much better than we are, can only know enough to die for their young or for the safety of the herd?

Her thoughts and inquiries turned more and more to nature.

Oak and hemlock, rose and fir, magnolia and cowslip, all draw something from the earth and transform the nourishment obtained into vastly different growths, colours and scents.

So we all draw something from the spiritual world and we all transform what we desire into vastly different characters, appearances and capacities. Can some help being deadly nightshade or stinging nettles?

The skies darkened as the war intensified. She compared the human race in its misery to a blackbird desperately knocking itself against the panes of a greenhouse when all the time the door is open. 'We are exactly like that bird. We think we are caught in some evil state of things we cannot get away from: we are frantic, fearful, flustered . . . and all the time there is some way out we are too hypnotised by our own terror to see.' The world was indeed depressing and the future of Europe seemed bleak.

Yet why not a deeper depression at so gloomy a prospect? If I live, I can quite believe it will be exhilarating to see here, then there, some little unexpected change for the better, a metaphoric crocus or snowdrop raising its head from the frozen soil.

The aerial bombardment stopped in May 1941 and did not resume till 1944. So she and Freddy returned to a flat in London, having been obliged to empty their Harley Street house for reasons of economy. Financially, Ruth and Freddy, once so well-to-do, believed themselves to be more severely embarrassed than was in fact the case. They did, however, have to raise large sums, including loans from the bank, to pay the debts of their elder son whose 'incredible imbecilities' would otherwise have bankrupted him; and their younger son's wife was also proving expensive far beyond her husband's means. Wartime taxes were cruelly high and, convinced that their income was inadequate for their bare needs, they sold most of their silver and Freddy's well-chosen collection of pictures, putting into store valuable furniture to await more favourable markets for a sale.

Ruth had a grandchild, Joseph Hoare, who was constantly in her thoughts, whom she had cherished from his nursery days and to whom she wrote weekly for some twenty-five years. His father was a diplomat so that he and Joseph's mother were usually abroad. She, the Cavendish-Bentincks' elder daughter, was intelligent and attractive. But she had suffered severely from tuberculosis as a girl, was constantly worried, and was not always the height of efficiency. Ruth therefore considered herself *in loco parentis* most of the time and though she frequently apologised to Joseph for the sermons she feared she was writing to him, she did offer much sound grandmotherly advice. She found in him a child on whom she could lavish affection greater than she had ever lavished on her own children with the exception of her younger son, Bill, though his marriage had created a rift between mother and son.

This was a typical letter to Joseph:

> I put out my hand to reach something I want. I don't get it. What of that? I (ape-like) catch sight of another desirable bauble and forget the first. I've missed something important. Do I frustrate? Not at all: I seize my knapsack and go a lovely tour full of joy at the strength of my legs and at all the marvellous beauty my eyes can gaze upon.

She worried incessantly about Joseph's health and sent both him and his mother copious advice, some of which the medical and dental professions might have questioned. For instance: 'You'll have a succession of colds if you put no milk in your tea and do not eat sweets and sugar; and not only colds, but also a succession of boils owing to a poor diet.'

When her daughter Joan said that a certain proposal was plain horse-sense, Ruth replied: 'Why horse? An ass is a far cleverer animal than a horse. A horse is apt to be temperamental.' This verdict did not, however, prevent her from taking a more than casual interest in the classic races at Epsom and Newmarket.

The war ended, her children were scattered and in due course Joseph joined the R.A.F. or as Ruth, who detested aeroplanes, called it, 'Satan's Aviary'. Freddy passed his ninetieth year and grew monthly more feeble. Her lifelong affection for him, at once a contrasting and a complementary personality, was evident as she sat beside him, holding his hand, sometimes rewarded by a smile as he lay in pain and discomfort. She compelled herself to regard death with equanimity.

It is the fear of life not death, which possesses us all, either for ourselves or for others. Despair has no place; courage must remain enthroned, as imperturbable as the grand Lao Tze in the Victoria and Albert Museum (or, shall we say, as an old shoe on the beach, quiescent, waiting till the next high tide washes it away).

Freddy died in November 1948, after a prolonged decline. She had never wavered in her devotion to him, nor he in his to her. Her absence even for a few days had always distressed him. Now having gazed once, and once only, at his body, she wrote to Joseph that it was

> as though some glorious dragon-fly had shot away and I was asked to look at the empty and shrivelled chrysalis it had left behind. Just as water is said to find its own level (to me a mystery), so must goodness go back to goodness and to the element of goodness.

All her life had been spent with him since she was nineteen and now, at eighty-one, she had neither strength nor desire to begin all over again. He had been so patient, so amiable, so diligent in years of unpaid hard work for the Middlesex Hospital. She by comparison had been the tempestuous and sometimes aggressive one. It can have been no accident that at the time of his death she copied out this simple poem which had been carved on a marble urn at the end of an avenue at Bulstrode:

> As by each rose we see
> A thorn there grows,
> Strive that no thorn shall be
> Without its rose.

She said sorrowfully to Bill: 'After sixty years of marriage, alone one withers.' Yet it was not Ruth's way to surrender. Her friends and contemporaries were almost all gone and she wrote that 'I feel more than ever as though I were in a dull station waiting-room and my train was delayed, whereas all my friends have gaily caught theirs and gone on.' Still, there were her children, Bill happily remarried to a wife whom both Ruth and Freddy had found sympathetic and understanding, and Ferdy now, after many difficult years, tall, bewigged Speaker of the Parliament in Kenya and a power in that still peaceful colony. There was Joseph, there was Brinsley Ford, there was her unflagging interest in public affairs at home and abroad; and while strength allowed there were still plays to be seen and exhibitions to be visited.

When Ruth died there were 'no comets seen'. *The Times* printed no obituary until Brinsley Ford sent them an eloquent tribute. Yet if her beliefs have any substance, an unusual collection of atoms was reunited with the Life Force, or It, or the Universal Law, on a cold February day in 1953, leaving behind the ashes of a woman of total integrity, intellectual as well as moral, who bestrode with equal pride the world of rank and fashion and that of poverty and deprivation. She made contributions to both those worlds. She was formidable and assertive, yet an altruist and a romantic. The word 'unique' is much abused, but the granddaughter of Edward Adolphus, 12th Duke of Somerset, and John Swan, labourer, of Higham near Bury St Edmunds, was a unique phenomenon by birth and not one to be disregarded as she went her way through life.

# 11
# The Cavendish-Bentincks

The story of the Cavendish-Bentinck family, though less sparkling than that of the Seymours and the Sheridans, includes men of significance in both political and military affairs and several notable eccentrics. The family tree has so many twigs and branches that it is almost impossible to see through it.

The Bentincks emerged into historic daylight in the Netherlands Duchy of Guelder during the fourteenth century. They acquired extensive properties, occasionally distinguished themselves on the field of battle, were created barons and eventually became Counts of the Holy Roman Empire, that Hapsburg Peculiar which was, in the imperishable words of Lord Acton, neither Holy, nor Roman, nor an Empire.

William, the youngest son of Bernard, Baron Bentinck and Anne de Bloemendale, was a handsome youth. He was born in 1649, a few months after the execution of King Charles I, who was the grandfather of William, Prince of Orange. Young Bentinck was appointed page of honour to the Prince, his near contemporary, whose intimate friend and confidential adviser he became. He played a prominent part in the betrothal of Prince William to Princess Mary of York, and when they later came to England as King William III and Queen Mary II, Bentinck accompanied them in a position of dominating influence.

Many leading Englishmen, including Sir Edward Seymour, the still powerful former Speaker, thought that while James II must certainly go, his elder daughter Mary should be Queen and the Prince of Orange only Prince Consort. This did not satisfy William, who was determined to rule, and so Bentinck made it clear in London that the acceptance of William as King, if necessary joint-sovereign with his wife, was the prerequisite of his willingness to lead a military expedition to the British Isles. Bentinck showed skill in the negotiations and proved himself a successful kingmaker. He also extracted a pledge from the

German principalities close to the Netherlands not to take any nefarious advantage of William's absence abroad.

As a diplomat and also as a soldier, twice wounded in the King's service, he was pre-eminent in British politics during the last decade of the seventeenth century. He was the architect of a peace treaty with France and for two years, at the turn of the century, a distinguished British Ambassador in Paris. The King heaped lands and honours on him and he was created Earl of Portland as soon as William and Mary were safely installed in London. The holding of office also provided opportunities for personal enrichment (it was rare to find men such as Sir Edward Seymour who thought it wrong to take advantage of the fact): Bentinck became a large landowner and exceedingly rich.

He disliked the English, failed to understand the feelings of the people or their traditions of government, and spoke the language badly. The English for their part, though apparently not the French, found his manners as bad as his looks were good. He was dour and he took no pains to make himself agreeable. He was soon detested by one and all at the Court of St James where his unpopularity was shared, to a lesser extent, by the King's other favourite, Arnold van Keppel, Earl of Albemarle, who was Bentinck's equally handsome, lighter-weight but more amiable compatriot. King William himself, able, diligent but devoid of charm, was only marginally more popular with his new subjects.

Before leaving Holland Bentinck married an English girl, Anne Villiers, sister of the Earl of Jersey. She died, to his genuine grief, shortly after their arrival in England, but she left him a son, Henry, who was heir to the estates that his father had accumulated all over England. Curiously enough the main family seat was Bulstrode, which was later the home of the Somersets and had formerly been the property of the infamous Judge Jeffreys of Bloody Assize notoriety.

Henry made an appropriate marriage with Lord Gainsborough's daughter, an heiress of some significance, backed the right dynastic horse and in 1716 was created Duke of Portland by George I. However, he did not prove a faithful steward of the fortune he inherited, for he was rash enough to speculate heavily and lose a lot of money in the unhappy episode of the South Sea Bubble. In consequence he felt obliged to economise by accepting the office of Captain General and Governor of Jamaica, an island where death from yellow fever and other afflictions was a common fate. He duly died there ten years after being made a duke.

Henry's successor, William, brought off a matrimonial coup. That insatiable schemer and grand acquisitor of Queen Elizabeth's reign, Bess of Hardwick, gaoler of Mary, Queen of Scots and of Lady Arabella Stewart, was by her marriage to Sir William Cavendish the ancestress of two Cavendish potentates, the Dukes of Devonshire and of Newcastle. Largely thanks to Bess they owned vast territories; but the death of Newcastle's son, the sickly youth Lord Ogle, whom the old Dowager Countess of Northumberland had briefly married to her granddaughter Elizabeth Percy, meant that the Newcastle possessions descended to his niece, the pretty and lovable Lady Margaret Harley, daughter of the last Earl of Oxford.

William, 2nd Duke of Portland, married her. Thus when her mother died he secured possession of Welbeck Abbey with thousands of acres and tons of coal beneath them. Lady Peggy also brought to the Bentincks valuable and extensive property in Marylebone, which a later Duke's daughter, Lady Howard de Walden, eventually inherited. William moved his headquarters, somewhat reluctantly, from Bulstrode to Welbeck and lived contentedly, but not at all illustriously, for thirty-five years. His wife, Peggy, who preferred her husband's house at Bulstrode to her own at Welbeck, is better commemorated than him by the poetry of Matthew Prior, and by Harley Street, Oxford Street, Margaret Street and Cavendish Square.

Their son, the next Duke, was of course a Whig. Only lesser county gentlemen, Jacobites, fox-hunting squires and some mayors and corporations were Tories. The nobility, with a few eccentric exceptions, were all Whigs, and under the dominating leadership of a new Duke of Newcastle, a Pelham rather than a Cavendish, they felt it their duty to ensure that the great landowners, and not the King or the middle classes, ruled the country. The majority of the seats in the House of Commons were in their gift.

This new Duke of Portland fell in love with the beautiful Lady Waldegrave, niece of Horace Walpole; then with the less beautiful Duchess of Grafton (whose husband was being horrid to her); and finally with the least beautiful, but most benign, of the three, Lady Dorothy Cavendish, daughter of the Duke of Devonshire. Having married Lady Dorothy, he settled at Bulstrode, which he much preferred to Welbeck, devoted his attention to politics, and in due course changed the family name to Cavendish-Bentinck.

There were many brands of Whig. There were Bedford Whigs (known as the Bloomsbury Gang), there were Chatham Whigs, there were Shelburne Whigs and, most potent of them all, the Rockingham Whigs, political heirs of the Duke of Newcastle. It was to them that Portland attached himself, becoming second-in-command and eventually leader. When he did so the Rockingham Whigs became the Portland Whigs, and although each group waged war against the others, they were united in their determination not to submit to royal control and in their hatred of the King's favourites, Lord Bute, the Duke of Grafton and Lord North.

Portland was honourable and high-minded, but he was also timid and an atrocious public speaker. Pepys had called Sir Edward Seymour 'proud and saucy'. Horace Walpole called Portland 'proud though bashful'; and Lord Malmesbury complained that he had 'rooted habits of procrastination'.

His properties may have been substantial but he was frequently harassed by financial difficulties. To begin with, his grandmother, the Countess of Oxford, who owned Welbeck and the London properties until such time as her daughter, the Duchess Peggy, should succeed her, was inconveniently long-lived. Then he had a long and costly law suit with Sir James Lowther which threatened the Portland estates and parliamentary patronage in Cumberland. On appointment as Lord Lieutenant of Ireland he had the formidable expense of establishing a suitably grand Viceregal Court in Dublin. Finally he felt in duty bound to support his younger brother, Lord Edward Bentinck, popularly known as Jolly Heart.

In a society where primogeniture rules, the younger sons of rich men sometimes console themselves for their smaller expectations by flamboyance and extravagance, indulgences for which, unlike the heir, they have no eventual means to pay. Jolly Heart, a cheerful, feckless and happy-go-lucky man, went further than other younger sons on the road to ruin and was a severe drain on the resources of his affectionate brother. At times Portland, whose political activities left him little time to improve the management of his estates, was hard put to it to pay his servants' wages, and he was deeply indebted to his brother-in-law, the Duke of Devonshire, who put Burlington House freely at his disposal in London.

In 1783 the war with the American Colonies ended disastrously. Lord North was discredited and George III, who had a large share of the responsibility, was disconsolate. Rockingham formed a Government and promptly died. Charles James Fox suggested Portland as successor, for although he was devoid of popular or parliamentary gifts, he was known to be hard-working and straightforward. George III agreed with an ill grace, declaring that his new administration was 'the most unprincipled coalition the annals of this or any other nation can equal'. A year later the King, by direct royal intervention in the matter of a Government of India bill, destroyed Portland's Government and sent for the twenty-four-year-old William Pitt. Portland should have been relieved that somebody else was burdened with the task of gathering together the flotsam and jetsam left by the American War of Independence.

When the excesses of the French revolutionaries drew Britain into war with France, Portland decided that it was the patriotic duty of his band of Whigs to support Pitt. Fox and Sheridan thereupon rejected Portland's leadership, but he stuck to his guns and the Portland Whigs were merged with Pitt's Government, thus becoming in effect Tories.

Portland was appointed Home Secretary. At a time when feelings ran high both in England and Ireland, and revolutionary infection was spreading across the English Channel, he conducted the affairs of the Home Office with competence and quiet discretion. He did, however, have to suspend the Habeas Corpus Act and take strong measures against sedition, so that Fox and Sheridan complained that the liberty of the subject was being suppressed. But his main worries were in Ireland where Wolfe Tone and Lord Edward FitzGerald, who may be regarded as the Founding Fathers of Sinn Fein and the I.R.A., inspired and led a nationalist rebellion. In the light of the subsequent history of Ruth and Bill Cavendish-Bentinck, it is a curious coincidence that one of the principal abettors of the rebellion was an Irish priest called Quigley or O'Coigley.

In 1807 the war was going badly, Pitt had died and the coalition 'Ministry of All the Talents' which succeeded him was in total disarray over the question of Catholic emancipation, to which

Portland was as ardently opposed as George III. So Portland proposed himself as Prime Minister and this time the King welcomed him with pleasure and relief. He formed a Government with brilliant individual membership and no cohesion whatever. He was not an inspiring leader; he suffered acutely from the stone, having it painfully removed by an abdominal operation without an anaesthetic; and during two years as Prime Minister he never once made a speech in Parliament. In 1809 he had an apoplectic fit in his carriage on the way to Bulstrode and there he died. He was certainly not a great statesman; but none doubted his integrity and sense of duty. He scarcely deserved Lord Rosebery's crushing description of him as 'a dull, dumb duke'.

The eldest of his four sons had scientific pretensions and was elected a Fellow of the Royal Society, though he had none of the qualifications of his contemporary, Edward Adolphus, Duke of Somerset. He sold Bulstrode to Somerset a few years after his accession since – unlike his father and mother – he much preferred Welbeck. In contrast to Somerset he had no liberal sentiments. When a member of the House of Commons, he argued against the abolition of the slave trade and later on, in the Lords, he was a leading opponent of the repeal of the Corn Laws. However, he did restore the family's finances and added to their wealth by marrying Henrietta Scott, whose father was the best-known gambler of his generation but who none the less brought as a dowry the largest estate in Ayrshire. By her he had, like his father, four sons and several daughters, including Lucy who married Lord Howard de Walden. With three brothers and four sons of his own he must have supposed the Portland dynasty to be as securely established as any in the land.

None of the four sons married. One, Lord George, was a Member of Parliament whose prime concern was for racing and who, like his father, strongly opposed the repeal of the Corn Laws, a measure vital to saving the Irish peasantry from starvation. He did, however, play the principal role in bringing Disraeli to notice and to influence, a debt to the Cavendish-Bentinck family that Disraeli never forgot. Another son, Lord Henry, was also a Member of Parliament and sponsor of Disraeli. He left a trust which did much to save some of his collateral heirs, who feature later in this book, from grave pecuniary embarrassment.

The strangest of the four was William John, subsequently 5th Duke of Portland. He was a handsome eccentric who on being rejected by Adelaide Kemble, daughter of a famous actor and herself an opera singer of repute, resolved to avoid both people and daylight. He built vast subterranean apartments at Welbeck, including a gigantic ballroom, and had them joined to Worksop by a tunnel over a mile long, broad enough for two carriages to pass each other. He was alleged to be at one and the same time Duke of Portland and Mr Druce, owner of a large shop in Baker Street. It was only after a much-publicised lawsuit and the eventual opening of Mr Druce's coffin, both of which events took place after the Duke's death, that this fantasy was finally discredited.

He was a good and careful landlord, despite his astonishing building extravagances: but some of his habits were bizarre. He employed several thousand men to build his underground palace at Welbeck as well as a riding school, connected to the house by a tunnel 1,000 yards long, which was lighted by 4,000 gas jets and was the second largest in the world. He provided his employees with umbrellas and also with donkeys on which to ride to work.

He himself occupied a small suite of rooms at Welbeck with two letters boxes, one for incoming and one for outgoing mail. Here he would sometimes shut himself up for days while guests invited to shoot did not even meet their host. It is recorded that one morning his valet found an outgoing missive which read:

> I have got the tooth-ache and a loose tooth likely to come out, and can't speak. I am going by mail-train tonight to London to see a dentist and think you had better come with me, and you can return by the first train without leaving the station. I shall only want rice pudding at one.

On this and other occasions when he went to London he would be driven along the underground carriageway to Worksop station in a wagonette with postilions and outriders, the side curtains tightly drawn to ensure his privacy. On arrival at the station the wagonette would be loaded on to the train with the Duke still inside.

After all the 4th Duke's sons had died unmarried, the London property went to their sister Lady Howard de Walden, and the dukedom went to a descendant of one of the three uncles, younger sons of the Prime Minister. Unlike their nephews they had all three married. The eldest of them, Lord William, was a well-known General in the Napoleonic Wars and subsequently an outstanding Governor General of India. He had no children, but his brothers, Lord Charles and Lord Frederick, did.

The elder, Lord Charles, had a son who took holy orders and married as his second wife Miss Caroline Louisa Burnaby. Their daughter, Cecilia, would have succeeded as Duke of Portland, had she been a boy. She did better: she married Lord Strathmore and was the mother of Queen Elizabeth, the Queen Mother.

In addition to his son in holy orders, Lord Charles had another, Arthur, who was Colonel of the 7th Dragoons and a major general. He produced an heir, William John Arthur Charles James, who succeeded as 6th Duke when he was twenty-two, before the days when death duties created havoc. He dropped his whole row of Christian names and was thereafter just called Portland, even by his wife and his oldest friends. He married a beautiful girl, Winifred Dallas-Yorke, with whom he fell in love at first sight when she was standing on a railway station platform.

Freddy Cavendish-Bentinck was fond of his cousin, the Duke, and was always welcome at Welbeck despite Ruth's radical vagaries of which the Duke and Duchess disapproved. Honest in his opinions and incapable of dissimulating, Freddy declared to his family that the Duchess, Winnie, was stupid and affected. In her own social circle she was regarded with benevolent amusement, but she worked hard for the welfare of the Nottinghamshire miners, from whose labours much of the Portland fortune derived. 'My miners', as she insisted on calling them, responded with warm affection and were genuinely touched by her strenuous efforts to improve their lot. The Duke, for his part, became Master of the Horse, held many non-political offices, including the Chancellorship of the Order of the Garter, lived in great state and was an excellent landlord.

Arthur, the Colonel of the 7th Dragoons, married twice and by his second wife had three more sons as well as a daughter, the celebrated Lady Ottoline Morrell. Of her brothers one married but had no children, one won a D.S.O. in South Africa and died unmarried, and the third produced only daughters. However, their elder half-brother, the 6th Duke, had two sons and so the succession still seemed secure.

It was not. The younger of the two, Lord Morven, was a musician of quality, a man of notably good artistic taste and a delightful companion. He was not, however, disposed to marry and he died when he was fifty, widely lamented but still a bachelor. His elder brother, Lord Titchfield, for more than twenty years a Member of Parliament, was not an outstanding politician, but he was well liked as a good-natured and public-spirited man. He married Ivy Gordon-Lennox, a granddaughter of the Duke of Richmond, and by her had two daughters. He succeeded his father during the Second World War, and when he died in 1977 he left Welbeck and his estates in Caithness to his elder daughter. Since though intelligent and attractive, she was unmarried, the ultimate heir to the Portland properties was, under her father's will, the son of her younger sister who had married an Italian and died regrettably young.

Neither of the sisters, nor the Italian grandson, could inherit the dukedom. It accordingly reverted to the descendants of the Prime Minister Portland's fourth and youngest son, Lord Frederick, whose only child was that jovial and likeable scapegrace George, Ruth's father-in-law. George did, indeed, have two legitimate sons, but the elder, who was Member of Parliament for Falmouth, married an American lady with a certain amount of money and died in 1909 leaving only daughters. There remained but Ruth's husband, Freddy.

Thus it was that when the 7th Duke, formerly Lord Titchfield, died in 1977 he was succeeded by Freddy's childless elder son, Ferdy, who was not far from his ninetieth birthday. Three years later Ferdy died, far away in Kenya, and his younger brother, Bill Cavendish-Bentinck, became the 9th, last and landless Duke of Portland.

# 12
# The Diplomatic Ladder

Ruth, like Georgiana Somerset, was a better grandmother than mother. Had she bestowed on her four children the care and affection she later gave her grandson, Joseph Hoare, she would have had a happier family. It was all very well for her to write in her old age: 'I don't like children clean. It's not natural. I prefer seeing them snatched out of the coal-hole': none of her own children was encouraged to frequent coal-holes. She was firmly set in her ideas and too immersed in Socialist and suffragist endeavours to pay full attention to the upbringing of her family or even to ordering the food (a task delegated to her husband). She once wrote 'The most difficult thing to tolerate is just intolerance', but more often than not that fine sentiment was disregarded in the handling of her sons and daughters.

Her elder son, Ferdy, called after the father she could not remember, inherited the St Maur good looks and some of her father's instability. He developed at an early age the extravagant instincts of his paternal grandfather, the amiable but feckless George. At Eton he made friends with the least steady and studious of his contemporaries and was allowed by the inadequately vigilant authorities to contract debts which were breathtakingly large for a schoolboy. He went to Sandhurst, joined the 60th Rifles, fought with gallantry during the retreat from Mons, was seriously wounded and won the Military Cross. He married young and unhappily, lived far beyond his means and caused his parents deep anxiety when they felt in honour bound to pay off large debts and save him from bankruptcy. 'Ferdy never liked his father and has been a grief to us all his life', wrote Ruth in one of her not infrequent overstatements.

In middle age the devil departed from him. 'C.B.' as he was known in East Africa, where he made his home, was first an uncompromising leader of the white settlers in Kenya and Tanganyika, impressive in appearance but forbidding in manner.

He made a happier second marriage and finally became a handsome and distinguished Speaker of the Kenya Legislative Council, respected by Europeans and Africans alike and knighted by the Queen. His critical mother began to think better of him and even brought herself to stomach his extreme Right-wing political views. At the age of eighty-nine he became for the last two years of his life the 8th Duke of Portland.

The two daughters, cherished by their father, were subjected to their mother's over-critical appraisal. The elder and better-looking, Joan, was loyal and courageous, but she suffered more than her share of ill health and to Ruth's frequently expressed indignation inherited the Duchess Georgiana's untidy, unpunctual habits. When her husband, Sir Rex Hoare, a diplomat of some distinction, died after treatment in the London Clinic, she ventured further along the path the Duchess had blazoned by going to war with the Clinic over her husband's treatment and the fees they charged. She pursued the charges vigorously in court and only abandoned them when the House of Lords pronounced against her. The other daughter, Barbara, was the victim of her mother's Socialist principles. Growing up in the First World War, she was not 'brought out', had none of the Seymour or Sheridan good looks and had little opportunity to make friends of her own generation. She did valuable war-work in London during the 1940 blitz, with ambulance and fire brigade, and was impervious to the falling bombs; but she died unmarried after a life that was seldom a happy one.

There remained Bill, born in 1897 and christened Victor Frederick William. Of all Ruth's children he was the one most capable of standing up to her, disregarding her angry tirades, amusing her by his cynical comments and impressing her by the prospect of a brilliant diplomatic career. She criticised him, but she loved him.

Distressed by the inability of Eton to cope with Ferdy's vagaries his parents sent Bill to Wellington where he was well taught but for which he conceived no lasting affection. In 1914 he went to Weimar, in the twilight of Imperial Germany, and acquired an embryonic knowledge of the language in which he later became fluent.

He was seventeen when war broke out and in the following year he applied to join the Grenadiers. He was rejected as unfit and so a post was secured for him as an attaché to the British Legation in Christiania, as Oslo was then called. There, during two years of patient slogging in the scarcely stimulating atmosphere of a small neutral capital, where daylight is a scant commodity for much of the year, he served a commercial and economic apprenticeship. The main task of His Britannic Majesty's Legation was to devise methods of inconveniencing the Germans by shipping controls. This obliged Bill to acquire a wide knowledge of both commercial practice and international law.

Late in 1917, in good health and better grounded in practical business matters than most of his contemporaries, he sailed home through the U-boat infested waters of the North Sea and again applied to join the Grenadiers. This time he was accepted, trained and commissioned; but before he reached the trenches on the Western Front the war was over.

Inspired by the starry idealism attending the birth of the League of Nations, which the Americans sponsored and then refused to join, he applied for membership of its Secretariat in Geneva; but the British contingent was already too large. So with his experience in Norway to his credit, he decided to try for the Diplomatic Service. Entry was fiercely competitive, even after a long war when the academic requirements were temporarily reduced; but he was a natural linguist, brought up to speak French almost as soon as he could speak English and with a knowledge of German that was already adequate. He was accepted, appointed a Third Secretary and at the end of 1919 dispatched to Poland, a posting which had an unforeseeable effect on his later career.

The world-famous pianist Paderewski was, of all unlikely people, the Polish Prime Minister and Warsaw vibrated with pride in the country's newly restored independence. The Poles were, however, beset by frontier disputes. There were problems with the Czechs about Teschen, problems with the Germans about Silesia and, above all, pressing problems with Bolshevik Russia in the East. Lenin and Trotsky believed that the workers of the world could only unite if the Red armies crossed Poland to join hands with Communist revolutionaries in Germany. 'Our next step on the path to world victory is the destruction of Poland,' wrote Trotsky; and he nearly achieved it.

In the summer of 1920 the Poles in a mood of over-confidence invaded the Ukraine. They reached Kiev, but did not ingratiate themselves with the Ukrainians, whom they despised. They were soon short of supplies and the Russians reacted strongly, driving the Polish army headlong back to the banks of the Vistula, only a few miles from Warsaw. Then it was the turn of the Poles, under the leadership of Marshal Pilsudski and with the tactical skill of the general commanding their northern army, the heroic Sikorski, to rally their forces and rout the Red Army. The disappointed Lenin and Trotsky were obliged to accept a frontier far to the east of the Curzon Line which had been proposed by the Western allies and called after the British Foreign Secretary. In the Treaty of Riga the Soviet Government resentfully agreed to a frontier delimitation which embraced many Ukrainians within the new Poland.

Warsaw was, in those hazardous days, a hive of diplomatic activity. There was a French military mission under General Weygand, who made a valuable contribution to organising the defences, and M. Jusserand, a stern French diplomat of the old school who had been Ambassador in Washington throughout the war. There was also a British mission which included a valiant soldier, Adrian Carton de Wiart, and was led by Lord D'Abernon.

D'Abernon had a startling career. One of his forbears gambled away the ancient family estates at Stoke d'Abernon, and so Sir Edgar Vincent, 16th baronet, was a penurious young man glad to be given humble employment in Turkey after a brief military career. He rose, by a mixture of cunning and ability, to be Governor of the Ottoman Bank, winning renown by his claim to have fought with a cutlass, single-handed and successfully, some Armenians who attempted to rob the bank in Constantinople. Whether or not this melodramatic claim had substance, he certainly made a fortune, partly, so it was said, by booking favourable investments to his own account and unfavourable ones to the Ottoman Bank; and in due course he was rich enough to buy back his ancestral lands. He married the outstandingly beautiful Lady Helen Duncombe, Ruth's cousin. As she could have no children and he had no heir, many considered that his strenuous, if unorthodox, efforts to recover his property had been in vain. A commanding personality, tall and white-bearded, he moved majestically from banking in Turkey to remunerative employment at home and ended as Ambassador to Germany. In 1914 he had been made a viscount and when Bill reached Warsaw, D'Abernon, together with Weygand, dominated the scene.

Bill was at once immersed in the hectic activities of a diplomatic mission in a beleaguered city. When the Russians admitted defeat the Anglo-French mission had no reason to remain. There was to be a jubilant and emotional farewell party, which was not the kind of thing Lord D'Abernon enjoyed. He announced that he was ill and must remain in the comfortable train where his mission resided. Bill inquired after his health and was told by the clerk accompanying him: 'If you ask me His Lordship is swinging the lead.' Shortly afterwards the train drew out of the station to the accompaniment of various national anthems and Bill noticed Lord D'Abernon watching from a window and laughing heartily.

The French took their representational duties more seriously. At another official dinner given by the Anglo-French mission Bill was instructed to arrange the correct placing of the guests. The new Polish Prime Minister, Paderewski's successor Witos, spoke no word of French or English, and so Bill thought it sensible not to place him next to the heads of the mission, but between two high-ranking Poles. M. Jusserand, to whom he submitted the *placement,* said sternly: 'It doesn't matter whether the Polish Prime Minister enjoys his dinner or not: protocol must be observed.'

Bill was sent to Danzig where the new Polish State was given access to the sea through the Polish Corridor. Together with the American military attaché he was delegated to supervise the departure of the Germans. He noticed that in one city, Bromburg, where the Polish troops sent to take over from the Germans were thin on the ground, the cavalry rode round and round, passing repeatedly along the same streets, like soldiers in an opera, to give the German inhabitants a false impression of their numerical strength.

From Bromburg he went to Berlin to report. At the German frontier he commented sympathetically to the officer in charge on the poor physique of his undernourished men. The German officer seems to have had prophetic gifts. He said: 'You have made a hard peace, but the spirit of the army will remain and we shall have a clandestine military nucleus, described as Fire Brigades, Gymnastic Societies and so on. It will be as it was after Napoleon's victory at Jena. In a few years you will be tired of sitting on top of us. We shall gradually rearm more openly and then a leader [*ein Führer*] will appear.'

Back in Warsaw Bill noticed Red Russian prisoners in British uniforms which had been captured from General Denikin's White Army and still bore the British royal arms on the buttons. He went to inspect a prisoner-of-war camp. At the camp hospital, where many of the inmates had typhus, he reported that Red Russian orderlies were refusing to give water to the White Russian sick. In their civil war the Russians, never renowned for their humanity, set no bounds to their contempt for it. He also found time to make Polish friends in a still feudal society, cosmopolitan, owning huge estates and set on restoring its lavish pre-war standards. It represented everything that Ruth held in contempt; but for a young diplomat there could have been few more agreeable posts than Warsaw. Among Bill's diplomatic colleagues was Arthur Bliss Lane, a Third Secretary at the American Embassy, who was to be a close colleague in more difficult circumstances a quarter of a century later.

Having won good marks at the Foreign Office for his conduct in Warsaw, he was recalled to London early in 1922. A few months later Bill was chosen to accompany the Foreign Secretary, the formidable Lord Curzon, to the international conference at Lausanne summoned to negotiate a peace treaty with Turkey. A companion on this journey, for whom he developed admiration and affection, was Harold Nicolson. He also developed an admiration and a certain affection for 'the Marquess', as Curzon's staff dubbed their sometimes over-dignified Secretary of State. Curzon was frequently in pain from his back and was obliged to wear a steel corset. When the pain was acute he believed every man's hand was against him and that his staff were useless. When it eased slightly, he concluded that the foreigners were irritating and tiresome, but that his own faithful staff were given him splendid support. When there was no pain, Bill found him as agreeable company as could be desired and revelled in his spellbinding descriptions of India and his anecdotes gathered over years of variegated experience. At that time 'the Marquess' still had Prime Ministerial aspirations.

It was at this conference that Mussolini first appeared on the international stage. The train bearing Curzon and the French Prime Minister, Poincaré, drew into the station at Lausanne, where Bill had already arrived to arrange accommodation for the delegation, to be met by a message that Mussolini was not going to

Lausanne but would meet Curzon and Poincaré at a station on the Swiss-Italian border. They agreed to go on there and had a nocturnal meeting with Mussolini, after which they returned to their railway carriages. To their surprise they then heard that Mussolini would accompany them back to Lausanne. He had wished to show off to the Italian public that the British and French Ministers came to meet him.

The following morning a meeting was to take place in Curzon's drawing room at the Beau Rivage Hotel. Poincaré arrived. They waited, but there was no sign of Mussolini. Bill was sent to find him. His secretary, Mauro Panza, who unexpectedly turned out to be an Old Harrovian, inquired whether Curzon and Poincaré were ready for the conference. Bill informed him sharply that they were waiting. Whereupon he said 'Then I will inform the Duce.' Mussolini excelled at stage management.

Curzon gave a large dinner party for all the delegates to the conference, a festivity complicated by the initial unwillingness of the Greeks and Turks to sit at the same table. When that was resolved, Bill asked the Secretary of State whether he wished the transatlantic innovation, cocktails, served before dinner. 'Bentinck,' said the frowning Marquess, 'does your father have cocktails served in his house?' 'No, he would never hear of it.' replied Bill. 'Then why should you expect me to have them served at *my* dinner party?'

Curzon was a skilled negotiator, and he was capable of concentrating on more than one thing at a time. To cover the Lausanne Conference the *Daily Express* had sent a diplomatic correspondent who brought with him a young lady from Vienna. She succumbed to the charms of a secretary in Mussolini's delegation. Returning from news gathering, the *Daily Express* correspondent found his Viennese girl friend in bed with the Italian. He seized the bedside lamp and broke it on the Italian's head, deeply cutting his ear. The Italian was taken to hospital, the aggressor and the Viennese lady to the police station.

Two days later, in full conference, Curzon spoke eloquently on behalf of the persecuted Armenians. 'Do you mean to tell me, General Ismet Pasha,' he declared, 'that in your vast territories there is not one nook, not one cranny, for these unhappy folk?' While this oratory was having its effect, he turned to his second-in-command and asked which of the Italians present was the adulterer and which ear it was. During his speech he had been scanning the audience for the damaged ear.

He then left Lausanne to join the British delegation to the Reparations Conference in Paris, but was so disturbed by the amorous activities of a Roumanian couple in the room next to his at the Ritz that he had no wink of sleep and was incapable of giving proper attention to his conference duties on the following morning. As his colleague, Mr Bonar Law, was mortally ill, the British delegation had nothing to contribute. The conference broke up without making any decisions, and the French, refraining from consultation with their allies, proceeded to occupy the Ruhr until the reparations they demanded should be duly paid. By such accidents is history made.

In 1923, promoted to Second Secretary, Bill was posted to the British Embassy in Paris. The Ambassador was Lord Crewe, Asquith's most trusted counsellor in the pre-war Liberal Cabinet. He was married to Lord Rosebery's witty and impressive daughter, Peggy, but his first wife, whose early death had desolated him, was that Graham cousin to whom Ruth was particularly devoted, Sibyl Houghton. Thus, though there was no blood relationship, the Ambassador had a natural interest in Bill.

The Embassy staff included men of future distinction. The Minister was Eric Phipps, afterwards Ambassador in both Berlin and Paris; and the Head of Chancery was Rob Hudson, married to an attractive American and subsequently Minister of Agriculture in the Second World War. There was another, who was strikingly different. He was able, ambitious and possessed of all the social graces. His name was Charles Mendl and his matrimonial designs had a decisive effect on Bill's career.

Mendl was a Bohemian Jew whose shrewdness matched his charm. What he lacked was a fortune. His father had settled in London and made enough money to send his sons to Harrow. Charles then went to Buenos Aires as a grain merchant and graduated to arms salesman. On the outbreak of war he became an army interpreter, was badly wounded and worked for Admiralty Intelligence in Paris. In Buenos Aires before the war he had exerted his never-wearying charm on Señora Grace de Duggan, subsequently Marchioness Curzon and wife of the Foreign Secretary. She, with the support of Sir George Graham, an influential member of the Diplomatic Service, persuaded Lord Derby, Lord Crewe's predecessor as Ambassador, to attach Charles Mendl to the Embassy. He remained there, a brilliant newsgatherer, an entertainer of everybody who mattered and an expert in arranging useful contacts, until forced to fly from Paris in 1940. In 1923 he was still embarrassingly short of the funds necessary to maintain his status.

An heiress was the obvious solution. The European ones were unlikely to think him grand enough, but in 1924 he was knighted and he hoped an eligible American might be impressed both by the charm which had so appealed to Señora de Duggan and by his new title.

Just then there arrived in Paris from Oklahoma a Mrs Quigley and her two daughters. Her father had founded a bank in Texas, she was the widow of a Kentucky lawyer, and she had two brothers of significance in Oklahoma. One of them had been the right-hand man of Governor Charles Nathaniel Haskell, who had made a large fortune in railroads and had been the runner-up for the Democrat candidature in the 1920 Presidential election. The Governor was over sixty, but the elder of Mrs Quigley's daughters, Dorothea, had been what the Americans used to call his Great and Good Friend, and Charles Mendl believed that she had been handsomely endowed from the railroad profits. Mrs Quigley herself had been put in funds by her brother, Governor Haskell's campaign manager, who had given her inside information about a deal affecting the stock market. A compulsive and usually unsuccessful speculator, she made enough on this occasion to bring her two daughters to Europe in order to bestow their hands on suitable noblemen. She was, according to Ruth, 'a bird of prey though she looks like an old sheep'.

Charles Mendl, moved by the thought of the elder Miss Quigley's fortune, persuaded Mr and Mrs Rob Hudson to give a dinner party for the two young ladies to which Bill Cavendish-Bentinck was invited as a partner for Clothilde, the younger and unendowed sister. The dinner party was a great success, though Sir Charles soon began to have disturbing doubts about the size of Governor Haskell's alleged endowment.

A few days later Ruth and Freddy arrived in Paris on a visit. Bill met them at the Gare du Nord and told his mother he was engaged to be married. 'I hardly believed it, but I asked who to? and he said: "Her name is Clothilde Quigley." I thought it was a joke.'

It was not a joke. Bill had been struck by a thunderbolt of infatuation and nothing that Ruth, Freddy or Lord Crewe could say about his youth, or his not having known her long enough, would dissuade him. They were married and though Ruth at first did her best to like Clothilde, she failed entirely; nor did Clothilde make an effort to endear herself to her parents-in-law. As the years went by Ruth's pen became increasingly violent against 'that strangely poisonous Clothilde'.

Clothilde was largely to blame. She and Bill were happy for a time and they had a son and a daughter, but she was quarrelsome and she was determined to flout all the conventions, diplomatic as well as social. She was recklessly extravagant so that Bill eventually had to be rescued financially by his parents, already distressed by his brother Ferdy's huge debts. She was headstrong and impervious to argument and, as her own daughter has said, she equated discretion with hypocrisy. Before many years passed she was also unfaithful. She was a grave impediment to a rising diplomat.

Anthony Powell wrote in one of his novels that 'history is full of examples of hard-headed personages – to be expected to choose partners in love for reasons helpful to their own career – who were, as often as not, the very people most to embarrass themselves, even to the extent of marriage, in unions that proved subsequently formidable obstacles to advancement'. Bill was a hard-headed personage; and he fell headlong into the category described by Anthony Powell.

They were moved from Paris to The Hague and thence to London where Bill, increasingly approved for his professional abilities, joined the League of Nations Department. He was attached to the British delegation that in 1925 went with the new Foreign Secretary, Sir Austen Chamberlain, to Geneva and Locarno. France was represented by Aristide Briand, as able a statesman as Chamberlain. Together they confronted the German Chancellor Luther and his Foreign Minister, Gustav Stresemann, with proposals intended to free Europe from all threat of a future war.

Concord reigned supreme. France and Germany solemnly undertook never again to attack each other. The Treaty of Locarno was signed to worldwide applause. Mussolini, less bombastic than at Lausanne, arrived in time to initial it and for three or four years, till the great Depression descended, it really did seem that there was to be peace on earth. Germany became a member of the League of Nations and was welcomed back into respectable international society. But the 'shame of Versailles' still rankled with the German people, as it had with the French after their defeat in 1870, and Bill noticed that in his first speech at the League Gustav Stresemann spoke of Germany's rights with a shrill emphasis that gave rise to qualms.

While the delegations were at Locarno it was announced in the press that the raucous German agitator Adolf Hitler had been released from prison. Bill asked the Secretary of State at the German Foreign Office, Herr von Schubert, whether this might lead to trouble. 'No,' was von Schubert's reply, 'the man is just a fool.' It was a verdict Bill never forgot. However, in the prevailing euphoria there seemed every reason to disarm and to regard the League of Nations as the successful undertaker at the long overdue funeral of Mars, the God of war.

The Cavendish-Bentincks went back to the Paris Embassy in 1928. Bill was now a First Secretary, and the new Ambassador was a former Permanent Under Secretary in the Foreign Office, Sir William Tyrrell, of whom Bill had seen much at the Lausanne Conference. Nevile Henderson, Ambassador in Berlin ten years later at the time of Munich and a leading supporter of appeasement, was the Counsellor; and Sir Charles Mendl, architect of Bill's marriage, had at last found a rich wife for himself.

She was Elsie de Wolfe, with a fortune made as an interior decorator in New York. She had exquisite taste, social ambitions and a large bank balance. She was a hostess at her house in Versailles and her Paris apartment rivalled by few and excelled by none. The fact that she was a notorious lesbian was of no account either to Paris society or to Sir Charles Mendl. She wanted the title of 'Lady'; he wanted the affluence she offered. He retained his flat in the Avenue Montaigne so as to entertain politicians, diplomats and businessmen who would not fit into his wife's café society parties at Versailles. They were always entirely well disposed to each other and also to Bill and Clothilde.

Lady Mendl became one of the leaders of the Edward VIII/ Wallis Simpson set, proclaiming (in the author's pained hearing) that she had been invited to redecorate the Belgian suite at

Buckingham Palace 'which David and Wallis will use when Wallis is Queen'.

During the four years of the Cavendish-Bentincks' second term in Paris, world depression struck first America and, two years later, Europe. There was a lull in international dissensions while Governments and peoples reeled before the shock of share market catastrophe, bank failures, shattered fortunes and crushing unemployment. Then came the National Government in Britain, the New Deal in America, the Front Populaire in France, Japanese aggression against Manchuria, the downfall of the Spanish monarchy and the death throes of the Weimar Republic in Germany. Life in the British Embassy was scarcely ruffled, for every foreign Government was introspectively intent on its internal worries. But Bill had his own worries, for loyally though he stood by Clothilde, he could not fail to observe that she was disliked by his colleagues and by the influential Ambassador. It was a relief to move to new surroundings and new faces at the Legation in Athens.

Venizelos and his Liberals still ruled Greece, though a movement to restore the King was gathering strength. While Bill was there, national introspection was rudely interrupted. The Far East was in turmoil, Hitler came to power in Germany and Chancellor Dolfuss was murdered in Austria; but the United States, and to a lesser extent the United Kingdom, remained majestically isolationist, and the shock waves were only mildly felt in Athens where the Turks and perhaps the Bulgarians were regarded as the sole potential disturbers of the peace.

Bill devoted his energies to negotiating a successful settlement of the intricate Greek debt problem, an achievement which added almost enough to his reputation in the Foreign Office to compensate for what Clothilde was busy subtracting from it. She viewed the British Minister, Sir Patrick Ramsay, with distaste and showed it. He was indeed somewhat unkempt, surly and indifferent to the social graces. A psychiatrist would doubtless have accounted for his occasionally uncouth behaviour by the fact that when he was eight years old, he had an alarming experience on the family yacht at Cannes. His father, Lord Dalhousie, shot his wife in a moment of unwarranted jealousy and then committed suicide. The yacht returned to England with the corpses of the Earl and Countess laid out in the saloon and the orphaned children in the care of the captain. Little Patrick was then handed over for safe-keeping to his uncle, Lord Tankerville, and spent a lonely childhood with the famous herd of white Chillingham cattle as companions until such time as a good education and his native wit earned him a place in the Diplomatic Service. This was not the ideal background for His Majesty's Minister in Athens, but as far as Clothilde was concerned she was only expected to be polite to the head of her husband's Mission. She was not.

Unfortunately she was equally antagonistic, and indeed rude, to Lady Ramsay whose good looks and manners made amends for her husband's social deficiencies. She chose Athens as a place to display her contempt for the conventions. Women did not go unescorted into the bar of the Hotel Grande Bretagne. Clothilde did. Women did not go cruising on yachts with unattached gentlemen, even if they were undemanding homosexuals. Clothilde did. Athens buzzed with scandalous rumours which were by no means without foundation, and soon London did too. Bill, mindful of his young son and daughter, remained stolidly protective, but the Ramsays were outraged, the Foreign Office took note and in 1934 the Bentincks were banished to Santiago, the capital of Chile.

Chile is a beautiful country, but it was then a diplomatic backwater unlikely to advance the career of a man who had the qualities required to reach the summit of his profession. Bill and Clothilde were there for three years, lavishly entertained by the hospitable Chileans, but as far as Bill was concerned tediously underemployed, though he did score a success by persuading the Chileans to cooperate in sanctions against the Italian invaders of Abyssinia and even to offer to send a Chilean cruiser to the Mediterranean. The Ambassador was Sir Robert Mitchell whose wife was the daughter of a Chilean diplomat. Clothilde was as unpleasant to her as she had been to Lady Ramsay.

One day Mrs Corrigan arrived in Santiago on a visit. Laura (pronounced Lowra) Corrigan was an American with a passion for entertaining important people in London and with ample means to do so. She was delighted by Bill and when she returned to England she told all and sundry that it was a scandal such talent should be wasted on the Chilean air. Amongst others she made representations to Lord Halifax, on whom she professed, doubtless with exaggeration, to have great influence. Be that as it may, in 1937 Bill was recalled to the Foreign Office and appointed Assistant Head of the Egyptian Department. For two years, while the clouds darkened, he busied himself with the affairs of the Nile delta, the Sudan and British troops in the Canal Zone, all of which at least had greater relevance to the developing world crisis than the leisurely activities of the Chancery in Santiago.

Clothilde remained tempestuous and her extravagance unrestrained. To Ruth's uncontrollable fury, and Bill's embarrassment, she talked freely in London of the prospect that she would one day be Duchess of Portland. Bill began to have doubts about her sanity. His mother characteristically went rather too far... 'It looks', she wrote to Joseph Hoare, 'as though the Life Force occasionally peppers the world with grains of pure evil (Clothildes, Hitlers etc.)...' Even poor Mrs Quigley was abused publicly by her daughter and the children were witnesses of constant rows and rages, by no means least those instigated by their paternal grandmother, Ruth. Despite all Bill could do, his home was increasingly unhappy. He himself plodded daily through St James's Park to the Foreign Office, leading his Kerry Blue terrier, Angus, and crossing the Horse Guards Parade at precisely the same time as the Household Cavalry; for right up to the outbreak of war members of the Diplomatic Service started work at 11 a.m., by which time the telegrams had been deciphered and the correspondence distributed from the registries. They did, by contrast, work late.

In August 1939 the family was at Coton, lent to them by Bill's aunt, Venetia James. When Bill, newly appointed Chairman of the Joint Intelligence Committee in succession to Sir Ralph Stevenson, returned to London, Clothilde accompanied him for the day. It was agreed that she should return to Coton, where the children were left in the care of a Hungarian maid, and in due course take their son, Billy, back to Eton.

Early in September, a few days after war broke out, Bill and Ralph Stevenson were sitting in a room at the Foreign Office discussing the handover of Bill's new duties. The telephone rang. Ralph Stevenson was hoping that his wife would not be coming back from the South of France, since he had an emotional entanglement in London. He feared it might be her, announcing her return. Bill, on the other hand, hoped it might be Clothilde as he wanted to discuss his family's wartime plans. It was neither: it was the Hungarian maid from Coton announcing in scarcely comprehensible English that two days previously Clothilde had taken the children to Liverpool in order to embark for America. She had left no letter or message for Bill; she had merely decamped with his children.

He had new and important professional preoccupations and the pre-war Foreign Office hours had drastically changed. But he did find time to make inquiries how best to institute divorce proceedings. Clothilde for her part arrived safely in New York, dumped the children on Mrs Quigley and set off for San Francisco where her lover was established.

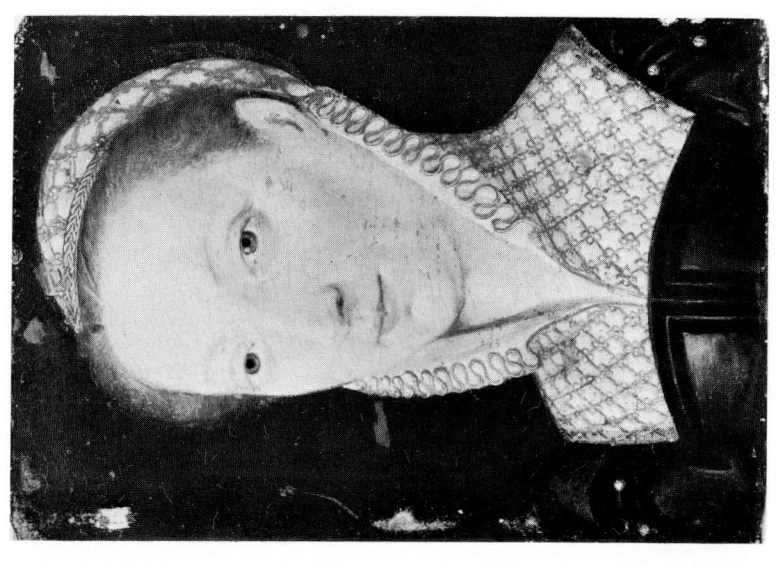

Anne Stanhope

Catherine Fillol

*Elizabeth Sheridan, by Gainsborough*

*Frances Crewe, by Downman*

*The Queen of Beauty*

*Ferdinand St Maur*

*Rosina Swan*

*Ruth*

*Bill*

# 13
# Exacting Assignment

A shrewd assessment of the enemy's designs is essential to the planning of strategy. Intelligence, which enables that assessment to be made, is in most respects an inexact science demanding the gathering and interpretation of information, comparison with that from other sources, judgement of its reliability and, finally, delivery to those who can make the best use of it. This sequence of activities was hampered between the two world wars less by the scarcity of information than by jealousies between the Departments of State. The Navy saw no need to cooperate with the Army or the Air Force, and the Foreign Office, with the Secret Intelligence Service subordinated to it, regarded itself as the only valid repository of information about foreign powers.

This was not peculiar to the British. The French had their celebrated *Deuxième Bureau*, which concerned itself with the Army alone; the Germans had a variety of organisations of which the *Abwehr*, also controlled by the Army, was the dominant; the Russians were believed to have spies everywhere, but were eccentric in the use they made of the reports they received; and the Americans had nothing at all. Probably the best all-round players in the game were the Poles.

In Britain Naval Intelligence was a law unto itself, Military Intelligence was only a little more forthcoming to other Whitehall departments and Air Intelligence was primarily concerned with the designs of other countries' aeroplanes and engines. Then there was the Secret Intelligence Service, to be distinguished from MI5 which was responsible for internal security. It only came into existence in 1909; but thanks to books like *The Thirty-Nine Steps* and *Bulldog Drummond*, which were read all over the world, the mere name of the British Secret Service inspired awe abroad and respect at home to an extent unjustified by its achievements.

In general, Intelligence was confined in unconnected and uncommunicating compartments; but there was a notable exception. An organisation called the Industrial Intelligence Centre had for many years before the Second World War amassed information about industry and commerce in foreign countries. It was ungrudging in its cooperation with all the departments in Whitehall, which was a great deal more than could be said for any of the other intelligence gatherers.

After the German military reoccupation of the Rhineland in 1936, the British Chiefs of Staff and their principal satellite, the Joint Planning Staff, concluded that Intelligence covering more than one of the three service departments would be convenient. So they created the Joint Intelligence Sub-Committee of the Chiefs of Staff with a mandate to provide the information required. The Industrial Intelligence Centre dutifully supplied the J.I.C., as it was invariably called, with facts about foreign industry and commerce; but the Foreign Office, convinced that all military men came from lesser breeds, apart from those happy few appointed to be service attachés at embassies abroad, did its best to ignore this upstart body. The Committee seldom met, and when it did the three heads of the Intelligence Sections in the Service departments sent junior officers to represent them.

In January 1939 the War Office, believing war to be unavoidable, convinced the Chiefs of Staff that blood should be pumped into the anaemic circulation of the J.I.C., provided, of course, that the independence of the Services' Intelligence Departments was unassailed. As none of the three armed forces could conceivably be expected to accept a chairman from one of the others, it was suggested that a diplomat should take the chair, thus ensuring that Intelligence from Foreign Office sources would be amalgamated with that from the Army, Navy and Air Force and the ever-obliging Industrial Intelligence Centre. Ralph Stevenson, of the Diplomatic Service, was for a short period selected to be chairman.

The Foreign Office was not at all enamoured of this arrangement, but to their dismay, six weeks before war was declared, Foreign Office chairmanship was endorsed by the Cabinet. It was at once asserted that no member of the Diplomatic Service senior to the rank of Counsellor could be spared. However, on reflection, they decided it was expedient that the chairman they were being coerced into providing should be a man of proved ability even though he would only have to preside over a committee of military dunderheads. They were wrong in their assessment, for the dunderheads turned out to be men of quality, but they were right in selecting as their representative the assistant head of the Egyptian Department, Mr V. F. W. Cavendish-Bentinck. The challenge was one which in the event he answered triumphantly, though his success was not acclaimed, publicised or rewarded.

At first it was an alarming assignment, for Bill knew nothing of Intelligence matters, and such men as Admiral Godfrey, Director of Naval Intelligence, were not only senior to their new chairman in rank but had long experience and formidable personalities. Nor was there any precedent for coordinating the product of different Intelligence departments, introspective by tradition and frequently jealous of each other. The duties formally notified to Bill and his committee were to assess all information received from abroad, to provide the data required by the Chiefs of Staff and Joint Planners and 'to consider measures necessary to improve the efficiency of the Intelligence organisation of the country as a whole'. The committee's function was to coordinate Intelligence, not to discover it.

During the early months of the war the J.I.C., despite its impressive mandate, did little but issue daily situation reports, which were usually dull, and weekly summaries which were only slightly more readable. However, in March 1940 the Chiefs of Staff pronounced that the committee should see and comment on all planning papers before they themselves considered them, and in May a representative of the Ministry of Economic Warfare, into which the peacetime Industrial Intelligence Committee had been expanded, joined their ranks. The Secret Intelligence Service and MI5 started to attend meetings. The J.I.C. was at last in business.

Bill had not wasted the preceding months. His unusual, often indirect, method of handling awkward situations, his acute intellect, his sly and cynical sense of humour and his patience in listening to all points of view, however foolish they seemed to him, won first the confidence and then the affection of his committee members and of the Joint Planning Staff. With them, during the long winter months of the 1940-1 blitz, he would dine off tinned soup, sardines and sausages, served by Marine orderlies in the cramped underground mess of the Central War Room at Storey's Gate.

The air-conditioning was, by later standards, primitive, and dining frugally, well below ground level, was an experience more congenial to dedicated submariners than to senior civil servants and high-ranking military officers. But few of those hard-pressed men had time to spare for a blackout walk to a club in Pall Mall where, in any case, an unappetising dinner was all that could be expected to the accompanying crash of anti-aircraft fire and the periodic whistles of falling bombs. The lack of comfort in the Central War Room mess was compensated for by freedom from the nerve-shattering noise of aerial bombardment and by intelligent, well-informed conversation among a group of men who had no need to restrain their words or their views; for they were all members of a select and high-powered secret circle. In these unprepossessing surroundings Bill became well acquainted with the Secretary of the Cabinet, Sir Edward Bridges, with the Prime Minister's closest military adviser, General Ismay and his able staff, with Major Desmond Morton, former head of the Industrial Intelligence Centre and now a member of Churchill's personal entourage and with the Prime Minister's private secretaries.

Clothilde's unheralded departure to America with his children had freed him from immediate domestic worries and he could concentrate his whole attention on his official responsibilities. Service rivalries all but evaporated under his chairmanship and by the end of 1940 the J.I.C., which had been unable to provide useful advice or information in the Norwegian campaign in the spring of that year, or at the time of the Dunkirk evacuation, was in a position to make a worthwhile contribution to deliberations in Whitehall. Already, in October 1940, Bill was declaring, in opposition to the members of his own committee, that Hitler would abandon the plan for an invasion of the British Isles and would divert German energies to an attack on the Soviet Union.

Bill was right and his colleagues were wrong. It was precisely in October that Hitler put the invasion preparations into mothballs and gave orders to prepare for a whirlwind campaign against the Russians. When that succeeded, as he was confident his inspired projects always must, Britain would in due time be gathered as a windfall in the orchard. However, the Service Departments in Whitehall remained convinced that Germany could only win the war by invading Britain. Perhaps they were right; but they were totally wrong in supposing that it was an immediate danger. They persisted in so thinking until a few weeks before the actual German attack on the Soviet Union in June 1941.

Bill, for his part, having concluded as soon as Hitler himself that an invasion of Britain was no longer practicable, noted a number of significant indications in support of his belief from the intelligence his committee received. Thus, for instance, he learned that urgent work had started on the lengthening of the runways on Polish aerodromes. That, he remarked, was unlikely to be for the benefit of the German commercial airline, Lufthansa.

He held to his opinion. The time would never come, insisted the War Office, when it would be safe to declare that the invasion of the United Kingdom was off. As early as October Bill wrote to say that this assertion was irrational and that so cautious an attitude would cripple military and political strategy. The Director of Military Intelligence closed the argument by saying that in anything affecting matters of strategy the Chiefs of Staff knew best; and so for weary month after month the War Office continued to maintain that Germany's primary aim was to invade and destroy the United Kingdom. One of the few people who shared Bill's prescient view that Russia was a more likely target was the Prime Minister; but there were many layers of uniformed officers between him and the chairman of the J.I.C.

Earlier in the year 1940, a new, dramatic and increasingly valuable source became available to British Intelligence. Towards the end of May, just as Lord Gort, with nothing but his own judgement to guide him, decided to lead the British Expeditionary Force northwards to salvation from Dunkirk rather than southwards to destruction on the Somme, the brilliant Code and Cipher School at Bletchley broke the German Air Force cipher in a form suitable for immediate use. Since January, largely thanks to help provided by the Poles, there had been intermittent success in breaking it; but the signals were only available for study days or even weeks after they had been sent. From the end of May onwards German Air Force signals were deciphered and translated within hours of transmission and an unceasing flow of information was available to those entrusted with it. The contents were principally of value for such purposes as identifying the enemy's order of battle, rather than of immediate tactical or strategic significance; but a year later the German naval cipher was broken and in 1942 that of the Army. For most recipients of the information derived from this exciting discovery, the messages were said to originate from 'Boniface' whom many, even in the intimate circles of Whitehall, were encouraged to think was a well-placed agent of the Secret Service.

For a whole year this most deadly of secrets was restricted to the few, including the J.I.C., whose duties required their indoctrination. Most members of the Cabinet were kept in ignorance and although, up till the collapse of France, the French cipher breakers had been abreast, if not ahead, of the British, they kept their mouths valiantly closed when the Vichy Government came to power.

Nothing was said to General de Gaulle and his supporters, who were notoriously indiscreet; and it was not until 1941 was well advanced that the Americans were told the secret in return for sharing with the British their skill in breaking the Japanese diplomatic cipher. By the summer of 1941 American warships were venturing far out into the Atlantic to relieve British escorts on the latter stage of convoy crossings. That was just at the time the German naval cipher was broken at Bletchley and it was only commonsense to impart to the helpful American naval authorities information which was almost as important to them as to the Royal Navy. Not a word was said to the Russians though much was imparted to them without indication of the source. Luckily neither Burgess nor Maclean, neither Philby nor Blunt, were privy to that most closely guarded of treasures.

It is remarkable that for more than twenty years after the war none of those concerned with these matters, whether at Bletchley or among the users of Bletchley's precious product, breathed a word about it. Indeed, it was not until Wing-Commander Winterbotham chose to write a book called *The Ultra Secret* (which was not wholly accurate), that the triumph of the Code and Cipher School became public knowledge.

Boniface was a major addition to Bill's steadily increasing sources of information. Already the Service departments had taken to laying their Intelligence deductions on the table; the Foreign Office was more cooperative than formerly; photographic reconnaissance yielded a better harvest every year; documents were captured and prisoners of war talked; neutral cities such as Lisbon and Berne were fertile centres for espionage; the Special Operations Executive flew agents in and out of occupied Europe;

the Americans, with the Office of Strategic Services, forerunner of the C.I.A., entered the Intelligence field with vigour though not, at first, with much success except in occupied France; and all the European Governments exiled in London, Poles and Czechs, Free French, Dutch, Belgians and Yugoslavs, had means of obtaining valuable information from their beleaguered countrymen at home.

It was a lot to coordinate and there were many contradictions to resolve; nor were the J.I.C.'s deductions by any means always correct. In May 1940 they had given no indication of the German plan to invade France through the mountainous forest of the Ardennes, believed to be impenetrable; but nor had the still better placed French *Deuxième Bureau*. In February 1941 they believed the Germans would invade Turkey and Syria rather than send Rommel to save the Italian army in North Africa. Bill was right, though all but alone, in insisting that General Franco would not allow the German army to march through Spain to besiege Gibraltar. Almost to the last the J.I.C. as a body maintained that Hitler's evident military build-up against Russia was bluff, though some weeks before 22 June 1941, when the invasion in fact took place, Bill, supported by the Foreign Office, told them he was entirely sure that a genuine attack was Hitler's intention.

Shortly before Hitler launched that attack, the Foreign Secretary, Anthony Eden, summoned Bill to his room to explain to the Soviet Ambassador, Ivan Maisky, that the danger was real and immediate. Both Eden and Bill did their best, but they were inhibited from telling Maisky the reasons for their conviction which were the information distilled from Boniface. Maisky refused to heed the urgency of the warning: he did not think Hitler intended to invade. When the German axe fell, the few who disbelieved the J.I.C. and War Office forecast that Russia would be conquered in four to six weeks included Winston Churchill and Bill Bentinck.

Failures were compensated by successes and in April 1941 the Chiefs of Staff were sufficiently impressed by the quality of the work produced by the J.I.C. to invite their chairman to attend their meetings once a week. As the war progressed, and Allied arms began to prosper, the subjects demanding assessment by the J.I.C. grew rapidly. So did Intelligence reports from liberated countries and from ever more rapidly deciphered enemy signals and diplomatic telegrams. So did the desirability of cooperating with allies, and in particular with the Americans, who admired Bill's finesse, moderation and disinclination either to boast or exaggerate.

In 1942 he added to his other responsibilities that of Foreign Office representative with the Directors of Plans, whose task it was to prepare strategic proposals for the Joint Planning Staff and ultimately for the Chiefs of Staff.

As early as May 1943, the Permanent Under Secretary for Foreign Affairs recorded that whereas the Foreign Office did not believe an Italian collapse was impending, Bill Bentinck disagreed. He had deduced that the Germans would only reluctantly continue to support their wavering ally.

It was the task of the Joint Planners to draft answers to the proposals, sometimes shrewd and sometimes a little too imaginative, that were fired like cannonballs from 10 Downing Street. In the autumn of 1944, when the defeat of Germany was almost, but not quite, in sight, it occurred to the Prime Minister that the widespread use of poison gas by the Allied armies, though inhumane in itself, might in the end be the most humane way of bringing the war to a quick end and avoiding another winter of death, misery and destruction. The Directors of Plans, instructed to draft a reply, reported that the use of gas would be militarily ineffective, would invite reprisals and would not, in their view, finish the war any quicker. Bill felt it his duty to add a rider pointing out that the moral effect on Britain's friends and allies, and on all neutral countries, would be deplorable. This elicited an inquiry in red ink on the finished paper: 'Who are these uniformed, psalm-singing defeatists?' But no gas was used.

Nobody, during nearly six years, challenged Bill's chairmanship of the J.I.C. Ministers came and went, as did admirals, generals, and air marshals, but Bill was one of the few who retained the same position throughout the war. He, a diplomat, succeeded in convincing the military establishment of the major part the coordination of Intelligence must play in their affairs, and he laid foundations on which a strong bastion was erected after the war. The Foreign Office, in those days seldom quick to recognise merit, did promote him to the rank of Under Secretary in 1944, although in their post-war use of his services they showed no imagination. He deserved a knighthood; but he did not receive one. For the

Foreign Office was much addicted to the all too well-established principle of 'Buggins's Turn' and there were members of the service senior to Bill who were still awaiting their spurs.

A greater tribute to his achievements was paid by one who knew as much about Intelligence as any man in any country, Major General Sir Kenneth Strong, Eisenhower's trusted adviser and the Chief of his Intelligence Staff at Allied Headquarters. When the war ended he was chosen to be head of the newly formed Joint Intelligence Bureau. Strong wrote: 'To my mind there is no doubt that without Cavendish-Bentinck's unobtrusive guidance the British Intelligence structure, and thus the total war effort, would have operated at a considerable disadvantage.'

# 14
# Warsaw

The summer sun shone brightly in August 1945 when Bill Bentinck arrived in Poland as British Ambassador to the Provisional Government of National Unity. It was the only thing that did shine. Warsaw was a heap of rubble, the people were close to starvation and the Russian Secret Police, the N.K.V.D., were assiduously instructing Polish recruits in the skills of their profession.

Bill had been offered the choice of political adviser to Field Marshal Montgomery in Germany or Ambassador to Poland. After almost six years of close association with the Chiefs of Staff organisation and its subordinate committees, a further term as adviser to the military did not appeal to him, and he wanted to stay in London till his matrimonial affairs were settled. He pleaded that Montgomery was known to regard with distaste any who had been closely associated with either the Chiefs of Staff organisation or with Eisenhower's Supreme Headquarters of the Allied Expeditionary Force.

As far as the Warsaw embassy was concerned, he pointed out that having served in Poland twenty-five years before under an entirely different regime, and having retained old friendships from those distant days, he might well start his new assignment with a black mark against his name. He would certainly be approached by distressed Poles obnoxious to the new rulers. The Foreign Office brushed his arguments aside. If he did not wish to give political advice to Montgomery, Warsaw was the only post available: to Warsaw he must go.

He would at least have strong support. His second in command, already established as Chargé d'Affaires, was Robin Hankey, eldest son of that legendary adviser to successive Cabinets and Committees of Imperial Defence, Maurice Hankey. He spoke Polish well and had been Head of Chancery in Warsaw for three years immediately preceding the war. Another member of his staff was an able and vigorous diplomat of the younger generation, John Russell, son of a highly esteemed administrator of Egyptian affairs, Russell Pasha. Bill's instructions were to ensure that the forthcoming Polish elections should be 'free and unfettered and held on a basis of universal suffrage and secret ballot'. This was the pledge that had been given by the British, American and Soviet leaders at the recent Yalta Conference. Bill commented with justifiable cynicism that to achieve such a desirable end the presence of several British and American army corps would probably be required.

The unhappy Poles, their country three times partitioned in the eighteenth century, their efforts to reassert their freedom ruthlessly suppressed in the nineteenth, had at last seen their independence restored at the end of the First World War. They had then been a little too grasping. After their victory over the Red Army invaders they had by the 1921 Treaty of Riga extended their frontier eastwards to embrace large numbers of Ukrainians and White Russians. Then in 1938, when the Germans began the process of carving up Czechoslovakia, the Poles forfeited much sympathy in the West by seizing from the demoralised Czechs parts of the province of Teschen, containing important coal-mines, which had been Czechoslovak since 1919. All the same they certainly did not deserve the fate that had befallen them; and as none knew better than the former Chairman of the Joint Intelligence Committee, it was largely to Poland that Britain owed the provision of that invaluable aid to victory, the Enigma machine, procreator of Boniface.

One thing was clear in the summer of 1939. Hitler could not take an unworried plunge into war if he was threatened from the east as well as from the west. Without Russian connivance in his proposed invasion of Poland, it would be long-term folly to confront the French and British Empires. By a performance of historic melodrama he was able, in the last few days of August 1939, to unite German Nazis and Russian Communists in an unholy alliance, the infamous Ribbentrop-Molotov Pact. A new Ribbentrop-Molotov Line, which coincided closely with the Curzon Line proposed by the Allies after the First World War, was drawn across the map and the two miscreant powers declared that the independent state of Poland had ceased to exist.

Though crushed by the strength of the invaders, the Poles remained undaunted. Their surviving soldiers slipped away across the Carpathians and formed six divisions in France where in the following spring they fought much better than the French themselves during the German onslaught on the West. Those who then escaped death or imprisonment contrived to cross the English Channel, so that by the end of 1940 there were two well-trained Polish divisions on British soil. A few years later there were no less than five fighting with the British armies. Meanwhile in Poland itself a Home Army was formed secretly and equipped with arms and supplies flown in by moonlight from Britain. Soon thousands of resolute patriots were awaiting a call to arms against the German oppressors. This was far from being agreeable to the Russians, for the Home Army owed allegiance to the exiled Government in London, which though not reactionary was dominated by the wholeheartedly anti-Communist Peasants' Party.

Conscious of implacable Polish hostility, the Russians took steps to lessen the risks. In 1941 they murdered at Katyn, near Smolensk, some 14,000 officers whom they had taken prisoner after the Germans had destroyed the Polish army. When the mass graves were discovered in a forest, under freshly planted pine trees, they blithely accused the Germans of the atrocity. However, this re-enactment of Genghis Khan's methods did nothing to deflect recruits for the Polish Home Army which by 1944 numbered over 40,000 men in Warsaw alone.

There then took place the blackest act of treachery and deceit in modern European history, an act beside which even the Ribbentrop-Molotov pact and the Katyn massacre fade into comparative insignificance. At the end of July 1944, when the advancing Soviet armies were but a few miles from Warsaw, Moscow radio called on the Polish Home Army to rise. They did so, whereupon the Russians halted their advance and watched while the desperate insurgents in the city fought week after week against continually reinforced German units. At the beginning of October, despite frantic efforts by the R.A.F. to drop arms and supplies from distant bases in Italy, the Germans had killed at least 200,000 Poles and reduced what was left of Warsaw to ashes.

The Soviet Government refused urgent requests that British and American supply aircraft be allowed to refuel in Soviet territory. Shortly after the end of the war John Russell, riding in the forest on the far side of the River Vistula, came upon the wreckage of a R.A.F. plane and the graves of its crew, carefully tended by the local peasants. It was a grim reminder of the self-sacrificing efforts made by the R.A.F. to succour the Polish Home Army during the weeks of Russian treachery. In 1944 it had fallen to Bill to convey to the Polish Ambassador in London, Count Edward Raczynski, the bitter news that with the best will in the world the R.A.F. and U.S.A.A.F. could deliver no more supplies to the besieged insurgents.

The Americans, after participating in an initial appeal to Stalin, became alarmed at the prospect of serious disagreement with their Soviet allies during the run-up to a Presidential election; and Molotov justified the Russian decision to let the Poles be massacred by declaring that the Polish Home Army, which Moscow Radio had called to arms, was an 'adventurist' and irresponsible group. When the Germans had methodically burned the city and completed the task of annihilation, the Soviet armies resumed their advance and occupied Warsaw.

In retrospect it is hard to understand the waves of gratitude and affection which rolled from the United States, Britain and France to Moscow in 1945; but roll they certainly did. The British had been more realistic than their American allies in political preparation for victory. Knowing that for the Russians possession was the whole of the law, they had put pressure on the Polish Government in London under its spirited Peasant Party Leader, Mikolajczyk, to accept an eastern frontier which might conceivably be acceptable to the Russians if it left the Ukrainians and other minorities in Soviet territory, and if the city of Lvov, with a population two thirds Polish, but coveted by the Russians, was sacrificed to the new Soviet imperialism. As the name Ribbentrop could no longer be mentioned in combination with that of the hero Molotov, the Ribbentrop-Molotov Line established when Poland was dismembered in 1939 reverted to its old title, the Curzon Line. This, modified in Russia's favour, was the line which, without much conviction, the British hoped to see accepted as a genuine frontier between a democratic Poland and the Soviet Union. The Poles would receive in compensation lands as indisputably German as Lvov was Polish.

The Americans took a more starry-eyed view of Russian intentions. President Roosevelt, already a stricken man, and many of his State Department advisers really did believe that the Soviet Union, purified by the fire of war and experience of international alliances, would thenceforward cooperate in the establishment of world peace through the new United Nations Organisation. The Russians would, they thought, be more powerful and worthwhile friends than the British, who were exhausted by a war they had been waging two years longer than their allies and were suspected in Washington of being primarily concerned with retaining their vast Empire. Not all American officials held this belief and prominent among those who did not was Eisenhower's influential Chief of Staff, General Bedell-Smith. He told Bill that he saw no prospect of the Anglo-Saxon powers being able to cooperate with the Russians.

Whatever the differences between the British and the Americans in their assessment of their Russian ally, they had two overriding preoccupations at the Yalta Conference in February 1945. The first was to ensure that Germany did not rise aggressively again, as she had been allowed to do after her defeat in 1918. To this end a close understanding with Russia was vital. The second was to have a guarantee of Soviet help in defeating the Japanese, who at the time of Yalta were expected to go on fighting long after the German war ended. There were some who even feared a repetition of the hideous Molotov-Ribbentrop pact, the Japanese foreign minister being substituted for Ribbentrop. These considerations, judged to be of immense importance by the Anglo-Saxon powers, outweighed the matter of unhappy Poland's fate. Morality, as it so often does, bowed down in the temple of expediency.

The Russian view was a simple one. Whatever might have been implied, or even promised, at the Tehran and Yalta Conferences about the future of Poland, they would by fair means or foul impose a regime chosen by themselves and would create a *cordon sanitaire* between the Soviet Union and Western Europe. Since the Poles were by an overwhelming majority hostile to them, the means would undoubtedly have to be foul.

Against this sombre and threatening background, with not many instructions and certainly no army corps, Bill Bentinck arrived in the Warsaw rubble where even the most sparse accommodation was hard to find and ˙rats were the most flourishing element in the community. He did however, find there a colleague of happier days, Arthur Bliss Lane, who arrived in

Poland a few weeks before him as American Ambassador. Bill and Lane proceeded to keep closely in step; but the ground over which they marched was consistently rough going.

There was the problem of British subjects, Polish by marriage, who were refused exit visas. There was that of the Embassy's Polish employees, many of whom were mercilessly interrogated and blackmailed by the political police, increasingly well-trained imitators of the N.K.V.D. and the Gestapo. Above all there was the task of impressing on the Polish Government that, under the terms of the Yalta agreement, Britain and America had not merely a right but an obligation to interfere in domestic affairs to the extent of ensuring freedom of speech and action as precursors of the promised elections.

Bill's second in command, Robin Hankey, was greatly impressed by his new chief. 'In thirty-eight years as a diplomat', he wrote, 'I never had a better chief to serve.' He found him enterprising and imaginative, but careful not to overstep the limits. Bill was well aware that the British Ambassador must not intervene in cases of hardship imposed by a ruthless regime on its own citizens; nor must he in any circumstances assist the persecuted to escape to happier countries. So he rigorously rejected appeals from his family and friends in Britain on behalf of entrapped Poles, even those who, precisely because they had fought in the Polish Home Army against the Germans, were illogically and, to Western minds, incomprehensibly labelled by the Communist regime as Fascist reactionary agents of the former Gestapo.

The fact that such accusations went beyond the bounds of absurdity did not diminish the intensity with which they were pressed. Writing to his sister Joan, Bill said:

> If asked, and I hope not to be asked too often, I am prepared to inquire how and where relations of individual Poles may be, but I regret that I cannot employ them, bring them money, take over their houses and carry out all the miscellaneous requests that are made of me.

A few months later, in reply to insistent pleas to help Poles escape, he wrote:

> I have enough attacks on me both here and by Members of Parliament in London and cannot afford to trail my coat by

allowing British ships under the control of the Ministry of War Transport to be used for clandestinely taking out Polish citizens from this country... I am having a hard tussle to get a passport to leave this country for Mary Ciechanowiecka although she is a British subject by birth, born of British parents. Much as I should like to, I can do nothing for Sophie Grocholska.

Bill had wisely decided that in the prevailing circumstances he must tread warily and though one of his legitimate tasks was to obtain and report home as much intelligence as he and his staff could procure, he took pains not to allow the Embassy to be enmeshed in the arcane activities of MI6 and the British Secret Service.

Shortly before his arrival the Russians had arrested and imprisoned sixteen representatives of the genuinely democratic Polish political parties who had travelled to meet them under a safe conduct. The safe conduct was disregarded once they were in Russian territory and the sixteen were put on trial, on a variety of invented charges, a few days after the unflinching Peasant leader, Mikolajczyk, and a handful of his supporters arrived in Moscow to discuss forming a Government of National Unity. The trial of the sixteen was intended as a salutary warning to Mikolajczyk. One of them was later sentenced to fifteen years' hard labour on the charge of having given treasonable information to Bill and Arthur Bliss Lane, neither of whom had even set eyes on him.

Despite the crystal-clear intention of Stalin and Molotov to impose their will on Poland precisely as they wished, the British and American Governments agreed to recognise the so-called Government of National Unity; nor did they take impressive steps to show their displeasure at the suppression of freedom. Vast quantities of relief goods were poured into the country, almost entirely from America; surplus military stores were offered to the Polish Government; and no objection was raised when a Russian was appointed to distribute the thousands of tons of food, clothing and medicaments provided by the United Nations Relief and Rehabilitation Administration (UNRRA). Appeasement which in 1938 had stemmed from the weakness of France and Britain was now, in 1945, based on overwhelming Anglo-Saxon military strength, supported by a monopoly of atomic weapons, but atrophied by weariness, enfeebled will-power and touching, if misguided, faith in the basic goodwill of the Communist powers. Greater folly has seldom been recorded.

Ernest Bevin, the new British Foreign Secretary, was assured by the Polish President Bierut, a Moscow-trained Communist notable for his failure ever to look anyone in the eye, that the free elections would take place early in 1946. As that year advanced the British and American Ambassadors continually exerted pressure in Warsaw. They raised objections to the proposal that the names of the candidates should be included in a single bloc. Such a bloc would include a few members of Mikolajczyk's Peasant Party, but they would only be a small in-built minority, and electors would have to vote for the bloc as a whole.

The American Government made things easier for President Bierut and his Moscow-trained Government by granting Poland substantial credits, contrary to the advice of their Ambassador in Warsaw. Then a referendum was organised on a number of matters, including the total abolition of the Senate, a step towards totalitarianism on which Mikolajczyk advised his supporters to vote 'No'. That they did so with an overwhelming majority was shown when, by an administrative oversight, the votes in Cracow were counted and announced without the requisite chicanery. A negative vote of 84% was recorded. Doubtless many election officers' heads rolled in Cracow after that; but elsewhere in the country the necessary adjustments were made and a positive overall vote of 80% was declared.

Bill and Lane could only stand helplessly by, watch developments with increasing disenchantment, and report home to their largely uninterested Governments. Meanwhile they saw long, sad detachments of Polish Home Army Supporters led away by soldiers or police and driven eastwards through the forest outside Warsaw in wagons escorted, in John Russell's words, 'by real Genghis Khan types of Mongol troops. I nearly got my horse stolen and myself shot by a bunch of them one day.' They witnessed the deportation of six million Germans, with a minimum of consideration in a bitterly cold winter, from their homes in Silesia, Pomerania and East Prussia. They made unavailing efforts to refute officially inspired claims that Britain and America had agreed to the details of new western frontiers for Poland. They noted with impotent anger that such machinery as the Germans had left in Polish factories was being physically transported to the

Soviet Union. They heard the American Secretary of State, a dedicated Democrat, described as a Fascist.

Open letters were published in the Government-controlled newspapers demanding that all Poles should protest against Anglo-Saxon meddling in their affairs. The Polish people had changed masters and the main difference was that the new tyrants, unlike their Nazi predecessors, were able to establish a façade of indoctrinated Polish rulers. These were abhorrent to at least four-fifths of their fellow countrymen.

In August 1946 the two Ambassadors were authorised to deliver notes criticising the conduct of the referendum campaign, for which the British and American Governments wished to make it clear they held no responsibility, and expressing the hope that the forthcoming elections, for which they did have a responsibility, would be properly conducted. Ernest Bevin gave Bill instructions that the truth was to be fearlessly proclaimed.

The sources of information normally available to foreign embassies were lacking. Friendly discussions with Government officials were impossible, though Bill established a personal relationship with some of them and, indeed, with the Soviet Ambassador. Accurate figures and statistics were not available, suspect propaganda being substituted. Those Poles willing to talk and to comment went in fear of their safety and were invariably opponents of the regime. Bill did, however, think it fair to record that whatever the cruelty and tyranny might be, the Polish authorities were proceeding efficiently with the task of restoration and rehabilitation: bridges were being rebuilt, roads mended and large blocks of working-class flats and houses constructed.

Though Bill might think it only fair to give the devil his due, the Polish Government and their Soviet masters had no such inclination. They must by one means or another discredit the critical and captious foreign Ambassadors. It was necessary to pursue in Poland the policy so successfully inaugurated in other countries dominated by Soviet troops. In Roumania, Vyshinsky, at once inquisitor and judge in many so-called spy trials, had installed a Communist Government by threatening the King, at that stage too popular to dethrone, and deploying tanks in the streets of Bucharest. In Bulgaria the peasant leader Petkov's secretary had been barbarously tortured to extract evidence and Petkov himself executed after a derisory trial. In Hungary another peasant leader, Nagy, and a courageous Socialist lady, Kethly Anna, had been subjected to comparable treatment. In Yugoslavia Tito had committed countless acts of judicial murder against supporters of the anti-Communists. In Czechoslovakia the Russians and their supporters were already poised for the eradication of the democratic politicians. No nonsense could be tolerated in Poland or in the Russian-occupied zone of Germany.

The Soviet cause was indirectly aided by a visit to Warsaw of a delegation of British Members of Parliament, largely Socialist in composition, who were intent on seeing for themselves whether their country's representatives were sending home truthful accounts and whether the forthcoming elections were likely to be free and unfettered. These adjectives had different meanings for, on the one hand, Mr Phil Piratin, Communist M.P. for Stepney, or Dr Stephen Taylor, subsequently ennobled but at that time M.P. for Barnet, and, on the other hand, the only two Conservatives, Sir Tufton Beamish and Dr Conant. This band of legislators, some of them with preconceived opinions, descended on Bill in November 1946.

The *New Statesman* had an editor, Kingsley Martin, who persisted in believing, against the steadily accumulating evidence, that all the Russian satellite regimes in eastern Europe were conducted by honest liberal-minded men who were scandalously maligned by His Majesty's reactionary representatives abroad. When in Zagreb with a number of Left-wing British M.P.s and journalists, Kingsley Martin naively reported that inmates of a prison he and his friends visited had eagerly confessed to him the anti-state crimes they had committed and declared their terms of imprisonment to be inadequate in view of their heinous crimes. Some visitors might have been suspicious; but not Mr Martin and his companions. The British Consul General subsequently learned that the real prisoners had been evacuated for the occasion and replaced by earnest party members in prison garb. The *New Statesman* was the gospel of the Labour intelligentsia and some of the British parliamentarians who now arrived in Warsaw were as ingenuous as Kingsley Martin.

Others, no doubt, saw political advantage in doing their best to discredit His Majesty's Ambassador. For the so-called Fellow Travellers there was every incentive to do so, because the Foreign Office saw with the clarity of John Milton that the new Communist presbyter was but the old Fascist priest writ large. Neither Attlee nor Bevin needed much convincing of that. However, many of their supporters in Parliament had yet to recover from the deeply rooted belief held by members of the Labour Party between the wars that all things Russian were bright and beautiful. The British Communists and their fellow travelling allies wished to sustain and foster this view.

As the Roman Catholic Church in 1946, no less than before and afterwards, exerted a powerful influence, Bill arranged among other items in the delegation's programme, for them to be received by the courageous Archbishop Sapieha, later Cardinal, who had been for the Poles a light burning undimmed during the Nazi occupation. His Christian courage and resolution were still required and still revered. The Polish Government, already furious because Bill had provided trustworthy interpreters (whom the delegation were persuaded to say they did not need), countered the proposed interview with the Archbishop by arranging a cocktail party to meet the Trade Union leaders, all appointed by the Government and wholly loyal to the Communist party. None but Sir Tufton Beamish had the good manners to call on the Archbishop. Dr Stephen Taylor said to Bill 'I can't bear priests'; and when the party went to see how Silesia was being denuded of Germans to make room for Poles exported by the Russians, the absence of interpreters made the task of the Government's information officers an easy one.

As the date of the elections approached, the attacks on the Polish Peasant Party redoubled in vigour, arrests by the Secret Police were daily events and even the *New Statesman* felt obliged to admit that ten out of the Peasant Party's fifty-two electoral lists had been banned. Candidates and voters known to be hostile to the Communists lost their jobs, flats and ration cards, and were often moved to another area where their names would not be on the voting list. Others were taken night after night to police stations and made to stand with their hands above their heads while they were interrogated. The time had come for Bierut's Government to divert attention, and perhaps even win support, by involving a foreign power in accusations of espionage and thus emphasising the justice of their complaint that the Anglo-Saxons were interfering scandalously in Polish affairs.

Bill was the chosen scapegoat. Many years previously his sister Joan had made friends with an agreeable and cultivated family called Grocholski. It was Sophie Grocholska whom Joan had begged Bill to help escape, but for whom he had prudently said he could to nothing. As aristocrats the family were, of course, both obnoxious and expendable; as a courageous patriot, badly wounded when fighting the Germans in Warsaw with the Polish Home Army, Count Remi Grocholski was, in Governmental eyes, a Fascist beast. Despite the circumstances in which he was wounded, they described him as 'an agent of the Gestapo, an international spy working for the darkest forces before us today'.

The elections took place and were carefully rigged so as to provide a Governmental majority which bore no relation at all to the choice of the voters. A trial of Count Grocholski and two or three other sacrificial lambs was synchronised to coincide with them. It was alleged that Grocholski had been an intermediary, feeding secret information to Bill from a reactionary and terrorist group, though nobody tried to explain how such a group had access to the kind of information in which foreign embassies might be seriously interested.

Bill had indeed entertained his old friend Grocholski at the British Embassy and had listened to his views on the unhappy state of the country, as he had to those of many other Poles, including sympathisers with the Communist Government. The Secret Police saw and grasped their opportunity when Bill paid an innocent return visit to Grocholski's old mother in the country. The house was surrounded, the inmates forbidden to leave and Bill obliged to claim diplomatic immunity in order to do so. Count Grocholski was arrested and tortured until he agreed to say he was connected with an underground reactionary movement and that he had communicated secret information to Bill. He was sentenced to death and shot, the whole affair being so timed as to divert attention from the unpopular official results of the election.

Poor Grocholski had committed no crime. He was just a convenient tool for propaganda. It seems that the grains of pure evil with which, according to Ruth, the Life Force occasionally sees fit to pepper the world, had fallen thickly on the People's Democratic Republic of Poland.

In Britain those acting on direct orders from the Kremlin, and the much larger body of Labour M.P.s and supporters who, though not Communists, still thought highly of Stalin and were always ready to believe their own Government and its representatives in the wrong, demanded the immediate withdrawal of an envoy proved (in a Polish court) to have collaborated with reactionaries. Mr Gallacher, Communist M.P. for West Fife, rose in the House of Commons to demand his replacement by 'someone who will make social contacts more in keeping with the policy of the Labour Government'. Mr Morgan Phillips, National Secretary of the Labour Party, was still more offensive in his comments; and the radical press joined in. Fuel was added to the flame by the decision of the British and American Governments to show their disgust at the electoral travesty and the patent disregard of the pledges given at Yalta by instructing Bill and Arthur Bliss Lane not to attend the opening of the new Polish Parliament.

The Foreign Secretary, Ernest Bevin, paid little attention to these accusations. After Bill had made a brief visit to London to report on the elections and on the successful efforts to implicate him in a spurious spy trial, the *Daily Worker* indignantly declared that Mr Bevin's retention of him as Ambassador 'is seen as a deliberate gesture against the Polish democracy'. He did go back to Warsaw; but not for long, for his term as Ambassador there had run its course and he was clearly *persona non grata* with President Bierut's regime (as was his American friend and colleague). It was decided to post him as Ambassador to Brazil. He was scarcely fifty and had a full ten years' service ahead of him. He was so well regarded in official circles that after Rio de Janeiro he could reasonably expect to be offered Paris, Bonn or Rome. Perhaps even the Permanent Under Secretaryship of State might eventually have been within his grasp.

Leaving Warsaw for good, at the end of the exceptionally hard winter of 1946-7, Bill could but reflect sadly on the fate of those indomitable Poles, whom he would so much have liked to help towards a free, untroubled future. He could not have been expected publicly to advise the Polish people, as Jean-Jacques Rousseau had almost two centuries before, that if they could not avoid being swallowed up, they must at least prevent their enemies from digesting them. They have, in later as in former years, steadfastly followed Rousseau's advice.

# 15
# *The Crash*

Nobody, however hard-headed, however cynical he might appear, could be anything but distraught when proclaimed to be responsible for events leading to the torture and death of an old friend. Bill knew that no shred of blame attached to him personally for that travesty of justice, that Grocholski had committed none of the offences attributed to him, that the Moloch seated in Moscow required endlessly repeated sacrifices on his altar, and that those in Britain who obsequiously saluted Stalin as a human benefactor would one day awake to the stark truth. All the same, consciousness of personal innocence was little consolation for being publicly denounced, even if the Foreign Office and the great majority of Poles knew full well that he was but a scapegoat.

Accusing voices in the House of Commons and prejudiced extracts from the Left-wing press, however unjust, however wide of the mark, were jabs that evoked sharp images of poor Grocholski's cruel torment as well as agonising reflections on his own helplessness to rescue him. If it had not been Grocholski, it would have been another; if it had not been the British Ambassador, it would have been the American. The fact remained that the Polish Government and their British admirers insisted it was due to the machinations of Mr Cavendish-Bentinck that Grocholski had committed crimes deserving imprisonment and death.

These wretched thoughts and memories at first outweighed worries about his forthcoming divorce which would, he presumed, be quietly effected and provide release from a private burden that had become insupportable. He failed to take account of Clothilde's vindictiveness.

She and the children had returned from America in the summer before the war ended, while Bill was still Chairman of the Joint Intelligence Committee. He was, he told his sister Joan, pleasantly surprised by his son Billy and daughter, Mary Jane, whom he had not seen for so long. Billy, snatched from Eton in 1939 when he was only fourteen, and poorly educated during his five years in America, wanted to join the R.A.F.; but he was declared unfit for flying duties on the remarkable grounds that he had flat feet. Bill tried to have him trained as an interpreter in Japanese, for it seemed in those pre-atomic days that the war against Japan might continue for several years to come.

Clothilde and Bill only communicated through solicitors. The divorce proceedings he had set in motion at the beginning of the war, when she took his children away without warning, were well advanced. In the intervening years, deserted by his wife and alone in London, he had fallen in love with another woman. She was Kathleen Tillotson, a quiet, competent and good-looking Canadian, who was in all respects a contrast to Clothilde. Bill's parents and sisters had taken an immediate liking to her.

It soon became clear that Clothilde had no intention of letting matters proceed smoothly. She was determined to contest the suit for divorce and to demand instead a judicial separation, which would prevent Bill from marrying again. She was offered generous terms for a settlement. When she turned them down her counsel, the celebrated Sir Patrick Hastings, said that since she seemed primarily interested in destroying her husband's career, he would no longer act for her. Mr Seymour Karminski, K.C., who did not suffer from a comparable inhibition, took Sir Patrick's place.

Bill returned from Warsaw in March 1947, carrying the heavy Grocholski burden of unhappiness, only to find that when his divorce suit was presented in court, it received lurid publicity from the evidence Clothilde and her counsel ruthlessly presented. It was headline news. As Clothilde had been unfaithful to him for at least ten years before her departure to America, it would have been surprising if, long before he met Kathleen Tillotson, Bill had not sought consolation elsewhere. Every sensational scrap that could be raked up was supplied to the court, and of course to the newspapers. When details were lacking, innuendoes were called into service.

Despite this, Bill still hoped for a smooth solution of his matrimonial unhappiness, and he made no move to retaliate by recounting the details of Clothilde's delinquencies. She for her part fought like a tiger-cat to shift all blame from herself to him, even obliging her son to give dubious evidence against his father and deliberately dragging the name of Cavendish-Bentinck through the mud. Her case was skilfully presented, and in March 1947 judgement was given in her favour.

Bill appealed. The Court of Appeal reversed the judgement, disallowed Clothilde's demand for a judicial separation and granted a decree nisi. In July 1948 Bill and Kathleen Tillotson were married, and Clothilde, who had at the last been persuaded by her son Billy not to make an expensive appeal to the House of Lords, retired to America.

The fat, however, was in the Foreign Office fire. No member of the Diplomatic Service might marry without the approval of the Secretary of State, and divorce was taboo. An Ambassador was the King's personal representative with a foreign power. For the King's personal representative to be anything but strictly monogamous was unthinkable, both to the King and to his ministers. Members of the Government themselves would have been obliged to resign if publicly involved in a matrimonial dispute, a rule which averted a number of salacious scandals in high places. This was not the case when Lord Melbourne was cited as Caroline Norton's lover, but since then the long, morally severe reign of Queen Victoria had intervened.

It is true that after two world wars outlooks were changing. A well-known Under Secretary in the Foreign Office had married a divorced lady shortly before the second war began and had been allowed by the deeply devout Lord Halifax to go as Ambassador to Brussels. But the circumstances had been exceptional and the lady, an entirely respectable widow, had only sought a divorce after a brief, injudicious second marriage. Sir Ralph Stevenson, who had been sitting with Bill in the Foreign Office on that September morning in 1939 when the telephone gave such an ominous ring, had quietly divorced his wife during the war and had remarried, while Bill was in Warsaw, without official objection. The significant difference was that in neither of those two cases had there been the almost daily headlines which harassed Bill throughout his divorce proceedings.

Despite the publicity, perhaps the Foreign Office – where the Secretary of State, Ernest Bevin, was always a stalwart supporter of those he commanded – would have contrived to surmount the problem, had it not been for two unfortunate coincidences. The first was the Warsaw spy-trial which had made Bill an Aunt Sally of the fellow-travelling Left wing in the Labour Party. That, by itself, would not have deterred Ernest Bevin from defending him, though it was inflammable additional material for his detractors. But Lord Beaverbrook's championship of his cause, unsought by Bill, was disastrous to him. Beaverbrook and Herbert Morrison, a dedicated rival of Bevin in Mr Attlee's Cabinet, were the two men the Foreign Secretary could not abide. Beaverbrook, who scarcely knew Bill, was a consistent opponent of any royal or official sanctions against divorce. He was not divorced himself, but two of his children were, and he had been an ardent protagonist of King Edward VIII marrying the twice-divorced Mrs Simpson.

Mischievously enjoying, as he always did, an opportunity to upset any official applecart in sight, Beaverbrook and one of his ablest journalists, Sefton Delmer, gave prominence in the *Evening Standard* and the *Daily Express* to the Cavendish-Bentinck divorce suit and went into battle on Bill's side. Nothing could have been better calculated to move Bevin in the opposite direction. There were also those in the Foreign Office who warned him against sending Bill as Ambassador to a Roman Catholic country such as Brazil, for which he had already been selected, and there were some who declared that the glaring publicity had brought discredit on the service. 'Oh dear,' said Bevin to his private secretary, 'if 'is name 'ad been Smith I might 'ave saved 'im. As it's Cavendish-Bentinck, I can't.'

So Bill was dismissed from the Foreign Service without a pension, which was an unpardonable surrender to official parsimony after twenty-eight years. As a further mark of disapproval he was even denied the usual letter of thanks from the Secretary of State for his past services. The Foreign Office took no account of the contribution he had made to the department's good name in Whitehall and in the armed forces during his six years as Chairman of the J.I.C. His old friends in the Diplomatic Service remained loyal; but the official attitude was despicably mean.

He was now fifty years old and all but penniless. The divorce had cost a large sum. Ruth intended to leave him in her will what remained of her once considerable fortune and his aunt, Freddy Cavendish-Bentinck's immensely rich sister, Venetia James, had been fond enough of him to provide at one stage an allowance of £500 a year; but the immediate future was darkly overcast. With

# THE CRASH

no pension and scant prospects he must start a new life and earn a new living.

While he was striving to do so, a further misfortune befell him. Billy, whom Clothilde had scarcely allowed his father to see, at first made quite a favourable impression on his grandmother, Ruth. She judged him to be 'plausible, and rather cunning', but she wrote that she believed he might yet 'turn out the Corner Stone of the Temple'; and when he first married she considered the bride to be

> very pretty, very silly and also vulgar. In my experience it is far better to be a bit vulgar and amusing, than conventional and dull. Vulgar people often have kindly, generous characters.

She was disappointed. Billy, by nature extravagant, a defect inherited from both sides of his family, also drank too much, unlike Clothilde who was always strictly sober. The Royal Air Force commissioned him, but after an ill-judged escapade he was dismissed from the service under a heavy cloud. He saw little of his father, except when in grave financial difficulties, married in rapid succession three wives, from all of whom he was divorced, and died in 1966, the last, unhappy male heir of the four sons and three uncles of the 4th Duke of Portland whose line had seemed so well assured against all eventualities.

Bill thus had many burdens to carry, but he did not succumb to despair. His mother's buoyant philosophy was his too. Married at long last to Kathleen Tillotson, he had a peaceful and contented base from which to plan new endeavours. Many years before something else connected with the Cavendish-Bentincks, the magnificently decorated, dark blue Portland Vase, was smashed to smithereens by a lunatic in the British Museum. It was repaired with great pains and such skill that today the damage is scarcely traceable. Had it not been for a serene second marriage and the encouragement it brought him, Bill would have found no incentive, despite his natural energy and determination, to pick up the pieces of his own shattered Portland Vase.

# 16
## *Picking up the Pieces*

Poets in introspective mood often pronounce as generalisations sentiments which apply principally to themselves. Oscar Wilde, languishing in Reading Gaol and brooding on his own sorrows, wrote:
> For he who lives more lives than one
> More deaths than one must die.

Bill showed that, at any rate for him, this was untrue. It is an effort to divert interest and energy to new pastures, especially at the age of fifty, but in his case the result of so doing was revitalising.

He had neither the time nor the money to dwell on regrets for the lost opportunity of a sparkling, highly decorated career. He was obliged, in middle age, to build a new one. He had a varied experience and linguistic gifts to offer, as well as an acute brain, a pleasantly caustic wit and a basic training in commercial matters stemming from those plodding duties in the chancery at Christiania during the First World War. His qualities were recognised in many influential quarters where the frowns of Mr Bevin and the Foreign Office were disregarded. Thus Lord Kemsley offered him the foreign editorship of the *Sunday Times;* and Mr Leonard Ingrams, a business man of high repute in the City (one of whose sons rose to fame as a founder of *Private Eye*), invited him to join the Continental Assets Realisation Trust, with the probable reversion of the chairmanship. The Trust was, however, controlled by the Bank of England and the Old Lady, in process of being nationalised, did feel obliged to take account of Mr Bevin's frowns.

He declined Lord Kemsley's gratifying offer; for his new ambition was centred on a commercial career. In this he succeeded and the first step on the path to success led to others. He became chairman of a consortium established by all the leading British companies, and centred in the Unilever building at Blackfriars, to reclaim assets in Germany frozen or sequestered by the Nazi regime. Frequent visits to Germany were necessary as well as a fluent command of the language. As he was still more fluent in French, and by means of an impromptu harangue in that language had restored order at an unruly gathering of European industrialists in Brussels, he was pressed to join the European Committee of the International Chamber of Commerce. Familiarity with the methods and the mandarins in the Foreign Office, the Treasury and the Board of Trade was an asset of high value.

His main activities were in Germany where he not only recovered the sequestered assets of many British firms, but contrived so to arrange matters that all foreign companies were exempted from a heavy tax levied to meet the reparations bill presented to the Germans by their late enemies, and in particular by the Soviet Union.

Immersed as he was in German affairs, he soon became a German industrialist himself, chairman of several British-owned companies in Germany and of the subsidiary in the United Kingdom of the chemical giant, Bayer. This led to membership of the German parent company's own supervisory board, of which he eventually shared the vice-chairmanship with the Chairman of the Deutsche Bank. He was, indeed, the only Englishman, and perhaps the only foreigner, ever to sit as a full member of the supervisory board of a major German company, one that all but matched I.C.I. in size and significance.

At home, too, his abilities were recognised. During the war, while he presided over the Joint Intelligence Committee, he had worked closely with Sir Kenneth Strong, who wrote that laudatory testimony to his achievements. Strong, when Eisenhower's Chief of Intelligence, had as his military assistant Kenneth Keith, an officer in the Welsh Guards. With him Bill had visited the headquarters of Generals Patton and Omar Bradley and had established a warm friendship. Keith, whose initiatives in the investment and merchant banking field amazed and bemused the City of London after the war, invited Bill to be a director of the Philip Hill Investment Trust. In return he provided Keith with useful information and sound advice, for he was no guinea-pig director. Before long he was elected to the board of Rio Tinto-Zinc and he held Austrian and Belgian directorships as well.

He had travelled far up the hill since the day, fifteen years or so previously, that he had returned home rejected, pensionless and back at the bottom of a slope he had spent twenty-eight years in climbing. He had, against all the odds, established a new reputation. He was widely respected in commercial and financial circles and he and his wife, Kathleen, were much in demand socially. He could look back down the hill, not in anger but with satisfaction at fresh endeavours brought to fruition. In his mid-eighties, still Chairman of Bayer (U.K.), he was a daily attendant at their office and they showed no wish to let him go.

Thus at an age when all diplomats and almost all businessmen have retired, Bill remained active and miraculously energetic. Ruth had always told him that it was better to wear out than to rust. He was happy, adequately prosperous and domestically content: he had won the battle for his own self-esteem and he had pieced together the broken fragments of his Portland vase.

In 1977, when he was eighty, his cousin, the 7th Duke of Portland, died. His elder brother, Ferdy, aged eighty-eight, childless and still a resident of Nairobi, succeeded and travelled to London to take his seat in the House of Lords. Bill, granted the title and precedence of the younger son of a duke, became Lord William Cavendish-Bentinck. Three years later Ferdy also died and Bill succeeded as 9th Duke.

This uplift in rank brought neither his brother nor himself any material gain. Their forerunner, the amiable 7th Duke, had, like the son of the Proud Duke of Somerset, made no provision at all for his successors in the title. Indeed, he had taken steps to exclude them from any material acknowledgement of their succession by specifically changing the terms of a discretionary trust he had made ten years earlier, for the benefit of nephews, cousins and others he might select. It was ordained that nothing whatever should be provided for 'Ferdinand and Victor Cavendish-Bentinck and any wife or widow that they might have and all daughters and all issue of their daughters'. Why this was done was a mystery to Ferdy and Bill. The Duke's father had been a close friend of his cousin Freddy Cavendish-Bentinck, though he certainly had reservations about the radical Ruth, and there had been no family quarrel. Whatever the reasons, neither the 8th nor the 9th Duke of Portland possessed so much as an inkpot that had belonged to their predecessors in the dukedom.

There was nothing, however, to prevent Bill from being a constant attender at the House of Lords. In his maiden speech he spoke in support of the Prayer Book and the King James version of the Bible, opposing those bishops and others who were reconciled to the dimming of one of the brightest jewels in the English inheritance. He gave close attention to matters of which he had a lifelong experience, foreign affairs, commerce and finance. Had he been twenty-five years younger he must have been a prominent candidate for a ministerial appointment, perhaps, which would have been entertainingly ironical, in the Foreign Office.

So it came about that Victor Frederick William Cavendish-Bentinck, 9th Duke of Portland, still active in business and politics when past his eighty-fifth birthday, lives in a modest, well-appointed house in Chelsea, furnished in great part from his own earnings, and spends his summer holidays at his wife's Canadian home in the province of Quebec.

'The gardener Adam and his wife smile at the claims of long descent,' wrote Tennyson. Variety is more remarkable than length, and in Bill's case the variety is striking indeed: John of Gaunt and Harry Hotspur; the Protector Somerset and that austere author of Habeas Corpus, Sir Edward Seymour; Bess of Hardwick and Hans William Bentinck, Earl of Portland; Richard Brinsley Sheridan, ethereal Eliza Linley and Georgiana, Queen of Beauty. By contrast his grandmother was the tragic half-gipsy kitchenmaid, Rosina Swan; and he ends his days the holder of one of the most illustrious titles in England, rejected by the Foreign Office, in which he would assuredly have been an outstanding figure, and lacking any territorial or material connection with the dukedom of which he is the last holder.

It is a strange inheritance.

# Index

Aberdeen, 4th Earl of, 38
Acton, 1st Lord, 143
Ailesbury, Elizabeth, Countess of, 12
Albemarle, 1st Earl of, 144
Alexander II, Czar, 68–9
Alford, Lord, 48
Anne, Queen, 13, 16
Anne of Cleves, Queen, 4
Argyll, 10th Duke of, 133, 138

Baker, Mary Ann, 79
Baring, Mrs Charles, 84–5
Beamish, Sir Tufton, 185, 186
Beauclerk, Lady Diana, 76, 77
Beaverbrook, Lord, 192
Bedell, Bishop William, 21
Bevin, Rt Hon Ernest, 183–4, 186, 188, 191–2
Bentinck, Col Arthur, 150
Bentinck, Lord Charles, 150
Bentinck, Lord Edward ('Jolly Heart'), 146
Bentinck, Lord Frederick, 102, 150, 151
Bentinck, George, MP ('Big Ben'), 41, 54–6
Bentinck, Lord George, 103, 148
Bentinck, Hans William, Earl of Portland, 16, 143–4
Bentinck, Lord Henry, 103, 148
Bentinck, Lord William, 150
Bierut, Boleslaw, 183, 188
Blackwood, Lady Helen, 99–100, 102
Blackwood, Hon Mrs Price, *see* Dufferin, Helen, Lady
Blount, Lady Charlotte, 85, 87

Boleyn, Queen Anne, 2, 3
Bottomley, Horatio, 101
Briand, Aristide, 161
Bridges, Edward, 1st Lord, 170
Burke, Edmund, 30–2

Callender, Col James, 34
Cambridge, Prince George of, 55–6
Campbell, Gen Sir Colin, 70
Catherine of Aragon, Queen, 2, 3
Cavendish, Lady Dorothy, 145
Cavendish-Bentinck, Lady Anne, 151
Cavendish-Bentinck, Barbara, 153
Cavendish-Bentinck, Billy, 165, 190–1, 193
Cavendish-Bentinck, Cecilia, *see* Strathmore
Cavendish-Bentinck, Sir Ferdinand, 123, 141, 151–3, 196
Cavendish-Bentinck, Frederick, 102, 104–5, 108, 110, 113, 118, 122, 129, 138, 140–1, 151
Cavendish-Bentinck, Rt Hon George, 102, 103, 108, 151
Cavendish-Bentinck, Lord Morven, 151
Cavendish-Bentinck, Prudence Penelope, 103, 108
Cavendish-Bentinck, Ruth, 77, 81, 86–92; relations with grandfather, 92–6; 'coming out', 98–102; marriage, 103; on Mount Athos, 105–8; early friendships, 110; foreign travels, 111–13; Socialist convictions, 115–26; votes for women, 127–32; character and beliefs, 133–42; on

# INDEX

capital punishment, 134; on anti-Semitism, 135; pantheism, 136–38; and grandson Billy, 193; death of, 142; mentioned, 152, 160, 165, 192–3
Cavendish-Bentinck, V. F. W. (Bill), 9th Duke of Portland, 112–13, 140–1, 151; early years, 153–4; 3rd Secretary Warsaw, 154–6; on Lord Curzon's staff, 157–9; in Paris, 159–61; marriage to Clothilde, 161; at Locarno Conference, 161–2; in Athens, 163–4; Santiago, 164–5; Chairman of J.I.C., 169–75; Sir K. Strong's verdict on, 175; Ambassador to Poland, 176, 180–8; and judicial murder of Grocholski, 187–9; divorce, 190–1; dismissed from Foreign Service, 192; remarriage to Kathleen Tillotson, 191; rebuilds career and fortune, 194–5
Cavendish-Bentinck, Mrs V. F. W. (Clothilde), 161, 162–6, 170, 189–91
Chamberlain, Sir Austen, 161
Chamberlaine, Frances (Mrs Sheridan), 23–5
Charles I, 12, 143
Charles II, 12
Charlotte, Queen, 27, 31
Churchill, Sir Winston, 171, 173, 174
Clarendon, 4th Earl of, 68
Connaught, Duke of, 100
Conway, Lord, 16
Corrigan, Mrs, 164
Cowper, 6th Earl, 73, 78
Cranmer, Archbishop, 5
Crewe, Frances, 27, 29
Crewe, Marquess of, 159
Crewe, Marchioness of, 159
Crewe-Milnes, Lady Annabel, 110
Cromwell, Oliver, 12
Curzon of Kedleston, Marquess, 157–9

D'Abernon, Viscount, 155–6

D'Abernon, Viscountess, 99, 155
Delmer, Sefton, 192
Devonshire, Georgiana, Duchess of, 28, 31, 33
Disraeli, Rt Hon Benjamin, 35–6, 43, 57, 89, 103, 148
Douglas-Hamilton, Lady Charlotte, 18, 19
Douro, Marquess (2nd Duke of Wellington), 53
Druce, Mr, 149
Drummond, Mrs, 129–30
Dudley, John, Duke of Northumberland, 4, 8–10
Dufferin, Helen, Lady, 35–7, 40, 54, 75–6
Dufferin and Ava, 1st Marquess of, 36, 40, 54, 85, 92, 97

Eden, Sir Anthony, 173
Edward VI, 3, 5–11
Edward VII, 59, 67, 68, 87, 102
Eglinton, 13th Earl of, 44–8
Egremont, 1st Earl of, 14
Elizabeth I, 3, 4, 5, 11
Elizabeth, the Queen Mother, 109, 150
Elizabeth of York, Princess, 109
Erskine, Thomas, 1st Lord, 28–9
Erskine, Anne, Lady, 28

Fawcett, Mrs Henry, 128, 129
Feversham, Mabel, Countess of, 84
Fillol, Catherine, 11, 14
FitzClarence, Lady Amelia, 41
FitzGerald, Lord Edward, 27–8, 147
Ford, Brinsley, 89, 135, 141, 142
Fox, Charles James, 24, 28, 31, 33, 34, 147
François I (King of France), 2, 4
Frere, Sir Bartle, 63

Gainsborough, Thomas, RA, 27
Gallacher, William, MP, 188
Garibaldi, Giuseppe, 70–2
George I, 13
George II, 14
George III, 17, 27, 29, 30, 147–8

INDEX 201

George IV (The Prince Regent), 12, 28–30, 32, 34–5, 41
Gifford, Earl of, 37
Gladstone, Rt Hon W. E., 127
Glenlyon, Lord, 45, 47
Godfrey, Admiral J. H., 169
Gort, Field Marshal Viscount, VC, 171
Graham, Cunningham, 119
Graham, Sir Frederick, 57, 84
Graham, Lady Hermione, 57, 83, 84, 94, 96, 99
Graham, Sir James, 39, 40, 44, 71
Graham, Lady (Aunt Graham), 39, 83, 99
Graham, Sir Richard, 57
Grant, Sir Colquhoun, 43–4
Granville, 2nd Earl, 68–9
Grey, Lady Catherine, 11
Grocholska, Sophie, 182, 187
Grocholski, Count Remi, 187–9

Hankey, 2nd Lord, 176, 181
Hardie, Keir, 119, 123, 127
Hardwick, Bess of, *see* Shrewsbury
Harley, Lady Margaret, 145
Haskell, Governor C. N., 160
Hastings, Sir Patrick, KC, 194
Hastings, Warren, 30–2
Henri II (King of France), 7
Henry VIII, 2–4, 12
Hertford, Edward, Earl of, 11
Hitler, Adolf, 162, 170, 173
Hoare, Joseph, 121, 122, 125, 134, 139–41, 152, 165
Hoare, Lady (Joan), 122, 140, 153, 181
Hoare, Sir Reginald, 153
Holland, Queen of, 94
Holyoake, C. J., 132
Houghton, Sibyl, Lady, 57, 99, 101–5, 139
Howard de Walden, Lucy, Lady, 108–9, 145, 148, 150
Hudson, 1st Viscount, 159–60

Ingrams, Leonard, 194
Ismay, General Lord, 170

James, Mrs Arthur, 109, 138, 165, 192
James, Frank, 105
James I, 11, 14
James II, 13, 16
Jeffreys, Judge, 144
Johnson, Dr Samuel, 24–5, 28
Jusserand, Jean, 155–6

Karminski, Sir Seymour, KC, 190
Keith of Castleacre, Lord, 195
Kemble, Adelaide, 149
Kemble, Fanny, 34
Kemsley, 1st Viscount, 194
Kenney, Annie, 128–9
Keppel, Hon Mrs George, 119, 135
Kethly, Anna, 185
Khama, Seretse, 126

Labanoff, Prince, 54
Lane, Arthur Bliss, 157, 180, 182–4, 188
Lansbury, Rt Hon George, 127
Latimer, Bishop, 4
Leopold I (King of the Belgians), 38
Linley, Thomas, 25–6
Londonderry, 3rd Marquess of, 46, 47
Londonderry, Marchioness of, 44, 46
Louis Napoleon, Prince (Napoleon III), 46
Lowther, Sir James, 146
Luther, Chancellor, 161

Macaulay, Thomas Babington, Lord, 15, 31
McDonnell, Lady Elizabeth, 34
MacFadden, Elizabeth, 22, 23
MacIain, Murdoch, 21
Maisky, Ivan, 173
Malmesbury, 2nd Earl of, 56
Maria da Gloria (Queen of Portugal), 38
Martin, Kingsley, 185
Mary I, 3, 7, 9, 11
Mary II, 143
Mary, Queen of Scots, 7

Matthews, Major, 26
Melbourne, 2nd Viscount, 37–8, 41
Mendl, Sir Charles, 159–60, 162
Mendl, Lady, 162–3
Mikolajczyk, Stanislaw, 179, 182–3
Mitchell, Sir Robert, 164
Molotov, V., 122, 126, 179, 182
Montrose, Caroline, Duchess of, 48
Montrose, Violet, Duchess of, 57, 99
Morrell, Lady Ottoline, 110, 135, 150
Morton, Sir Desmond, 170
Mussolini, Benito, 72, 157, 158, 161

Nagy, Ferenc, 185
Nassau, Duke of, 43
Nicolson, Hon Sir Harold, 37, 157
Norfolk, 3rd Duke of,
North, Lord, 146, 147
Northumberland, Dowager Countess of, 13, 145
Northumberland, Duke of, *see* Dudley
Northumberland, Sir Hugh Smithson, Duke of, 14
Norton, Hon George, 35, 37–8
Norton, Hon Mrs George, 35, 37–8, 44, 74–6, 85, 128

Ogle, Earl of, 13, 145
O'Neill, Hon Arthur, 110
Onslow, 4th Earl and Countess, 104
d'Orléans, Ferdinand, Duc, 41
Outram, Gen Sir James, 69

Paderewski, I. J., 154
Palmer, Sir Thomas, 9
Palmerston, Lord, 57, 63
Pankhurst, Emmeline, 128
Panza, Mauro, 158
Parr, Queen Catherine, 24
Pearce, Col John, 71
Percy, Lady Elizabeth, 13, 145
Petkov, Nikola, 184
Phipps, Sir Eric, 159
Pilsudski, Marshal Joseph, 155

Piratin, Phil, MP, 185
Pitt, Rt Hon William, 29–30, 147
Poincaré, Raimond, 157–8
Pollard, Professor, 8
Portland, 1st Duke of, 144–5
Portland, 2nd Duke of, 145
Portland, 3rd Duke of, 30, 145–8
Portland, 4th Duke of, 108, 148
Portland, 5th Duke of, 149
Portland, 6th Duke of, 118, 150–1
Portland, 7th Duke of, 151, 196
Portland, 8th Duke of, *see* Cavendish-Bentinck, Sir Ferdinand
Portland, 9th Duke of, *see* Cavendish-Bentinck, V. F. W.
Portland, Winifred, Duchess of, 150
Portland, Earl of, *see* Bentinck, H. W.

Quigley, Clothilde, *see* Cavendish-Bentinck, Mrs V. F. W.
Quigley, Dorothea, 160
Quigley (or O'Coigley), Father, 147
Quigley, Mrs, 160, 165–6

Raczynski, Count Edward, 179
Raïsuli, 112–13
Ramsay, Hon Sir Patrick, 163–4
Ramsden, Sir John, 58
Ramsden, Lady Guendolen, 58, 63, 68, 79, 91, 96, 98–9, 102, 115, 128
Ramsden, Hermione, 93, 98, 100, 101–2, 115–16, 123, 130
Reynolds, Sir Joshua, RA, 27, 31
Rockingham, Marquess of, 30, 146–7
Roosevelt, President F. D., 179
Rousseau, Jean-Jacques, 188
Rudolf, Crown Prince of Austria, 110
Russell, Lord John, 54, 57, 63, 66
Russell, Sir John (1st Earl of Bedford), 3
Russell, Sir John W., 177, 178, 183

Sainte Beuve, 54

## INDEX

de Saint Maure family, 1
St Maur, Lord Edward, 58, 59–65, 68, 70–4, 76, 77, 96
St Maur, Ferdinand, Earl, character, 58–9; urged to marry, 65; military activities, 70–1; travels, 68, 73, 76–7; summoned to House of Lords, 76; matrimonial disappointment, 73, 78; meets Rosina Swan, 78; life in Tangier, 80–1; death, 82
St Maur, Harold, 81, 86–8, 93, 95, 97, 111
St Maur, Lady Henrietta, 85
Sapieha, Archbishop, 186
Schubert, Herr von, 162
Scott, Henrietta, 148
Seymour, Sir Edward, 11, 14
Seymour, Sir Edward, 1st Bt, 14–15
Seymour, Sir Edward, 2nd Bt, 15
Seymour, Sir Edward, 4th Bt, 15–16, 143
Seymour, Sir Edward, 5th Bt, 16
Seymour, Sir Edward, 6th Bt, *see* Somerset, 8th Duke of,
Seymour, Lady Elizabeth, 14
Seymour, Lord Francis, Dean of Wells, 17, 97
Seymour, Queen Jane, 2, 3–5, 12, 41
Seymour, Sir John, 2, 5
Seymour of Sudeley, Thomas, Lord, 2, 4
Shaw, Charlotte, 120
Shaw, George Bernard, 120, 124, 128, 136
Sheridan, Brinsley, 35, 38, 41, 43, 75, 85, 93
Sheridan, Caroline (Mrs Tom), 34–5, 39, 76, 83, 99
Sheridan, Charles, 47
Sheridan, Revd Dennis, 21
Sheridan, Elizabeth Anne, 25–7; affair with Lord E. FitzGerald, 28; at Warren Hastings's impeachment, 31; death of, 32; mentioned 34, 35
Sheridan, Richard Brinsley, 24, 25;
elopes to France with Eliza, 26; as playwright, 26–7; acquires Drury Lane, 26; gift for light verse, 28–9; given office, 30; trial of Warren Hastings, 30–2; decline and death, 33–4
Sheridan, Thomas (Swift's friend), 22–3
Sheridan, Thomas (actor), 23–6
Sheridan, Tom, 32–4
Sheridan, William, Bishop of Kilmore, 21
Shrewsbury, Elizabeth, Countess of (Bess of Hardwick), 11, 13, 145
Shuckburgh, Lady, 50–2
Sikorski, Gen W., 155
Smith, Lady Sybil, 129
Smith, General Walter Bedell, 180
Snowden, Viscount and Viscountess, 127
Somerset, Algernon, 7th Duke of, 13
Somerset, Algernon, 14th Duke of, 46, 85, 97
Somerset, Archibald, 13th Duke of, 49, 51, 85, 97
Somerset, Charles, 6th Duke of ('The Proud Duke'), 13–14
Somerset, Edward, 1st Duke of, The Protector, 2, 4–11
Somerset, Edward, 8th Duke of, 16–17
Somerset, Edward Adolphus, 11th Duke of, 17; academic achievements, 18; liberalism, 18; buys houses and property, 18–19, 39; death of, 57, 148
Somerset, Adolphus, 12th Duke of (Seymour), 19–20, 39–41; Lady Dufferin praises, 42; fights duel, 43–4; given office, 49, 52–3; expedition to Ionian islands, 54–6; view of Gibraltar problem, 54–5; enters Cabinet, 57; First Lord and KG, 62; pride in Lord Edward, 63; created Earl St Maur, 77; and Ruth, 89–90, 96; and religion, 92–3; last years, 95–7; mentioned, 128

## INDEX

Somerset, Georgiana, Duchess of, 35, 38; marriage, 39–40, 41–4; Queen of Beauty, 45–9; culinary problems, 50–2, Scottish adventure, 53; in Paris, 54; attitude to her elder son, 68, 73–4; quarrels with Caroline Norton, 74–6, 80; on death of Ferdy St Maur, 81–3, 85; kindness to Rosina Swan, 86–8; growing eccentricity, 89–92, 94–5; last years, 95–7; mentioned, 152–3
Somerset, William, 2nd Duke of, 11–12
Stalin, Joseph, 122, 126, 182, 188–9
Stanhope, Anne, 11
Stevenson, Sir Ralph, 165, 168, 191
Stewart, Lady Arabella, 11, 145
Stirling-Maxwell, Sir William, 38
Strathmore, Cecilia, Countess of, 109, 138
Stresemann, Gustav, 161, 162
Strong, Maj-Gen Sir Kenneth, 175, 195
Surrey, Earl of, 6
Swan, John, 79, 87
Swan, Nathan, 80
Swan, Rosina, 78–87
Swift, Dean Jonathan, 22–3

Taylor, Dr Stephen, 185–6
Teck, Princess May of (Queen Mary), 102
Thynne, Lord Henry, 58, 95
Thynne, Ruth (Pitt-Rivers), 93, 99
Thynne, Thomas, 13
Thynne, Lady Ulrica, 58, 81, 96
Tillett, Ben, 117

Tillotson, Kathleen (Duchess of Portland), 190, 191, 193
Tone, Wolfe, 147
Tournier, François, 86
Trotsky, Leon, 154–5
Tyrrell, Sir William, 154–5

Victoria, Queen, 40, 67, 101, 127, 128
Verulam, Frances, Countess of, 57, 99
Vetsera family, 105, 110
Villiers, Anne (Countess of Portland), 144
Vyshinski, Andrei, 184

Warwick, Earl of, *see* Dudley
Waterford, 3rd Marquess of, 46–8
Watts, G. F., 103
Webb, Beatrice, 116, 119, 122
Webb, Mary, 17
Webb, Rt Hon Sidney, 119, 122, 135
Wellington, Field Marshal 1st Duke of, 39, 103
Wentworth, Margery, 2
Weygand, Gen M., 155
Whitbread, Samuel, 33
Wilde, Oscar, 27, 194
William III, 13, 16, 143–4
William IV (Duke of Clarence), 19, 27, 38, 41
Williams, Dr Charles, 81–2, 86
Wittenham, Lady, 57
Witos, Wincenty, 156

Zedwitz, Baron, 52

Hans William, Earl of Portland, KG (1649–1709)
= (1) Anne Villiers    = (2) Jane Temple

Henry, 1st Duke of Portland (1682–1726)
= Lady Elizabeth Noel

William, 2nd Duke, KG (1708–62) = Lady Margaret Harley

William Henry, 3rd Duke, KG (1738–1809), Prime Minister 1783 and 1807–09
= Lady Dorothy Cavendish

William Henry, 4th Duke (1768–1854)      William (1774–1839), Governor-General of India
= Henrietta Scott                         = Lady Mary Acheson

William, Marquess     William John, 5th Duke (1800–79),     George, MP (1802–48)
of Titchfield         builder of underground Welbeck

Revd Charles                    Arthur (1819–77)
= Caroline Louisa Burnaby       = (1) Elizabeth Hawkins-Whitshed
                                = (2) Augusta Montague-Browne
Cecilia, Countess of Strathmore

Lady Elizabeth Bowes-Lyon = King George VI

Queen Elizabeth II              (4 sons and)
                                William John, 6th Duke, KG
                                (1857–1943)
                                = Winifred Dallas-Yorke

                William Arthur, 7th Duke, KG (1893–1977)      Morven
                = Ivy Gordon-Lennox

        Anne        Margaret (Parente)